HUMAN

COMMUNICATION

TECHNOLOGY

2nd Edition

Philip J. Salem

TABLE OF CONTENTS

Introduction

Bob Gratz and I began writing about technology in the late 1970s. Later, he would go on to be an active administrator at Texas State University, serving as a chair, dean, academic vice-president, and assistant to the president. I designed one of the first graduate classes about human communication technology in the early 1980s, and I have continued to research and write about this fascinating area.

When Bob and I first started writing about technology, we wrote about television, but we soon turned out attention to computer use. We both recognized the "concerns" people had about these technologies were similar, and I found some literature tracing current worries back to headlines and speeches about the telegraph. Lest we forget, many use "bookworm" as a derisive term with synonyms such as nerd, dork, geek, and weenie. We were a bit surprised at the strength of such dystopian views of nearly all technologies even though we knew "Luddites", a term to describe people opposed to technology, had its roots referring to those who led riots against using the new cotton machinery of the early 1800s.

Our motives were to present a more balanced view about new technologies but also to analyze how human communication might be changing in light of recent innovations, some of which were directed at changing how humans communicated. Communication studies is one of the "newer" academic disciplines, and, even today, people often confuse communication studies research with research from linguistics, mass communication, political science, psychology, sociology, and even neuroscience. In the nineteenth century, there were no academic departments with "communication" in the title, and nearly all areas of what we now think as behavioral and social sciences were in departments of rhetoric. By 1977, Wilbur Schramm, in an address to the International

Communication Association convention in Berlin, likened the study of communication to an oasis village in the desert of research about human behavior. "Everyone studying human behavior will need to pass through the oasis village at one time or another", he noted, "but some would stay to live there. I am happy to be addressing the people who stayed" (see Schramm, 1989). Bob and I grew up in the village, and we hoped to provide a unique perspective.

This book is about how humans communicate, and it examines the latest research about enduring issues related to human communication technology. These issues range from the nature of human information processing to humans' sense of reality. At the center of all these issues is how humans construct communication, and, in so doing, construct themselves, alone and together, and construct the world they inhabit.

Chapter One is about human information processing. It presents a brief history of information from a mathematical representation of relative variety to how humans make sense. The chapter explains how data becomes information and how information becomes knowledge. The chapter emphasizes the active engagement of the receiver of information in creating information. The chapter also includes contemporary material about Fear Of Missing Out, attention, multitasking, continuous partial attention, and cyberchondria.

Chapter Two describes communication as a social process in which individuals in a social relationship make messages as part of an ongoing episode. This is a process of emergent and mutual sensemaking. The chapter introduces basic terms necessary for other chapters. It uses social network sites and texting examples to demonstrate some of the unique features of human communication.

Chapter Three provides traditional explanations of technology and introduces terms for the attributes of current human communication technology. The chapter introduces seven categories of human communication technology and describes the most controversial "effects" of using the technology. The chapter ends by presenting alternative explanations for the effects.

Chapter Four describes Rogers's famous model of diffusion. Key concepts include the stages in the process, the perceived attributes of technology, various forms of communication related to the process, and the importance of personal networks. The chapter uses the adoption of mobile phones or features related to mobile phones as primary examples. It uses the latest literature on who adopts and does not adopt the latest technology and why.

Chapter Five starts with the story of an event that led to my own systematic study of human communication technology. The chapter explains how human communication constructs a person's sense of self. Topics include richness of self, presentation of self, self and relationships, and the development of self in interaction. The chapter highlights unique technological challenges such as anonymity and privacy, the Proteus effect, deindividuation, self-disclosure online, and Internet addiction.

Chapter Six begins by presenting old material on communication competence and applying it to digital behavior. There are special sections on effective behaviors, appropriateness, and mindfulness. The chapter then focuses on ten specific online bad behaviors: flaming, cyber-ostracism, bullying, cyber-hate, online harassment, lying, deceptive or abusive personas, trolls, predators, and commercial intrusions.

Chapter Seven is about communication technology networks. This material starts with the nature of relationships and how they develop. The chapter is careful to describe how people use a mix of technology to begin, sustain, or end relationships. The chapter explains some features of general social networks, and then focuses on personal networks and the different networks that emerge from using various technology. The final part of the chapter emphasizes social network sites and the types of networks that emerge from those sites.

Chapter Eight explores issues related to human communication technology and close relationships. Does using the latest human communication technology alter our sense of friendship? What does it mean to have a romantic relationship today? Does the latest technology change the meaning of intimacy? When do we disclose or just perform? How does the latest human communication technology relate to loneliness?

Chapter Nine explains how individuals create social resources through communication and how using various technologies might change that. The chapter highlights the creation and use of seven resources: information, emotional support, validation, instrumental support, diversion, escape, and pleasure. The chapter ends with material on obtaining support online and online support groups.

Chapter Ten begins with an explanation of civic engagement and contrasts the traditional ways people engaged with digital ways. The chapter describes the ways people have used technology to perform various civic activities and how people have used technology to organize group activity. The chapter describes the uses of digital technology for political activities and civic unrest. The chapter ends by explaining how the nature of community has changed.

The final chapter distinguishes between unmediated, simulated, and virtual realities. It describes how individuals may have difficulty making these distinctions using the current technologies. The chapter describes difficulties associated with distinguishing various forms of news and with distinguishing various forms of self, especially using virtual and simulated digital sites such as Second Life. The chapter explains the importance of thinking critically about both public and private concerns and being more mindful in a hybrid reality.

Current uses of human communication technology favor breadth over depth. This is true for aspects of self, making messages, social networks, close relationships, social resources, civic engagement, and our collective sense of reality. This greater breadth means variety is rushing into the system, and the diminished depth means the rush of variety is so great that there is a lag integrating what is new with what is old. This is an unstable period as people decide what new and old things to retain, how to adjust old structures, and how to create new structures using what they have retained. Adopting the new human communication technologies has also meant new communication practices, newer ways of seeing others, and seeing ourselves.

References

Schramm, W. L. (1989). Human communication as a field of behavioral science: Jack Hilgard and his committee. In S. S. King, (Ed.). (1989). *Human communication as a field of study: Selected contemporary views* (pp. 13-26). Albany, NY: State University of New York Press.

Chapter One: Information

This book is about human communication and technology. It is about communication and contemporary technologies such as computers, the Internet, and mobile phones. It is about how we use those technologies, how our communication behaviors affect that use, and how that use affects our communication. Those who write about these technologies often refer to them as information and communication technologies (ICT), and Chapter Three contains material exploring the unique features of these technologies.

> If you are an average American, you have spent about 70% of your waking hours in 2009 consuming information. During these 11.8 hours per day of reading or viewing or listening to what is now charmingly called "content," you consumed, per person, about 33.8 gigabytes of data, and 100, 564 words . . . The average American's information consumption has more than tripled since 1980. So, are we smarter than we were a year ago, or than people were in 1980? What, 3.6 zetabytes and 10,845 trillion words later – the combined US annual total for 2009 – have we learned? (Faulk, 2009).

William Faulk is an editor at the *The Week*, a news magazine, and he was commenting on how much information we process compared to our predecessors. Most of us can understand the comments about words, but is just over 100, 000 words a lot of words? The quotation itself is nearly 100 words. What are bytes? What do 33.8 gigabytes and 3.6 zettabytes mean? Is that a lot? What does "consume" mean? Does looking at a Facebook alert mean I consumed it? How well? In this Chapter, I want to explain information and how humans process information. Information is a broader concept than communication, and as you will see, human communication is one way we process information.

Differences and Variety

A recent history of information traced the idea back to African drums, and that history weaved its way from prehistoric times through the Industrial Revolution to the present (Gleick, 2011). Although there have been many important figures in that history, there can be little doubt that the seminal figure contributing to the way we think about information today was Claude Shannon. Although several of his ideas were original ones, like all great thinkers, he borrowed and cobbled the ideas of others to develop *The Mathematical Theory of Communication* (Shannon & Weaver, 1949/1998).

Figure 1.1 Claude Shannon

Shannon was a prodigy who was interested in engineering. The 21-year-old Shannon completed his master's degree from the Massachusetts Institute of Technology by writing a thesis about designing electrical circuits (Shannon, 1938). In the process, he demonstrated how a series of switches could represent nearly anything, including symbolic logic. Many years later, Negroponte (1995) would popularize the expression "Bits is bits" to express the way all things become digital.

Bit is shorthand for binary integer. An integer is a number, and a binary integer indicates how many choices of two (binary) are part of an event. More bits mean an event has more differences or more different things that are part of it. For example, flipping a coin has two possible outcomes, and it has the same number of possibilities as choosing between a paper or plastic bag at the grocery line since this involves a choice of two. However, picking from among four apps involves a choice of four, twice as many possibilities as the previous examples. The coin and the grocery bags involve one bit, but the choice of apps involves two bits.

Shannon's mathematical description of choices of two was to use a logarithm with a base of two. Such a logarithm produced a binary (choice of two) integer (number). The typical logarithm converts a number using a base of ten, and so the logarithm for 10 is 1, for 100 it is 2, for 1,000 it is 3 and so on. Using a base of two converts 2 to the logarithm 1, 4 to 2, 8 to 3, 16 to 4, and so on. As I noted earlier, 100 with a base-10 logarithm becomes 2, but 100 converts to a base-2 logarithm of 6.64.

Why did Shannon use base-2 logarithms, and not just base-10 logarithms, or for that matter, why not just count the number of differences in an event? Why is 6.64 better than 100? Shannon was an engineer interested in electrical switches that could be either on or off, and so the natural way to measure differences was by choices of two. A bit involves a choice between two alternatives. The number 6.64 suggests that 7 switches could represent an event with 100 alternatives. In fact, 7 switches could represent 128 alternatives.

An event might have the potential for many alternatives, but a specific occurrence of that event might display fewer bits. For example, the English language alphabet has 26 letters, 4.7 bits, but the word "alphabet" does not contain all 26 letters. Indeed, for an engineer, "alphabet" is an array of eight specific events (the letters) not 26 events, and some events are repeated. Using Shannon's formulas reveals the word has 2.9 bits when considering the actual differences displayed in the word "alphabet" instead of what could have been.

Bits of what? Shannon called what he was measuring "information." The classical use of information is the amount of differences in a given event relative to the probabilities for possible differences. *Information is the relative variety in an event. More differences mean more information.*

When Negroponte had written his book, the circuits had gone from switches to transistors to liquid and even gas circuits. Engineers found it more convenient to use bytes instead of bits as a standard measure. A byte is a choice among eight alternatives – 3 bits. Table 1 displays the common ways we talk about the size of computer programs, pictures, music, games, and files of all sorts. More bytes and bits mean more differences. More bytes also mean more electricity needed to process or use the device.

Table 1.1
Amounts of Data

Bit, a choice of two

Byte = 8 bits

Kilobyte = 1000 bytes

Megabyte = one million or 1000^2 bytes

Gigabyte = one billion or 1000^3 bytes

Terabyte = 1000^4 bytes

Petabyte = 1000^5 bytes

Exabyte = 1000^6 bytes

Zettabyte = 1000^7 bytes

Yottabyte = 1000^8 bytes

This chapter is less than one megabyte, and it contains fewer than 7,000 words. This book has eleven chapters of about equal length. In a technical sense, the average person "consumes" the equivalent of over 11, 000 chapters like this per day – 917 books.

What Shannon did was demonstrate how engineers could reduce anything to bits. They could digitalize things like pictures or sound, but they could also break down logic into a series of yes-no decisions – sort of a hyper variation of the game of Twenty Questions. Once they could analyze something this way, they could convert it to electricity or some signal to send and receive. The bit now joined the meter, the inch, the gram, etc. as a basic unit of measurement. As a master's student, Claude Shannon had found a way to reduce every thing, motion, thought, and feeling into bits, and he gave us a fundamental way to talk about ICT. He was not done.

Information Processing

American Telephone and Telegraph (AT&T) employed Shannon, and he published a monograph in the *Bell System Technical Journal*. Later, Warren Weaver helped him write a now famous piece for *Scientific American*. In 1948, Shannon noted the following:

> The fundamental problem of communication is that of reproducing at one point either exactly or approximately a message selected at another point. Frequently, the messages have *meaning*; that is, they refer to or are correlated to some system with certain physical or conceptual entities. (p. 31, Shannon & Weaver, 1949/1998).

Shannon sketched several versions of Figure 1.2 before it became part of a publication. Later he and Weaver would refer to the first part of the quotation as the "technical problem" and the second part as the "semantic problem" (p. 4, 1949/1998). The model focuses on the technical problem, but it displays much about the semantic problem as well. The model describes information processing as one of reproducing the original form of message in a different place or time. However, "reproducing" has many meanings, and the process involved matching or mapping one form of substance with another repeatedly to produce a "copy" of the original form.

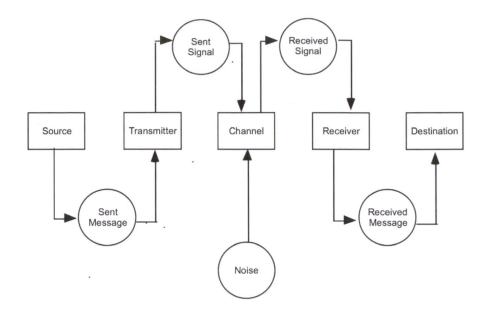

Figure 1.2 Shannon's Diagram of a Communication System

The easiest way to apply this diagram is to think about a telephone system, what AT&T hired Shannon to think about. The sent and received messages are sounds, and the sent and received signals are telephone signals, electrical signals. The source could be anyone sending a message, and the person speaks into one end of the telephone, the transmitter. The transmitter changes the sounds into electrical signals, and the channel transforms the sent signals into received signals until it reaches a receiver. The receiver then transforms the received signals back into sound.

Figure 1.2 begins with someone speaking into a phone, the sent message, and the system reproduces the sound at the other end, the received message. It is as if the system had copied the sent message as a received message in a different place. However, we all know the sounds coming out of the phone are not the original sounds from the voice at the source. The received message may sound like a voice, but we all know it is not a true or exact copy. Some things are happening between.

It seems a bit of a stretch to say the transmitter "copied" the sent message as a sent signal. Rather, the transmitter converts the message into a signal by pairing up sounds with electrical switches. The transmitter is matching sounds to electricity. A given set of sounds becomes equivalent to electricity that will represent the sounds throughout the process until the receiver matches electricity back into sounds. A digital camera does the same thing, but the input is light, and your eyes do similar matching processes. People often refer to the process as mapping since the same basic processes could apply to a host of inputs and outputs.

Shannon had been interested in secret codes and breaking codes since he was a child, and the United States military hired him to do just that during World War II. Cracking a code means you discover the rules for changing one set of things in an array, such as letters in one language, into the set of things in another array, the letters in the alternative language or "code". *Coding* was the more natural term to describe matching one set of things as equivalent to another set of things. Each mechanism in an information processing system has its own coding system. *Encoding* meant that an information processor changed the original message, sounds in phone system, into something, electricity in this instance, for transmission. *Decoding* means changing the energy and form of the transmission array back into its original array.

Information processing is about coding. It involves copying, matching, and mapping. The transmitter changes the sounds into electrical signals by matching sounds with signals – matching sound waves with electrical waves. The channel transforms the sent signal into a received signal by continuously mapping one set of electrical signals onto another set of signals throughout the system until it reaches a receiver. The receiver then decodes the received signal back into sound.

One important thing to understand is that nothing really moves from one place to another. There is just a sequence of coding. The original sound remains at the point of origin, the sequence occurs, and a sound emerges at the other end. When you "give" someone a piece of information, you just set off a sequence; you stimulate a process.

Secondly, there will be errors. The sent message will have less than the maximal information, because people will not use all the sounds available to them to create a message. People will only use the sounds consistent with what they are trying to say and how they are trying to say it. What Shannon discovered was that the information in the array of sounds was less than the information in the sent signal, the information in the sent signal was less than the information in the received signal, and the information in the received signal was less than the information in the received message. As the sequence progressed, there were unwanted increases in variety.

Shannon focused on noise, one type of error. *Noise* is the variety in the received message the sender could not predict. Equivocation is the second type of error, and *equivocation* is the variety in the received message the receiver could not explain. His diagram seems to suggest that the channel is the source of these errors, but his monograph was about both noise and equivocation.

Why do the errors occur? Some information processors have more capacity than others, and error happens when the input exceeds capacity. We all know about this because we use Internet connections with different capacities and speed. When a download is slow, it is because what we are downloading exceeds the capacity of the system we are using, and we all hope it downloads everything we wanted.

Another reason error occurs is that all systems involving copying or matching anything will have errors. It is inevitable. The chances for error increase when the original message is more complicated (more bits) and when processing involves longer sequences of matching. There is a greater chance for confusion if you try to manage conflict (complicated messages) using text messaging or the 140 characters on Twitter, than if you told friends where and when to meet you (simple message) using the same technology. There is greater chance for error if you try to relay a message to your boss through several people (longer sequence) than if you talk to the boss directly.

Shannon called the way to overcome errors redundancy. *Redundancy* is anything you can use to reinforce a message. Redundancy involves repeating a message, but it can involve repeating a message in a different way such as sounds plus pictures. Redundancy can mean saying less in any one message but sending several messages. Redundancy can also involve structuring a message so that one part of the message leads to another part. For example, one text message read as follows: "sent Sam a cake. your name is on it. chocolate mouse" (Kaelin & Fraioli, 2011).

When you increase the redundancy in a message, you decrease the chances for errors, but you also inform less in the message. Basically, you are constructing a message you believe the receiver will understand better because of the redundancy. You could overdo it. You could be so redundant as to be boring. You want the messages to have enough information (differences) to be interesting, but enough redundancy (similarity and reinforcement) to reduce error.

Shannon found a way to describe information as differences, and he gave us a way to describe and measure the basic features of our technology. He described the technical aspects of information processing and noted how error can occur and how to correct for error. The efforts to apply much of this work to human information processing began almost immediately, but there would be errors.

Reducing Uncertainty

Most of us think about information as something that helps us understand what is going on. We discover something that peaks our curiosity, and the actions we take to satisfy that curiosity leads to information. We check a web site, we read a magazine article or a post, or call a friend, and we get information. Information becomes anything that satisfies that curiosity.

The way to connect our informal understanding of information to our technology and Shannon's classical work is through the concept of uncertainty. Uncertainty is doubt. More precisely, *uncertainty* is an inability to describe, predict, or explain something (Salem & Williams, 1984). There are stories that Shannon wanted to call his basic formula for describing the potential amount of differences in an array "uncertainty", but his colleagues talked him out of it (Campbell, 1982). The idea was that any circumstance presents a person with many choices – uncertainty, and when a person makes a particular choice, the choice has a particular amount of information. In this way, information became that which reduces uncertainty. One reason Shannon might have rejected these suggestions is that to explain things in this way took him away from the technical problems and into the semantic problems, something he did not want to do.

We reduce our uncertainty by creating information and integrating it into what we already know. The world contains a buzz of phenomena, but all of what is going on is not accessible to us. *Signals* are the potential phenomena we could access from what is going on. *Data* refer to the signals we access, the phenomena at any one time we are uncertain about. *Information* is the sense we make of the data, and information reduces our uncertainty about specific phenomena. *Knowledge* is the result of adding information into what we already know, but we create our knowledge by organizing information in a way that makes sense to us. We make sense of information by fitting it into our mental models of how the world works generally. Distinctions like these are part of the knowledge management literature that began in the late 1980s (Boisot, 1998; Salem, 2007). The quotation at the start of this chapter is more about data than information or knowledge.

Mindfulness is an awareness of and attention to our information processing and communication activities. *Mindlessness* utilizes old frames of references and scripts to make sense, and there is very little attention to detail (Langer, 1978, 1989). Mindful people are thinking about how they are thinking and acting, as they are thinking and acting. A person can be too mindful and become wary or self-conscious (Berger & Bradac, 1982), but mindful people are prepared more to deal with differences and with different people than those who are less mindful (Weick & Sutcliffe, 2001). We are more likely to choose technology suitable to a task when we stop to consider the differences in the situation than when we just act on reflex (Timmerman, 2002).

Considering information in this way makes information more about what we bring to a situation than what is in the situation. In the previous section, information was about differences in sounds and signals, actual physical things. In this section, information is about *perceiving* differences and patterns of differences. In the previous section, hardware, like a transmitter and receptor, had coding rules, but in this section, the coding rules are in the heads of people.

How uncertain are you about "7H15 M355AG3 53RV35 70 PR0V3 HOW OUR MINDS C4N D0 AMAZING 7YHINGS"? If you just glanced at this message you might wonder what it meant, and some might have a difficult time making sense of it. However, if you had experiences with the English language and some sense of the linguistic structure and rules of the language, you would be less uncertain. The more past knowledge you brought to the data, the quicker you would be able to process it.

The world contains a universe of books, part of what is going on. The books you can access are part of the signals you can access. When you buy or download a book, you are creating data. Reading the book, taking notes about it, and talking to others about it help to create information related to the book. You might just think the information related to the book is just an instance of what you already know, or you might connect the information to past explanations and expectations in some novel way. You are adding to your knowledge. The basic process of going from signals to knowledge is similar to Shannon's description of information processing, but there are some remarkable differences.

Human Information Processing

Human information processing is similar to all information processing in that it is a coding process involving copying, matching, and mapping. *Human information processing* (HIP) is a process of connecting what we already know to what we do not know. The process converts signals into data, data into information, and information into knowledge. This process continues until we no longer have uncertainty about what we do not know. The function of information processing is to reproduce messages, but the function of HIP is to reduce the tensions that come with uncertainty.

Weick's model of making sense provides the best description of this process (Weick, 1969, 1979, 1995). He described making sense as a process of framing. A *cue* is a general term for what you don't know, what you are uncertain about, a *frame* is part of your knowledge, what you already know, and a *connection* is a way you relate the frame to the cue. *Framing* is a process of connecting cues to frames, and we repeat the cycle until we are comfortable with the result. At some points in the overall process, framing will access cues as signals and convert them into data, framing will make sense of data as information, and framing will process information into knowledge. In other words, HIP involves cycles of framing within stages.

Enactment is the stage where we make data. The world may contain a buzz of phenomena, but we come to it with some already established explanations and expectations, and nothing happens until we act. Your phone may buzz, but nothing happens unless you hear or feel it. If you are expecting a message (a frame), you may be more likely to react to the signal.

If you are expecting an *important* message (frame), you may have put the phone in a place that you could hear or feel it better. Indeed, if the signal comes at an unexpected time or place, you may be more likely to react. If you had no uncertainty about the signal, you may not react at all. Nevertheless, the minute you sense the signal and react to it, the minute you pick up the phone to look at the message, you are converting the signal into data. The buzz or ringtone was the cue, your expectations were the frames, and you started to connect the two by looking at the message. How will the message match your expectations? How uncertain will you be about the data?

With electronic ICT, some people react to every signal nearly instantaneously. Some have called the emotional reflex to every alert as FOMO, fear of missing out (Wortham, 2011). It is a kind of anxiety, a sense that you will be inadequate or left behind if you don't react. In other words, FOMO is more about the uncertainty people feel about themselves than about the topics of the alerts. The alerts can come from social network sites like Facebook, but they can also come from commercial sources such as your favorite shopping site, or a news source sending a bulletin, emergency alert, or sports score. FOMO helps us understand enactment better because FOMO is an instance of how we create our own environment. *We create the differences we are uncertain about.* People with greater FOMO create a situation with more signals and more chances to begin HIP. However, those with greater FOMO spend time scanning and discarding more data from the alerts rather than time processing less data into information. For those with greater FOMO, constantly checking on alerts is a way of reducing the uncertainty they feel about themselves.

Selection is the stage where we make information. Data act as the initial cues into this stage, and we search for the matches in what we already know. We always have more frames than data. That is, our minds can create more explanations for things than there are things! When we look at a text message, we make sense of it by embellishing what is there with what we know. Seeing "LOL" and hearing "laughing out loud" is a simple example. However, we might wonder why is that other person LOL? Did I say something funny? What is so funny about the other part of the text? And so, we try to answer the questions by searching for more matches. In other words, the data acts as the initial cue, we try to connect it to some frames, but the framing may result in incomplete information. We are still uncertain. The incomplete information acts as a cue for another cycle of framing, and so on until we are comfortable with the answers.

Selection is typically the longest stage of human information processing. If we are uncomfortable with the results of several cycles of framing, we may enact more data in an attempt to make additional information. If we are uncomfortable with the answers from one site, we might search several web sites, visit a commercial site, or call a friend. We may infer some common themes in the data and see some data as more redundant than information. Alternatively, additional enactments may just lead to more differences, and we can confuse ourselves.

The longer this stage takes, the more the results are about the person making sense than the object of making sense. Good things seem better than they were when we experienced them, and bad things seem terrible. In interpersonal conflict, people often over-think their problems, they mull over the difficulties, and simple conflict becomes intractable (Cloven & Roloff, 1991). Like all information processing, HIP is more likely to experience some form of error when the original message is more complicated (more bits) and when processing involves longer sequences of matching. Sometimes, over-thinking could lead to poetry, but in other cases, it could lead to depression!

The Internet is a wonderful source for data about a host of topics, but we must remember that we, the users, make it into information. Over 60% of Americans are "e-patients", people who regularly go online to get health data (Fox & Jones, 2009), and over 50% use their mobile phones to do this (Fox & Duggan, 2012). Usually, e-patients also consult professionals and friends about what they find online, but e-patients are also looking for commentary from others who have similar health concerns or experiences (Fox & Jones, 2009). Cyberchondria refers an unfounded escalation in anxiety after searching online about health concerns. People who already have higher levels of health anxiety than others are likely to increase their anxiety when they search online (Muse, McManus, Leung, Meghreblian, & Williams, 2012). The frames users bring to gathering online data are more important to developing cyberchondria than the data itself.

Retention is the final stage of making sense, and we integrate information into our already existing body of knowledge. Retention is also about storing what we have learned so we can retrieve and use it later. Retention is as if you have completed a document on your computer, and you need to save the file in some way. You search for some frames to label the document, and sometimes you may already have a file with the label you need. Your new piece of information is just another variation of the other file, and so you create a new folder and label both files accordingly. In other instances, the new document may be a subcategory of a folder you have already, and you may need to create a new "folder within a folder" for the new document. The labels for the folders at the bottom of the hierarchy are more specific than the ones at the top. Your filing system gets more complicated.

Table 1.2

Human Information Processing

HIP is a process of matching, mapping, or copying what is not known onto what is known.

HIP creates data and coverts data into information and information into knowledge.

HIP involves a process of connecting a cue to frame.

Different people

- have different knowledge and different frames
- have different ways of connecting cues to frame
- collect different signals
- enact different data
- have different doubts
- embellish differently
- make different information
- organize information into knowledge differently
- organize knowledge differently
- remember differently

Information is more about you and your processing than about what is there.

As we learn, we generally increase the complexity of our thinking. *Cognitive complexity* refers to ways people organize their information and knowledge about a given area (Crockett, 1982; Delia, O'Keefe, & O'Keefe, 1982; Schroder, Driver, & Streufert, 1967). *Scope or breadth* refers to the absolute number of discriminations. A more complex folder, for example, would include more subfolders or more documents than a less complex folder. *Depth* involves the hierarchical organization of the information and knowledge. A more complex folder would involve more folders within folders than a simpler folder with no folders within, one level of complexity. Hierarchies generally involve movement from more general information to more specific information in lower levels and subfolders. Finally, *configuration* refers to the interconnectedness of cognitions. A set of folders becomes more complex as more and more categories relate to other categories. We may have greater complexity about one type of knowledge than another. We retain some things better than others.

We create data, we discover differences, we organize those differences, and we use those differences as frames when we begin to make sense again. We develop explanations, and the explanations become expectations for framing new experiences. Table 1.2 summarizes some key points about human information processing.

Attention

One famous quotation from Noble laureate Herb Simon captures the importance of attention today.

> . . . in an information-rich world, the wealth of information
> means a dearth of something else: a scarcity of whatever it is
> that information consumes. What information consumes is
> rather obvious: it consumes the attention of its recipients.
> Hence a wealth of information creates a poverty of attention and
> a need to allocate that attention efficiently among the
> overabundance of information sources that might consume it"
> (Simon 1971, pp. 40–41).

With all the different signals available to us today, a traditional business approach is to challenge marketers to "get our attention" and "hold it long enough" to sell us the product or service (Davenport & Beck, 2001). With all the different signals available to us today and with the information we make more dependent on us than on the signals themselves, it is more important than ever that we become mindful of our attention.

Attention is focused mental engagement (Davenport & Beck, 2001). It means (a) narrowing and prioritizing of your mental activities, (b) deciding to engage or process the action, signal, data, information, or knowledge, and (c) overcoming distractions. Attention involves effort and, often, mindful effort. That is, in some situations you are aware you are trying to focus.

There are different levels of cognitive activity, and different levels involve different amounts of attention or effort (Kahneman, 2011; Pavlov, 1927). Lower-level thinking operates on reflexes, hunches, and intuition, and this kind of thinking is fast and requires very little effort. In higher-level thinking there has been a violation of expectations, there is greater uncertainty, and making sense takes longer. You must maintain attention longer, and it takes effort. Lower-level thinking might involve some symbolic activity such as reacting to the word "fresh" on the menu, but higher-level thinking involves symbols and abstractions. You can mix several lower-level activities to be done simultaneously – you can chew gum and walk at the same time. Operating at the higher level can squeeze out the lower level, and people can miss obvious signals and reflexes.

Attempting to do two or more higher-level tasks simultaneously means divided attention. Driving a car requires some higher-level mental activity, and so does talking, reading, and writing. You are four times more likely to get into an accident while talking on a hand-held mobile phone and 23 times more likely to get into an accident while texting than if you were not distracted (Olson, Hanowski, Hickman, & Bocanegra, 2009).

Multitasking is an attempt to accomplish several things during a given time. One way to do this well is to organize your work so that you can do one or more activities that can help multiple tasks. An example would be searching the Internet for a single piece of material you could use on two projects. Another way to multitask well is to plan the time you will spend on each project and then alternate the projects based on some criteria. For me, I get tired working for any longer than 90 minutes on one type of project. I lose effort, and so I must take a break and switch projects. Notice that to do multitasking well requires some planning – identifying tasks, budgeting time, etc.

There are problems without planning and mindfulness. You can encounter the serious problems with divided attention noted above, but you can also reduce the quality of accomplishing the task. Heavy technology multitaskers were more likely to be distracted and performed worse on switching tasks than those who multitasked less (Ophir, Nass, & Wagner, 2009). Trying to do any two tasks involving higher mental processes involves switching tasks. You will use extra time switching, and the chances for error increase. For heavy multitaskers, the probabilities for distraction increased. It was difficult to decide what was important and decide what to engage, and difficult to avoid other things. Just knowing your smartphone is available reduces available cognitive capacity (Ward, Duke, Gneezy, & Bos, 2017).

Several years ago, consultant Linda Stone coined the expression "continuous partial attention" or CPA to refer to what goes on when people have FOMO or a craving to connect just to be connected. Others have referred to the phenomena as constantly scanning streams of data, picking out the most relevant pieces, and scanning some more (Johnson, 2005). If it happens occasionally or purposefully, partial attention may increase the breadth of knowledge while sacrificing depth. Conversely, accomplishing any one task may be nearly impossible because of constant scanning while trying to complete a task. Scanning your phone or laptop while typing and trying to hold a face-to-face conversation increase the chances you may actually miss something important, need to type the same material again, and lose a friend. A recent newsletter about problems with multitasking and partial attention in business included the following post from a person doing management consulting:

> . . . doing any other task while someone is talking to you is being
> rude. If a person has come to you with a problem, you're telling

them "Whatever I am doing is at least as important as what you
are saying. You matter less to me than this." If they have any
self-respect whatsoever, they'll take offense. And rightfully so.
This behavior has become more socially acceptable than picking
your nose and farting. It's no less rude. . . . You're right that it
isn't possible to do two things simultaneously with full
effectiveness. There's plenty of cognitive testing to demonstrate
that. But even if you CAN do this-- even if it did not make you
worse at your job-- PEOPLE DON'T CARE. They're still going to
be hurt. (Beane, 2012).

Partial attention may happen continuously because of problems just
deciding to do the things required for full attention. A person may have
trouble prioritizing, and since everything is important, there is constant
reprioritizing. Nothing is a distraction, and so there is little effort to limit
unimportant potential signals. Instead of deciding to act, the person just
reacts. There is no attention, just lower-level activity.

Processing Information

This is an information age. Information is about differences, and when there
are more differences and variety, a technology processes more information.
Information increases by adding color, sound, and motion to a message.

Information processing is about coding one set of material from an array
onto another. Transmitters, channels, and receivers convert sent messages
into sent signals, sent signals into received signals, and received signals into
received messages. Just understanding the technical aspects of the
sequences in electrical circuits helps us appreciate the current ICT.

Any kind of information processing will have errors. The final received
message will have differences the sender did not intend, and the receiver
cannot explain well. Building in some sort of redundancy into the process
helps but reduces the amount of information processed at any one time.

Human information processing begins with uncertainty about something. Human information processing involves connecting what we do not know to what we know. We connect cues to frames and so map the unknown to the known converting signals into data, converting data into information, and integrating information into knowledge. The process moves through stages, but users enact the data and direct the entire selection and retention processes. People use technology to make information. People are more responsible for their information than the technology they use or the signals, data, information, and knowledge they process.

People and the ways they use technology are primarily responsible for any errors related to HIP. People can use the Internet to enact enormous amounts of data, but failing to be mindful of their choices can lead to difficulties. Planning and reflection can improve multitasking and improve the use of online health related data. Mindfulness about how you process information might reduce feelings of missing out and help to use your full attention on the things that matter. Mindfulness of your own information processing could help maintain a friendship and avoid an automobile accident.

References

Beane. G. (2012, December 10). On multitasking and motivating people in organizations (Web newsletter comment). Retrieved from http://www.linkedin.com/today/post/article/20121210172831-84166298-my-rule-2-for-motivating-people-and-organizations?ref=email.

Berger, C. R., & Bradac, J. J. (1982). *Language and social knowledge: Uncertainty in interpersonal relationships*. London: Edward Arnold.

Boisot, M. H. (1998). *Knowledge assets: Securing competitive advantage in the information economy*. NY: Oxford University Press.

Campbell, J. (1982). *Grammatical man: Information, entropy, language, and life*. New York: Simon and Schuster.

Cloven, D. H., & Roloff, M. E. (1991). Sense-making activities and interpersonal conflict: Communicative cures for mulling the blues. *Western Journal of Speech Communication, 55*, 134-158.

Crockett, W.H. (1965) Cognitive complexity and impression formation. In B. A. Maher (Ed.) *Progress in experimental personality research* (Vol. 2) (pp. 47-90). NY: Academic Press.

Crockett, W.H. (1982) The organization of construct systems: The organization corollary. In J.C. Mancuso & J.R. Adams-Webber (Eds.) *The construing person* (pp. 62-95). NY: Praeger.

Davenport, T, H., & Beck, J. C. (2001). *The attention economy: Understanding the new currency of business*. Cambridge, MA: Harvard Business Review Press.

Faulk, W. (2009, December 25). Editorial. *The Week*, p. 5.

Fox, S., & Duggan, M. (2012). *Mobile health 2012*. Washington, DC: Pew Research Center. Retrieved from http://www.pewInternet.org/Reports/2012/Mobile-Health.aspx.

Fox, S., & Jones, S. (2009). *The social life of health information*. Washington, DC: Pew Research Center. Retrieved from http://www.pewInternet.org/Reports/2009/8-The-Social-Life-of-Health-Information.aspx.

Gleick, J. (2011). *The information: A history, a theory, a flood*. New York: Pantheon Books.

Johnson, S. (2005). *Everything bad is good for you*. NY: Riverhead Books.

Kaelin, L., & Fraioli, S. (2011). *When parents text: So much said . . . so little understood*. New York: Workman Publishing.

Kahneman, D. (2011). *Thinking fast and slow*. New York: Farrar, Straus, and Giroux.

Langer, E. J. (1978). Rethinking the role of thought in social interaction. In W. I. J. Harvey, & R. Kidd (Eds.), *New directions in attributional research* (Vol. 2) (pp, 35-58). Hillside, NJ: Lawrence Erlbaum Associates.

Langer, E. J. (1989). *Mindfulness.* Reading MA: Addison-Wesley.

Muse, K., McManus, F., Leung, C., Meghreblian, & Williams, J. M. (2012). Cyberchondriasis: Fact or fiction? A preliminary examination of the relationship between health anxiety and searching for health information on the Internet. *Journal of Anxiety Disorders, 26,* 189-196.

Negroponte, N. (1995). *Being digital.* New York: Random House.

Olson, R. L., Hanowski, R. J., Hickman, J. S., & Bocanegra, J. (2009). *Drive distraction in commercial vehicle operations* (Report # FMCSA-RRR-09-042). Washington DC: US Department of Transportation, Federal Motor Carrier Safety Administration.

Ophir, E., Nass, C., & Wagner, A. D. (2009). Cognitive control and media multitaskers. *Proceedings of the National Academy of Sciences of the United States, 106*(37), 15583-15587.

Pavlov, I. P. (1927). *Conditioned reflexes: An investigation of the physiological activity of the cerebral cortex* (G. V. Anre, Trans.). London: Oxford University Press.

Salem, P. J. (2007). Making sense of knowledge management. *Vestnik. 5,* 47-68.

Salem, P. J., & Williams, M. L. (1984). Uncertainty and satisfaction: The importance of types of information in hospital communication. *The Journal of Applied Communication Research, 12*(2), 75-89.

Schroder, H. M., Driver, M. J., & Streufert, S. (1967). *Human information processing.* NY: Holt, Rinehart, Winston.

Shannon, C. E. (1938). A symbolic analysis of relay and switching circuits. *Transactions of the American Institute of Electrical Engineers, 57,* 1-11.

Shannon, C. E., & Weaver, W. (1998). *The mathematical theory of communication.* Urbana, IL: University of Illinois Press (Original work first published in 1949).

Simon, H. A. (1971). Designing organizations for an information-rich world. In M. Greenberger (Ed.), *Computers, communication, and the public interest* (pp. 40-41). Baltimore. MD: The Johns Hopkins Press.

Timmerman, C. E. (2002). The moderating effect of mindlessness/mindfulness on media richness and social influence explanations of organizational media use. *Communication Monographs, 69*(2), 111-131.

Ward, A. F., Duke, K., Gneezy, A., & Bos, M. W. (2017). Brain drain: The mere presence of one's own smartphone reduce available cognitive capacity. *Journal of the Association for Consumer Research, 2*(2), 140-154.

Weick, K. E. (1969). *The social psychology of organizing.* Reading, MA: Addison-Wesley.

Weick, K. E. (1979). *The social psychology of organizing* (2nd ed.). Reading, MA: Addison-Wesley.

Weick, K. E. (1995). *Sensemaking in organizations.* Thousand Oaks, CA: Sage.

Weick, K. E., & Sutcliffe, K. M. (2001). *Managing the unexpected: Assuring high performance in an age of complexity.* San Francisco: Jossey-Bass

Wortham, J. (2011, April 10). Feel like a wallflower? Maybe it's your Facebook wall. *The New York Times,* pp. BU3.

Chapter Two:
Human Communication

When Shannon published his famous monograph, the title was *The Mathematical Theory of Communication* (Shannon & Weaver, 1949/1998). In the first chapter, I used this material to describe basic ideas about information processing and the digital age. Information is a broad concept that includes both human and nonhuman coding processes. I often noted that human communication was just one way humans made sense of the world, and that individuals have the primary responsibilities for the information they process.

What about communication? There is no one best definition for communication. As many have noted, "Where you stand depends on where you sit." For me, this means that those who are from different disciplines, where they sit, explain similar phenomena in different ways. They stand on different sides of an issue or idea.

Defining communication is also like the old tale of the blind men and the elephant from the Indian subcontinent. John Godfrey Saxe (1816-1887) wrote a poem that captured the essential essence of the problem. In Saxe's poem, there are six blind men who touch different parts of an elephant and attempt to describe what they perceive. Each claims to have found the animal's essence from his or her own unique perspective. It is as if they each believed they enacted the same experience, but they failed to recognize the limitations of each person's ability to process information. In the end, Saxe concluded with "though each was partly right, and all were in the wrong."

What I found interesting is how the early uses of communication changed with the invention of print. The *Oxford English Dictionary Online* begins with the earliest uses of "communication" as something you have –

something you share or the means of sharing with others, sort of "common-in-cation". These early uses come from a translation of the Bible, and the authors were explaining having communication with God. The second use is of communication as "interpersonal interaction, and as social interaction, association, or intercourse". That would have been fine, but over the years, people have come to use communication to mean "the sending and receiving of information or the means of sending and receiving information".

People began using communication - an expression for a social and interactive process of sharing - to refer to what happens when one person does one thing, sending, and the other person does another, receiving. How did that happen? Print. Sending and receiving is just a step away from writing and reading. It is as if the grammar teachers of the world had decided their end of the elephant was the correct one, and they had a platform for advocating that - in the classroom. You can't have grammar teachers without grammar books, and so they taught "the grammar of communication" as the essential part of communication. Social interaction is not print, of course. I have described this in earlier work (Salem, 2013), and others have noticed how print alters our sense of communication (McLuhan, 1964). There will be more about print in the next chapter.

Over fifty years ago, Dance (1970) reviewed multiple definitions of communication, and things have not changed much. A good definition should be broad enough to encompass the phenomena, but it should be narrow enough to distinguish the concept from others. People define communication in a purposeful way, and the person defining wants to emphasize the aspect of the elephant that person is touching. A definition is a device to help focus. In this case, I need to help you focus on aspects of what I think are most important to explaining human communication technology.

This chapter begins with a picture that could be an extension of Shannon's model. Explaining the basic process of communication in this way will make it easier to see the connections between information and communication. The hard part is at the right of the model. Relationships and episodes are what separate human communication as a unique way to process information. The second half of the chapter will be the most difficult. Information may be about you, but communication is about us.

Human Communication and Human Information Processing

An *individual* can perform human information processing (HIP). Reading these lines, searching the Internet, thinking about something new, or meditation are all instances of HIP that only require one active mind. However, there are instances when we process information together, and some of those instances are human communication.

Figure 2.1 portrays human communication as a process of communicators (Cs) constructing messages (Ms) as part of an emerging relationship (R) and ongoing episode (E). The easiest way to think of this figure is that it depicts what goes on in a conversation. The title of the model, The Social Channel, reflects the idea that much of what is going on is an instance of HIP. Human communication is a process of mutual cueing.

Communicators are the source of messages, and Cs represent the unseen information processing mechanisms of humans. Inside each person are the collection of beliefs, attitudes, values, intentions, explanations, expectations, and mental models that many would refer to as perceptions. In the last chapter, I referred to the products of this internal buzz of making sense as data, information, or knowledge depending on how much HIP had occurred about a particular idea or feeling. Also, inside Cs are the unique cognitive ways each person performs HIP, the unique ways each person connects frames to cues and the unique ways individuals organize information into knowledge. During communication, Cs are the source for what a particular person is attempting to cue with a particular message – what a particular person intended to mean by a particular message.

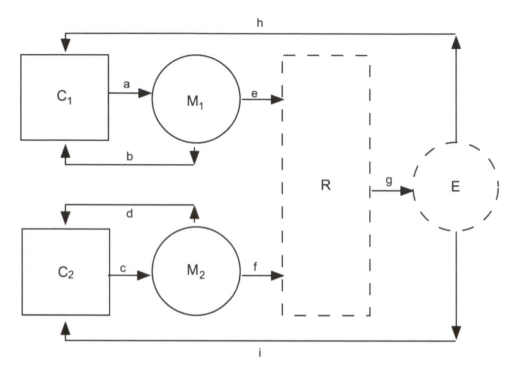

Figure 2.1 The Social Channel

There are two types of perceptions (Blumer, 1972). *Social perceptions* or social cognitions are perceptions of yourself, the other people in the communication, and the relationship(s) between you and other(s). Social perceptions include social information of how an immediate relationship and communication is occurring or should occur, and they include more general social knowledge of self, others, and social situations (Kunda, 1999; Moskowitz, 2004). Portions of social knowledge are the frames for ongoing interaction. *Object or technical perceptions* are perceptions of everything else. Technical information and knowledge include ideas and feelings about specific tasks, abstract concepts, and preferences for clothes, food, movies - everything that are not social perceptions.

When you listen to a lecture in class, the information you make about the class material is technical information, and the information you make about the speaker is social information. Similarly, when you go to a fan site for some musical group, the information about the group's songs, travel dates, and recordings is the technical information, and the impressions you form about the people in the group is social information. In a conversation, the additional social information is about how you see yourself with that other person.

Messages are symbols in some physical form - sounds, spatial arrangements, touches, etc. Messages are outputs with the potential to influence beyond their physical attributes. When someone says, "Come here," for example, the message is packaged as a sound, and although the listener will react to volume, rate, or pitch of the sound, the listener also will enact the message as some form of data and process the data into information. In this case, the receiver may process the sounds and words as an instruction or invitation for the listener to approach the sender of the message. The arrows from C_1 to M_1 and from C_2 to M_2 represent communicators constructing messages.

Messages are only what one communicator makes available to another to make sense. When communication is face-to-face (FtF), bodily appearance, grooming, gestures, facial expressions, and a host of other nonverbal behaviors are potential cues for another person. Talking on the phone limits potential cues, and texting limits even more. In this model, how people create messages is part of the hardware of communication technology.

Portions of messages can act as cues. *Content or technical cues* are the portions of the message that stimulate object perceptions, and *relational or social cues* are the portions of the message that stimulate social perceptions. The receiver associates content cues with frames about ideas, objects and tasks. The receiver associates social cues with frames about how the sender sees him or her self, how the sender sees the receiver, how the sender sees the relationship between the sender and receiver, or about any combination of these three social perceptions. This kind of distinction has been around for some time (Locke, 1998; Maturana, 1997; Watzlawick, Beavin & Jackson, 1967). Technical cues indicate what the message is about, and social cues indicate how to take the message.

Social perceptions and cues frame technical perceptions and cues. That is, people use the sense made of social cues as part of the frames for technical cues. The perceived style of the communicator frames the perceptions of the substance of the message (Norton, 1983). A person will perceive an utterance differently if s/he perceives the sender as argumentative than if s/he perceives the sender as friendly, for example.

The arrows from M1 to C1 and from M2 to C2 are displays of the ability of humans to monitor their own messages (Fisher, 1978). Individuals can hear themselves talk or watch themselves write to judge whether the output was what they intended. This is an important loop. It suggests that the only person who can evaluate with complete accuracy how well a message represented the intent of a message is the person who produced it.

The model shows communicators directing their messages to R, a relationship. A *relationship* is the set of shared or aligned perceptions about each other with each other. A *relationship* is the set of shared or aligned perceptions about how communicators will interact or are interacting with each other. That is, no one person knows the other person completely. One person knows the other person only as part of roles they play with each other as part of a relationship. Sue may know Emi as part of their family, and the ways Emi acts and thinks, as Sue's sister, Emi will be different from the way she acts at work or with her romantic partner. In fact, Sue does not want Emi to act with her as she would with those others. Sue constructs her message for Emi assuming she is talking to her sister. Sue has expectations about how to talk to Emi and how Emi might make sense of Sue's messages.

The lines around R are dotted lines to represent the emergent character of relationships. Individuals come with different expectations for how communication will occur and as they talk to each other, they will become aware of the specific aspects of their relationship or the novel nature of a new relationship that apply to this conversation. Their perceptions of the rules for this conversation will align. In some communication this will happen very quickly, but in other instances there will be very little alignment and very little communication.

There can be considerable confusion on a social network site. Typically, a site includes contacts from different previous or ongoing face-to-face relationships. The profiles and updates are messages, but they must appeal to the diverse audience that may include family members, high school classmates, college friends, and coworkers. Posting a message has the same challenges. It would be natural to post one message that appeals to one segment of the audience instead of another, and some episodes can develop through the public posting rather than a private chat or email option. There are also times when people develop episodes knowing others are watching, and this complicates matters even more.

An *episode* is a sequence of messages in which one message influences another. Sometimes nearly anyone could decipher this patterning in the messages, but at other times, only the communicators could recognize the patterning. In the latter case, this means that either the relationship is very personal or that the relationship is a social context that you, an observer or intruder, are not familiar with. Look at several sequences of text messages. Which ones might make no sense to people other than those who wrote them?

Notice that how people created messages could influence how people create episodes together. People could mix message formats. For example, one person could send a text message, and the second person could respond with a phone call. However, it would be strange if the first person listened to a voice mail message and then responded with another text message. People generally reciprocate message formats, and episodes with different formats develop differently.

The lines around E are dotted lines to represent the emergent character of episodes. At times, there is a tight coupling between messages such as at the start of most FtF conversation or during a question-answer sequence. At other times, there is a loose coupling as individuals might be struggling to find a particular way to say something or take something. A natural place when patterning becomes less predictable is when communicators introduce or change topics. The coupling between messages also reflects the perceptual alignment about relationships. When individuals are on "the same wavelength" about how to appropriately communicate with each other, conversations flow more smoothly.

Notice the lines going from E back to Cs. This depicts communicators making sense of each other's messages as part of the episode. Although an individual may be able to monitor the extent to which he or she produced a given message as intended by considering the message in isolation, an individual cannot evaluate the impact of that message without considering its place in the sequence. Look at text messages in isolation. Sometimes, such as a short "OK", it is nearly impossible to make sense of the message without considering the texts before and after the "OK".

A portion of a message does not become a cue until the receiver of the message enacts the message as part of an episode, attends to the message, and uses that portion to make meaning. The receiver may bracket the sender's message in the episode in a manner unintended by the sender. A sender may intend a portion of a message to prompt a particular perception in the other, but that portion of the message is only a signal until the receiver actively connects the sender's behavior to a frame. Furthermore, the receiver may select portions of the message display that the sender did not consciously or actively manipulate. Finally, any notion of the importance of consensual meaning falls when one recognizes that people need only enough information to respond. *Human communication involves mutual cueing, but each individual completes their own information processing.*

The model depicts human communication as HIP in several ways. First, the process is one of matching, mapping, or copying one array onto another. Individuals convert the patterns of their thoughts and feelings into messages. The shared thoughts of individuals communicating together, their relationship, converts and orders the separate messages into portions of an episode. Individuals use portions of the episode as cues to make sense and convert data into information, and information into knowledge.

Second, the information processors have limits on their capacities. The last chapter noted that individuals have varying capacities to process different information in different ways. What is important about the Social Channel is that relationships also have limits. That is, individuals have rules for their relationships that prohibit messages about certain topics, about using specific verbal and nonverbal behaviors, or about communicating in different styles. Messages reflect the internal states of individuals because the messages are the mapping of internal states onto observable behavior. Episodes reflect the mutual perceptions of individuals about each other since episodes are the mapping of individual behaviors into collective behavior.

Third, there will be errors. Individuals can't say all they are thinking. Individuals get to decide what parts of an episode are important and how another person's messages fit or do not fit those portions. Individuals get to choose what part of another person's message is important, and individuals will always have more explanations for a message than another person intended. In human communication, one person acts, and another person makes sense. Individuals can control their own thoughts and actions, but the individual shares the development of a relationship or episode with others, and everyone will make sense. Communication is different from other instances of HIP in that the social nature of communication increases the probabilities for error.

Recall that error is unintended or unexplained differences, and the emergence of these differences provides opportunities. The next section contains explanations of basic nuances that point to those opportunities. In human communication, we make sense of ourselves together.

Attributes of Human Communication

Not Communication

"You cannot not communicate" is an expression the writers of communication textbooks used for much of the last decade to emphasize various attributes of communication. The statement originated in one of the seminal works about human communication (Watzlawick, Beavin, & Jackson, 1967), the writer of a textbook would explain it for instructional purposes (e.g., DiVito, 1976), and then another writer reviewing theoretical approaches would use the textbooks as sources (e.g., Littlejohn, 1983). This kind of sequence is just the sort of thing Shannon described. There would be errors.

The most important error for me was the omission of various phrases limiting what appears to be the scope of a very broad statement. The original message was as follows:

> Now it is accepted that all behavior in an interactional situation[1] has message value, i. e., is communication, it follows that no matter how one may try, one cannot *not* communicate. Activity or inactivity, words or silence, all have message value: they influence others and these others, in turn, cannot not respond to these communications and are thus themselves communicating. (Watzlawick, Beavin, & Jackson, 1967, pp. 48-49).

The original message had a footnote about excluding their comments about "internal dialogues", but the footnote situated the statement as about behavior in an "interactional situation". The consequent textbook authors emphasized the potential message value, the potential for behavior, both verbal and nonverbal behavior, to be a cue, but most failed to explore "interactional situation". "You cannot not communicate" was more dramatic than "You cannot not message" or "You cannot not cue", but many readers made sense of the expression as a way to label all human behavior as communication.

I have already described human communication as a process in which individuals create messages as part of emerging relationships and ongoing episodes, and I have explained how the process is one of mutual cueing. However, the primary function of human communication is very different from the information aspects. *The function of information processing is reproduction, and the primary function of HIP is reducing uncertainty to manageable levels. The primary function of human communication is to create that interactional situation.* This book is about how we use technology to do that, and how using various technologies changes individuals, relationships, messages and episodes. In the next section, I will highlight various features of how I use the expression "human communication" as a unique phenomenon. Along the way, I hope to improve your understanding and appreciation for how humans come to communicate with each other.

Today, humans use a lot of text. There was quite a jump from typing, to email, to blogs, to text messages, and beyond. On December 3, 1992, Neil Papworth sent the first text message "Merry Christmas" to Richard Jarvis, one of his bosses at Vodafone. People sent over 8 trillion texts worldwide in 2012, about 15 million a minute (Gayomali, 2012). However, people tend to use text more as part of conversation than as writing (Baron, 2008). In what follows, I will contrast our uses of text with face-to-face conversations to explain how messaging can become communication.

Developing Communication

Many begin essays on communication by noting it is a process, but the idea soon vanishes from the rest of the material. Process is not an easy idea to understand or to depict since it is about time. *Communication is a process because it happens through time. There are sequences of connected activities.* In human communication individuals alternate between internal activities such as thinking and feeling and external activities such as their verbal and nonverbal behaviors. It gets more complicated when the sequence involves one set of simultaneous internal and external activities followed by another set. Figure 2.1 is my attempt to represent the process, but it is just a diagram seeking to represent the basic things going on during a sequence.

Listening and watching a conversation gives you a better sense of the flow. Imagine how many text messages it would have taken to capture what went on in the conversation. Looking over the list of past text messages you sent and received from a particular someone can show you how the process slows down when we chose to communicate this way. Reviewing the text messages might also lead you to a particular message in the sequence that was particularly meaningful. Notice when it occurred in the sequence. The flow is where the communication happens. One message – a vocal utterance or a single text message – is not communication. A message is just a part of the process.

Human communication is a *complex* process. Three particular features of human communication are similar to all complex processes (Salem, 2013).

First, human communication is iterative. An *iterative* process repeats processing rules. Individuals create messages, they make sense of episodes, relationships, and themselves, and they repeat the process. They come with frames they use and reuse as a sequence develops. When individuals develop an understanding of their relationship, adding new messages to an episode involves a reuse of those rules.

Second, human communication is recursive. *Recursiveness* refers to the way that outputs for one cycle become inputs for the next, and Figure 2.1 displays this with arrows coming from the episode back to the communicators who produce an additional message for the episode.

Third, human communication is multiplicative. *Multiplicative* means that the interaction can produce phenomena unique to interaction. That is, one or the other of the communicators could not have produced phenomena alone, and what is happening can be of much greater magnitude than without the process. People could not have produced a relationship alone, and they could not have produced an episode alone. What happens is that effects of each cycle of an episode - the sense people are making and their placement of each successive message as part of the flow – build the overall flow of the sequence to create cumulative effects. Additionally, the effects of one episode become the input for the next. Sometimes the cumulative effects happen in very surprising ways.

Consider the following text sequence.

A1: Who are you in a relationship with?

B1: What?

A2: Your facebook page says that your in a relationship!

B2: How would you know that?

A3: Becca has a facebook and she told Zinny and Zinny called daddy and daddy called me.

A4: Who are you in a relationship with? (Kaelin & Fraioli, 2011, p. 70).

You can see this very short episode building, and you can see the "behind the scenes" complexity in A3. What happened before this episode? What happened after? Sometimes what happened involved another technology. Human communication can get very complex.

Communication develops social interaction. Several distinctions will help to appreciate a minimally social situation. An *action* is one activity, a text message, for example. A *reaction* is an activity connected to the action. You glance at the message (reaction), and you process what you saw (a series of reactions). *Coaction* occurs when two or more people are reacting to the same signals, two people watching the same video, for example. A *response* is an activity directed at the source of the original action. Sending a text message back to the source of the original text is a response. *Feedback*, in a social situation, is a response that gets a response (Salem, 2013). Minimal *social interaction* occurs when there is a sequence of *responses* between two or more people. In the simplest case, A acts, B responds, and A responds. When B responds to A, there is a type of closure to A's action, but A must respond to B's response to give closure to B's action. There is feedback – responses that get responses. Others have called this minimum sequence of three connected behaviors a collective structure (Allport, 1962) or a double interact (Weick, 1968).

Much of our use of ICTs is not about social interaction, not about communication. There are sequences of messages, but the messages are not about each other. The blog post may be a reaction to the previous post, and the author of the previous post may not even read the reaction. When you see a series of comments after a news story, the comments may have been posted several hours before, and the comments could be all about the story or directed to the author of the article. The author does not need to respond. You don't need to respond and seldom do respond to all the people who post on your social network site. Many post arrays like this can have serious social and psychological consequences, but the reader of the array is more responsible for connecting them to each other than the authors of the messages. What is going on is a sort of assisted HIP, but not a mutual cueing.

Human communication is an emergent phenomenon. Emergence means that there are products of connected actions over time. Indeed, the connection of any actions to others over time involves the emergence of the sequence itself. Completing a task normally involves connecting behaviors step by step, and the product of the sequence is the emergent phenomenon. How you feel after watching a video is an emergent phenomenon, and how you feel about yourself and others after communicating with them is also emergent phenomena. For human communication, the most important developments are the emergence of the social relationships between the participants and the development of the episode itself.

Although some phenomena emerge at the end of a sequence, the emergence of relationships and episodes happen simultaneously as part of developing feedback. Consider the following exchange of texts between A and B.

> A1: Would you get the mail on your way in?
>
> A2: Mail please?
>
> A3: Could you get the mail?
>
> B1: this is the only thing you ever text me about.
>
> A4: No. Sometimes I ask you to get the garbage cans too. (Kaelin & Fraioli, 2011, p. 204).

A and B have exchanged text messages. A sent four of the five. Can you guess what type of relationship is between A and B? Notice that you would need to get to A4, the message that made the exchange a true episode, before you might have a good chance of pinpointing this relationship. How do you make sense of the social cues after A1? A2? A3? How does A see the relationship between A and B? How does B perceive her/himself when s/he texts B1? In what kind of relationships would a response like A4 be appropriate? Do you have a name for this type of episode? In what kind of relationships are these episodes common?

Human communication involves convergent social perceptions. When people begin to communicate with each other, they come with expectations of how they are with each other, and their first few messages attempt to establish the communication rules for the interaction. As these perceptions align, the dotted lines in Figure 2.1 become more distinct, and the communicators can "exchange" other information. At the end of *Close Encounters of the Third Kind*, a 1977 movie, the Earth scientists are trying to communicate with the aliens aboard a large spaceship. The scientists use a computer to send a series of tones to the ship as a way of suggesting a code for information processing between the two cultures. There are several slow sequences of tones between the computer and the ship until they find the common code. Then, there are alternative rapid turns in which both the computer and the ship produce coordinated sequences of tones. They make music together. In human communication, we cue each other about how we can construct our relationship and episode, and when there is minimal perceptual convergence, specific relationships and episodes emerge.

Without the minimal perceptual convergence there would be no human communication. Cooperation of any kind would be impossible if people did not co-orient on similar rules for cooperation and organizing (Farace, Monge, & Russell, 1977; Newcomb, 1961). People may work in the same organization for different reasons and goals, but the organization cannot function if they are not on the "same page" about how to deal with each other (Weick, 1979). Similarly, people have differences when communicating with each other, but no communication can happen if they do not converge on the appropriateness of topics, topic development, language, nonverbal cues, length of turn or text, timeliness of response, etc.

Human communication involves the emergence of coherent dialogue. *Coherence* refers to the extent to which messages seem to connect to each other in some meaningful or orderly way (Craig & Tracy, 1983). Coherence is another way to describe how messages hang together to make sense. Statistically, one message can follow another message in a very predictable way. There can be tight-coupling between actions as part of the interaction (Weick, 1979). However, the rules are not so strict in most conversation that individuals have just one way of responding. Usually, each person has multiple choices of messages to maintain coherence.

Conversations have different levels of coherence. The starts and ends of conversations can be predictable, but there are those periods when individuals introduce new topics, and they need to reestablish or change the rules for communicating about them. Most conversations are improvisations with varying degrees of coherence throughout.

You can see coherence and incoherence develop over a string of text messages. Sometimes, it is as if one "conversation" ended and another one began. You can also see what happens when episodes fall apart. It just takes one inappropriate or "stupid" comment, and there will be no response.

A1: where are you?

B1: home

A2: what are your gps coordinates? (Kaelin & Fraioli, 2011, p. 205).

When individuals intentionally create behaviors to have some consensual meaning for another member of a community that might recognize that intention, individuals are creating messages (Burgoon, Buller, & Woodall, 1996). However, these mindful and often strategic actions are not communication. Creating messages, messaging, is just a part of a larger process.

Table 2.1

Human Communication

HC involves both perceptions and behaviors.

HC involves both individual factors and social factors.

One person has direct control over his or her information processing and messages, and indirect influence of others in the episode.

HC is a *process* of communicators constructing messages as part of an emerging relationship and an ongoing episode.

- One person acts, and the action becomes part of the episode.

- A second person makes sense of the episode. That person responds, and the action becomes part of the episode.

- The first person makes sense of the episode, the first person responds, and it becomes part of the episode.

- And so on.

HC is a *complex* process. HC is iterative, recursive, and multiplicative. Messages and episodes can accumulate in sometimes surprising fashion.

At a minimum, individuals construct an episode by developing a feedback sequence of mutual responses. HC is about *social interaction*. Individuals make communication together.

Individual social perceptions about the rules for an episode *converge* as the process continues.

The contours of a relationship *emerge* as perceptions converge and episodes develop coherence.

Episodes have varying degrees of *coherence* reflecting varying degrees of convergence.

Making sense of the episode means making sense of ideas and each other.

It is more about us together than about you or me.

Although we might all like to believe that a specific strategic behavior would have meaning in an intended way, others can only perceive the behavior and make sense of it as part of the flow of other behaviors. Indeed, others may process some of our unintended behaviors as meaningful, and others may process our intended messages in unintended ways. We can control some of our messaging, but we lose the sense of it to others in the flow that is communication.

Table 2.1 displays basic ideas about human communication. *Process, complexity, social interaction, emergence, convergence, and coherence are attributes of human communication.* That is, when behaviors fail to exemplify these features, what is going on is not communication. When our messaging fails to encourage a feature such as minimal perceptual convergence about communication rules, we fail to connect with each other. It is as if two people were speaking different languages. Messages do not connect to each other in any meaningful way, and episodes never really develop. There may be a sequence of HIP behaviors, but the individuals will not connect to each other. They are not communicating with each other. "One cannot not communicate", but *we* cannot communicate.

Communication Practices

Communication, in the broadest sense, involves a set of procedures for creating social interaction. The focus in many disciplines has been on how individuals might achieve their individual goals through messaging as part of communication. There has been attention in other areas of study to how the creation of messages might encourage or discourage the development of sociality and social phenomena such as cooperation. Some have investigated the development of unique episodes such as conflict episodes to understand how participants make sense of differences, maintain relationships, and extend dialogue. A recent development has been the investigation of recurring episodes.

Communication practices are a set of repeated communication behaviors along with the rules for their enactment. Individuals often repeat message behaviors across different social situations, and communication style refers to these patterns (Norton, 1983). Some individuals repeat behaviors because they are more effective than others, and communication skills or communication competencies refer to these behaviors (Spitzberg, 1983). *Information practices* are the repeated individual information processing behaviors along with the rules for their use. In contrast, communication practices refer to the recurring **collective** efforts of individuals to construct episodes together.

Since individuals repeat their sequences with some variation, the commonalities suggest the participants have accomplished some perceptual convergence about the rules for creating these patterns. *Communication rules* are followable prescriptions indicating the obligated, preferred, or prohibited behaviors in certain situations (Shiminoff, 1980). The rules describe how to communicate in an appropriate way, but they also suggest that if you do not communicate this way, you cannot continue the episode or be part of the relationship.

We all become aware of the rules when we visit someone else's family for the first time or meet people from a different culture. As we develop intimacy with a romantic partner, we consider how the rules might be changing. Moving from one organization to another also heightens your awareness of the rules. If we are not mindful of rules and make no attempt to discover or cue differences in rule expectations, the minimal perceptual convergence for communication will not occur.

Some episodes are barely episodes or barely repeated. A *simultaneous monologue* refers to a minimally coherent episode in which people express their own interests with little or no references to each other. Sometimes, people may talk over each other and turn-taking breaks down. The co-worker I mentioned earlier was engaged in monologue. My favorite example of simultaneous monologue is when two of my aunts would start talking to each other at family gatherings many years ago. These sisters had not seen each other for a while and seldom talked on the phone. When they met, they bombarded each other with what had happened to their families. They just started talking with little time for the other to even ask a question. It was if they were two facing televisions turned to different channels.

An *impromptu episode* refers to instances in which people struggle to learn each other's rules. In these instances, people may develop coherence toward the end of the episode or abandon the episode altogether. This can happen when you meet someone from a different culture, but it can also happen when you join a new online discussion group or become a friend on a new social network site. What are the new rules?

Improvisation involves accepting but adding to the previous comments, responding in the moment, and placing comments within a sense of the emerging collective whole (Sawyer, 2001). Coherence varies within an improvised episode as people switch topics and cue each other to different rules. People know the general rules, but they can talk about many different things in creative ways. Most conversation is improvisation, and communication resembles jazz (Eisenberg, 1990). However, there is an underlying structure to improvisation, just as there is an underlying structure to jazz. The rules still define what is appropriate, and there are still ways to be inappropriate.

Most of our face-to-face conversations are improvisations. We match answers with questions, try to maintain coherence by extending topics, adjust rules, use a variety of time for each turn, help each other tell stories, and start and end in a variety of ways (Nofsinger, 1991). Most of our everyday conversations are about people and social situations (Dunbar, Marriott & Duncan, 1997), but this should not come as any great surprise since humans are social animals and our random thoughts are about people (Liebeman, 2013).

Social routines refer to intended, repeated sequences of behavior in which people refine interactions to better accomplish an outcome. In some instances, they may discard behavior, and in other cases they may expand their behavior. People may come to appreciate the limited use of some behaviors that were pervasive before. The development of tight coupling in a routine resembles trial-and-error learning as people improve their ability to accomplish outcomes (Rerup & Feldman, 2011). People employ rules, but the sequences may be so tightly coupled that they can also employ a script.

Consider the routine you and your friends might use for meeting for dinner. Twenty years ago, I might have telephoned a friend to invite them to dinner. We would have chatted about recent personal or public events, discussed where to eat, time, and place, and scheduled the dinner. Today, we are likely to contact each other via email or texting. We will exchange some messages about where to eat, time, and place, and schedule the dinner. We will probably schedule the dinner more efficiently. We will discard the chatting about recent personal or public events as part of the scheduling. We will save chatting for dinner.

The functions of routines differ. People help construct *instrumental social routines* to get a task done, but they perform *rituals* to express or reinforce relationships (Rothenbuhler, 1998). The differences between the two types of routines are similar to the differences between technical cues and social cues. Indeed, the social cues are more important in a ritual than the technical ones. The conversation you might have with a salesperson while trying to buy furniture is likely to be an instrumental social routine, and so is the ordering routine at the fast food counter. A couple I know gets together early in the morning before their kids are awake to read the paper and share some coffee. Although they will discuss the news, what is more important is that they took the time to be together before the day began. Just performing the ritual is more important than what is going on about technical information. Some rituals can be very formal, such as a religious ceremony, but most rituals are informal.

Routines generally have some room for improvisation, and they can serve multiple functions. When trying to buy furniture, the salesperson had better be ready for the customer's unique desires. Once the deal is closed, the rest of the routine becomes much tighter with payment and delivery. Some routines have a mixed character, with some subroutines being instrumental and another subroutine being more ritual.

Sometimes the same sequence can serve multiple functions. Consider the following text sequence, repeated often throughout a week.

A1: Made it.

B1: OK

A2: LvU

B2: ♥

I am not sure people could make any technical information out of A2 and B2. But are the first two messages really about making it to a destination? The whole sequence could be ritual. The ritual reaffirms who the participants are to each other with each other.

Routines can be a problem when people perform them mindlessly. The most common explanations for mindlessness are a tendency to generalize existing perceptions, premature commitment to a particular way of doing things, or a tendency to activate a performance based on few cues (Langer, 1989; Timmerman, 2002). People may perform a routine without recognizing how the situation is different from other situations, believe there is only one routine they can use to accomplish a function, or begin performing the routine before they recognize what they are doing will not work well. What happens is that people perform an episode that worked in the past, and they activate it on little data. There is a script, and they select a script with little thought.

One of my graduate students is a very savvy user of technology. She gets alerts and updates on everything, including anything going on with her friends on selected social network sites. One day in my office, she received a message from her boyfriend, and she asked to take the message. She went into the hallway and returned a few minutes later. She was laughing. She and her boyfriend had exchanged some intimate messages on her Facebook! She failed to realize the message was from Facebook, and her boyfriend also forgot how the routine began. Now "everyone" knew about them.

A Flow of Collective Creativity

Communication is one method people use to process information. Similar to all information processing there are factors related to coding, capacity, and errors. Similar to all HIP there are factors reinforcing how individuals make sense by connecting what they know to what they do not know. Many times, we use technology to begin communication but end it by only helping each other with HIP.

Humans communicate with each other as they develop their relationships and episodes together. Individuals come with differing expectations about how they will relate to each other. They cue each other about those expectations, and they come to an understanding about how an episode will proceed. In some cases, this understanding is minimal, and there is little communication. In other instances, they develop communication practices that serve multiple functions. These practices vary from improvisational episodes to highly structured formal routines or ceremonies. Understanding human communication and technology begins by appreciating what happens when people communicate regardless of the technology. There are intricacies to just preparing to communicate or constructing messages, and things get more complicated with the realization of how little else individuals control as they create social events. The new information and communication technologies provide users opportunities for greater information processing and social development, and there are challenges as well.

References

Allport, F. H. (1924). *Social psychology*. Boston: Houghton Mifflin Co.

Allport, F. H. (1962). A structuronomic conception of behavior: individual and collective I. Structural theory and the master problem of social psychology. *Journal of Abnormal and Social Psychology, 64*, 3-30.

Baron, N. S. (2008). *Always on: Language in an online mobile world.* Oxford: Oxford University Press.

Blumer, H. (1972). Symbolic interaction: An approach to human communication. In Richard W. Budd & B. D. Ruben (Eds.), *Approaches to human communication* (pp. 401-419). NY: Spartan Books.

Burgoon, J. K., Buller, D. B., & Woodall, W. G. (1996). *Nonverbal communication: The unspoken dialogue* (2nd ed.). New York: McGraw-Hill.

"Communication, n." In *Oxford English Dictionary Online*, December, 2012. Retrieved from http://www.oed.com/view/Entry/37309?redirectedFrom=communication

Craig, R. T., & Tracy, K. (Eds.). (1983). *Conversational coherence: Form, structure, and strategy.* Beverly Hills, CA: Sage.

Dance, F. E. X. (1970). The concept of communication. *The Journal of Communication, 20*(2), 201-210.

DeVito, J. (1976). *The interpersonal communication book.* New York: Harper & Row.

Dunbar, R. I. M., Marriott, A. & Duncan, N. D. C. (1997). Human conversational behavior. *Human Nature, 8*(3), 231-246.

Eisenberg, E. (1990). Jamming: Transcendence through organizing. *Communication Research, 17*, 139–164.

Farace, R. V., Monge, P. R., & Russell, H. M. (1977). *Communicating and organizing.* Reading, MA: Addison-Wesley.

Fisher, B. A. (1978). *Perspectives on human communication.* New York: MacMillan.

Gayomali, C. (2012, December 3). The text message turns 20: A brief history of SMS. *The Week*, Retrieved from http://theweek.com/article/index/237240/the-text-message-turns-20-a-brief-history-of-sms.

Kaelin, L., & Fraioli, S. (2011). *When parents text: So much said . . . so little understood*. New York: Workman Publishing.

Kunda, Z. (1999). *Making sense of people*. Cambridge, MA: MIT Press.

Langer, E. J. (1989). *Mindfulness*. Reading MA: Addison-Wesley.

Lieberman, M. D. (2013). *Social: Why our brains are wired to connect*. New York: Crown Publishers.

Littlejohn, S. W. (1983). *Theories of human communication* (2nd ed.). Wadsworth Publishing.

Locke, J. L. (1998). *The de-voicing of society: Why we don't talk to each other anymore*. NY: Touchstone.

Maturana, H. R. (1998). *Metadesign*. Retrieved December 8, 2012 from The Chilean School of Biology of Cognition, Santiago, Chile. Web site: http://www.inteco.cl/biology.

McLuhan, M. (1964). *Understanding media: The extensions of man*. NY: McGraw-Hill.

Moskowitz, G. B. (2004). *Social cognition: Understanding self and other*. NY: Guilford.

Newcomb, T. (1961). *The acquaintance process*. New York: Holt, Rinehart and Winston.

Nofisinger, R. E. (1991). *Everyday conversation*. Newbury Park, CA: Sage.

Norton, R. (1983). *Communicator style: Theory, applications, and measures*. Beverly Hills, CA: Sage.

Rerup, C., & Feldman, M. S. (2011). Routines as a source of change in organizational schemata: The role of trail-and-error learning. *Academy of Management Journal, 54*(3), 577–610.

Rothenbuhler, E. W. (1998). *Ritual communication: From everyday conversation to mediated ceremony.* Thousand Oaks, CA: Sage.

Salem, P. J. (2013). *The complexity of human communication* (2nd ed.). Cresskill, NJ: Hampton Press.

Sawyer, R. K. (2001). *Creating conversations: Improvisations in everyday discourse.* Cresskill, NJ: Hampton Press.

Shannon, C. E., & Weaver, W. (1998). *The mathematical theory of communication.* Urbana, IL: University of Illinois Press (Original work first published in 1949).

Shimanoff, S. B. (1980). *Communication rules: Theory and research.* Beverly Hills, CA: Sage.

Spitzberg, B. H. (1983). Communication competence as knowledge, skill, and impression. *Communication Education, 32,* 323-329

Timmerman, C. E. (2002). The moderating effect of mindlessness/mindfulness upon media richness and social influence explanations of organizational media use. *Communication Monographs, 69*(2), 111-131.

Watzlawick, P., Beavin, J., & Jackson, D. (1967). *Pragmatics of human communication.* New York: Norton.

Weick, K. E. (1979). *The social psychology of organizing* (2nd ed.). Reading, MA: Addison-Wesley.

Chapter Three: Technology

Information processing is a way to code one array onto another such that the processing system can produce the original array at a different space or time. Human information processing (HIP) is the way people code new phenomena onto old knowledge to reduce the uncertainty they might feel about the new phenomena. Human communication is the way for two or more people to cue each other to construct relationships together and cooperative behavior. Communication practices involve improvised and routine communication that accomplish tasks and fulfill social and psychological functions. In the broadest sense, what I have described in the last two chapters are forms of technology.

Technology can refer to three phenomena (Arthur, 2009). First, technology is a means to a purpose or function, a way to get something done. Throughout the first two chapters, I have tried to describe how various activities accomplish basic functions. Second, technology is an assemblage of practices or components. This use of technology highlights the various parts of a technology and the overall order or design of a technology. The various figures and descriptions of the first two chapters have emphasized these features. Finally, technology can refer to a collection of devices or practices available to a culture. This chapter will focus on current human communication technologies (HCTs), a collection of devices and practices.

A common way to describe any technology is to identify the hardware, software, and functions or effects of the technology. Hardware are physical components, and sounds, transmitters, and messages are just a few of the hardware in the last chapters. Software are the methods for executing the function. Hardware perform specific operations, and people organize hardware to perform these operations. The arrows in Figure 1.1 and Figure

2.1 give you a sense of the software of basic information processing and human communication. We generally refer to the programs or apps we use as software, but it is important to distinguish the design of the program, the software, from its physical manifestation, the electronic form of an HCT. Finally, people design hardware for a purpose, and accomplishing this purpose is one of the effects of using a technology. However, the design and use of technology often produce additional effects.

In the next section, I will describe seven types of information or communication technologies. I will provide a brief history of each type and characteristics that distinguish them. The second section describes various effects of technology, including how the current HCT might have changed the way we think about human communication. The last section provides some popular explanations for these effects.

Types of Information or Communication Technologies

Face-to-Face Communication (FtF)

Face-to-face communication refers to those situations in which the communicators are in the same space. At the most basic level, FtF is dyadic, between two people, but FtF also includes small group communication and public communication. Each of these FtF levels has its own unique characteristics, and an appreciation of these characteristics will assist out understandings of the other communication technologies as well. Most of our communication using other technologies is with people we have already communicated with FtF (Boase, Horrigan, Wellman & Rainie, 2006). FtF communication is the point of reference for understanding the characteristics of other HCT.

Public communication differs from dyadic communication in several ways. In public communication, communicators increase their reach while simultaneously reducing their interactivity. *Reach* refers to the number of people who could process a message (Gurak, 2001), and *interactivity* is the extent to which actions, especially messages, in a sequence relate to each other such that later actions relate to earlier actions (Rafaeli & Sudweeks, 1997). One of the earliest forms of public communication is storytelling (Gerbner, 1983; Fisher, 1987; Langellier & Peterson, 2004), and the storyteller speaks to a general audience. If the audience is small, such as when a grandparent tells a story to grandchildren, audience members may interrupt the storyteller with questions, and the storyteller and an audience member may develop a short episode in front of the remaining audience. Indeed, the storyteller should change the telling of the story to better suit the interests of the audience. The audience and the storyteller jointly construct the story because of the social interaction. Because there is a small audience, there is limited reach and some interactivity.

The storytelling example demonstrates feedback in an episode, and feedback is a type of interactivity. When a person pushes a key on a keyboard, when an image appears on the screen after pushing the key, and when the person looks at the image and pushes another key, there is interactivity. Such a sequence can go on for some time, and there can be the perception that a person and the computer are interacting or "communicating".

The development of feedback and coherence between any two or more participants becomes less likely as the audience size increases. A speaker does not interact with an audience but may interact with audience members as a separate performance for the remaining members. In many public communication situations, interaction will be limited to a separate "question and answer" session, and even in those situations, developing interactivity between the speaker and each audience member is unlikely.

Simply adding any people to a dyad can change communication in significant ways. If two people have been communicating and a third person enters the space, the members of the dyad have some difficult choices. On the one hand, whoever is speaking can continue to speak to the original member of the dyad and exclude the new person. Alternatively, the speaker can address the new person and ignore the other original member of the dyad. Finally, the speaker could change the language and style of presentation or even the topic to include the new person. This third choice, of necessity, will become more general and abstract than what was going on before the third party entered. The triad may negotiate a relationship that admits greater specificity, but the conversation could go on at the new level of generality. These challenges are ones of constructing relationships and episodes in a *diverse social space* (Meyrowitz, 1985).

The awareness of an audience may heighten *face concerns*. Face is the perception one person has of how others perceive him/herself. Face becomes a concern when there is uncertainty about how others perceive him/her, or when there is a perception that others might be perceiving him/her contrary to the way he/she wanted. People want others to see them positively, and they present themselves in such a way as to maintain or enhance their own dignity or self-respect (Goffman, 1967). Heightened face concerns can turn simple disagreements into intractable conflict (Folger, Poole, & Stutman, 2018). Communicators may recognize constituents or members of a personal network who are not present in a dyad as people who will hold them accountable for their actions, and communicators will act in such a way as to conform to those expectations (Rubin & Brown, 1975; Lewicki, Barry, & Saunders, 2010). What may start as open and responsive messaging may become dramatic and dominating when any communicator develops concerns for how an audience might see him/her.

Small group communication is the most complicated of the three levels. There are periods where a communicator addresses the group as audience, talks to the group as fellow members of a collective, and addresses specific others as the member of a separate relationship. The oscillation between dyadic, public, and dyadic performed for an audience magnifies the challenges of reach, interactivity, a diverse social space, and face.

Telephone (TEL)

Bell Telephone was born in 1877 and became American Telephone and Telegraph (AT&T) in 1885. AT&T might have owned all the telephones in America by 1919 (Davie, 2012). AT&T became a regional company, Southwestern Bell, when it lost its protected monopoly status in 1983. By 2005 Southwestern Bell had purchased most of the old Bell regional companies and changed its name back to AT&T. Another regional company, Bell Atlantic, began buying smaller companies in the eastern half of the United States. In 2000, it merged with GTE Corporation, the largest independent contractor in America, and became Verizon Company. China, the world's largest country provides fixed phone service to its population through state owned regional companies associated with China Telcom Corporation, and mobile service through state owned China Mobile. Today, AT&T and Verizon have the largest US mobile phone networks, but China Mobile has the largest number of subscribers (Davie, 2012).

There have been rapid advances in technology from telephone operators to rotary phones (1920s) to pushbutton phones (1960s) to mobile phones (1990s) and smart phones (2000s). The introduction of mobile and smart phones has had a profound change in how we communicate. Mobility was possible because of changes in phone systems and the use of the Internet. *Mobility* means that we no longer communicate from place-to-place, but now communicate from person-to-person, and smart phones add text, email, and social networking abilities allowing for hyperconnectivity (Rainie & Wellman, 2012). Mobility means people can contact nearly anyone at any time, and this potential connectivity can have the positive and negative effects later chapters explore.

One feature of moving from FtF to TEL is that there is a potential loss in signals. *Signal capacity* is the ability of a technology to provide phenomena others can access. Other ways to refer to this feature are as bandwidth, types of media, or richness. In electronics, bandwidth is the range of frequency variations a given communication medium has the capacity to accommodate (Williams, 1987). McLuhan (1964) placed technology along a continuum from hot media to cool media depending on the number of senses involved and the potential for personalization and interaction. The sharpest contrast was between oral FtF communication, very cool, and print, very hot because it involves only sight and standardized text. A dyadic TEL oral conversation is hotter than FtF with all nonverbal signals available, but a TEL oral conversation is cooler than exchanging several voice mail messages. Similarly, Daft and Lengel placed technology along a continuum from lean media to rich media, and their classification added the extent to which media use involved natural language and the potential for multiple cues (Daft & Lengel, 1986; Lengel & Daft, 1988). Fewer signals mean fewer phenomena are available to access as cues. Small group and dyadic FtF communication are richer than print or email.

The capacity of traditional phones limited themselves to features of the voice. Speech communication refers to messages involving voice and language (Dance, 1967). Voice can vary in many ways such as by pitch, rate, and volume, and communicators often access the nonverbal aspects, the non-language features, as social cues. Speech communication has the unique property of carrying potentially different levels of cues simultaneously with little effort or mindfulness because of the use of voice with language. The choice of language is important, but communicators are more likely to believe the nonverbal cues when communicators perceive they contradict the verbal ones (Burgoon, Buller, & Woodall, 1996).

Today's mobile TELs include video telephony, the ability to see each other as well as hear each other with applications such as Skype and FaceTime. Technologically, these are extensions of earlier efforts at teleconferencing. However, the quality and cost of personal video telephony vary, and many prefer that others not see them. A sizable minority of Americans prefers to text than to call (Smith, 2011). Although the latest

TELs have increased signal capacity, people choose to limit the types of signals they make available to others. Mobility may bring hyper connectivity, but people choose to limit the types of signals for the connections.

Writing and Print (WP)

Language is the systematic use of signs or symbols (Dance & Larson, 1972). Language represents phenomena in a way that does not require the direct experience of phenomena. Initial efforts represented phenomena as pictures, and then as symbols that were analogous to phenomena. Analog coding still exists, but the more popular codes are those that represent sounds using a specific language. That is, a person experiences phenomena, makes sense of it and codes what is unknown into what is known, codes the perceptions into some symbolic form, and codes the symbols into sounds. A phonetic alphabet codes the sounds into a visual form to represent the sounds. Many refer to digital coding as coding phenomena into representations that bear no physical resemblance to phenomena (Watzlawick, Beavin, Jackson, 1967). Symbol use becomes systematic by developing phonetic, semantic, and syntactic rules. A specific language describes the symbolic practice for the members of a culture.

People still write handwritten notes and letters to each other. Handwritten messages are more personal, and so the handwritten form is more about social cues than technical ones. President Barack Obama wrote a handwritten apology to an art historian, the White House staff offered the offended scholar an electronic version of the note, but she selected the original handwritten letter (Schuessler, 2014). Writing a handwritten note can provide as much pleasure for the writer as the reader, but people create many excuses for not writing a note by hand (Shepard, 2002). However, 45 of the 50 United States have adopted standards for education that no longer require instruction in handwriting (Shapiro & Voison, 2013).

Print improved the portability of language, and members of a culture could preserve representations of phenomena more easily from one generation to the next. Print also improved the reach of communicators, and the period from 1600-1750 included the first books, newspapers, and periodicals. McLuhan's analysis of print (1964) focused on the precise ways communicators placed symbols on a page and the ways communicators attempted to conform to a prescribed grammar. He claimed a culture dominated by any hot media, especially print, encouraged specialization, centralization, and nationalism while an oral culture was more flexible and tribal. He saw computer use as cool media, and he argued that society would become a global village.

Electronic Mail (EML)

In the 1960s, the US Defense Department began a project to link computers, military personnel, and researchers. The Advanced Research Project Agency Network, ARAPNET, became the Internet in the 1980s. At first, researchers dominated the use of the network, and they were the first users of electronic mail. Originally, EML use consisted of attachments and short typed messages similar to print. Using EML and other electronic messages have largely displaced written or printed communication.

Although today's EML can include nonlinguistic visuals, sounds, and animations, most EML is *text only*. Furthermore, EML use is more likely to conform to the use of more formal print than text messages, which are more similar to oral messages (Baron, 2008). Communicators face the challenges of providing signals in their EML they intend as social cues because they are limited to constructing a message using only text in a relatively formal linguistic manner (Freeman, 2009). Although poets can use language this way, most communicators are not poets.

TEL is a way to overcome space limitations, and EML is a way to overcome time limitations. *Synchronous communication* refers to communicators attempting to enact episodes during the same time, and *asynchronous communication* refers to communicators attempting to enact episodes at different times. Communicators can use TEL in an asynchronous way such as exchanging a series of voice mail messages, and they can use EML in a synchronous way by scheduling a time to exchange several messages. Most communicators use TEL as synchronous communication and EML as asynchronous. The lag between messages is an attribute of asynchronous communication, and so, all forms of asynchronous use of technology are leaner technology because of the delayed feedback. Exchanging traditional snail mail letters had even greater delays.

Baym (2010) contrasted synchronous and asynchronous uses of technology and concluded that the advantages of one become the disadvantages of the other. Synchronous use can enhance a sense of immediacy and intimacy similar to communicating FtF with a few people. Asynchronous use allows people in larger groups to communicate with each other, and asynchronous communication has the distinct advantage of allowing people more time to be strategic in their messaging and presentations of themselves.

The asynchronous use of technology can challenge the development of coherence in an episode. Postings on a blog or fan forum are often a reaction to the previous posting and exhibit little reference to the overall flow of messages. At times, such postings do enact an episode between a few of the participants in front of the remaining members of a site. Although people can use EML to provide news to many people, most EML messages are exchanges between a few people. Most EML users develop some sense of coherence by being more mindful of the history of previous messages between those people.

Private Electronic Communication (PEC)

Private electronic communication refers to communication between members of a restricted dyad or small group using contemporary electronic communication. PEC includes private chat, all forms of instant messaging, and text messaging. Most uses of PEC are in real time, and there is the expectation that responses will have only a short lag. Users tend to limit themselves to short text only messages, but they use language in inventive ways suggesting more oral messages than print ones (Baron, 2008). People use text messages for instrumental functions such as coordinating tasks and for relational maintenance (Kelly, Keaton, Becker, Cole, Littleford, & Rothe, 2012). Managing complex issues such as conflict can be difficult with such a lean technology (Lengel & Daft, 1988), and expectations for use can become a source of conflict (Duran, Kelly, & Rotaru, 2011).

Users can *store and replicate* PEC, similar to other new technologies (Baym, 2010). Furthermore, another user can edit the messages before reproducing them. Although we all seem to recognize this feature, we often seem to forget others could access hard drives, voice recorders, and the memory cards on our phones for legal matters. This is especially common when it comes to business matters (Freeman, 2009). Although storage and replication may assist memory of important PEC messages or episodes, law enforcement officials are pressuring legislators to require telephone carriers to store text messages for two years (McCullagh, 2012).

Public Electronic Communication (BEC)

Public electronic communication refers to those technologies in which communicators create interactions with an audience. BEC includes interactions on message boards, blogs, mailing lists, social network sites (SNS), and other online communities. Although some of these technologies allow private chat, instant messaging or email between a few participants, the defining feature of these technologies is that interaction occurs while others watch or listen.

Social media (SM) is another term for BEC, but it is important to understand that the "social" in these expressions is an audience and the opportunity to create messages for an audience (see Treem, Daily, Pierce &

Biffl, 2016). There is little communication on SM with most activity being postings of updates, pictures, or comments (Hampton, Goulet, Rainie, & Purcell, 2011). Most postings in the message streams on Twitter are about personal or social topics rather than sports or politics (Naaman, Boase, & Lai, 2010). However, most SM members lurk, preferring to watch or listen rather than post any type of message (Nonnecke & Preece, 2000). SM messaging may stimulate communication in other ways or no communication at all.

More people used SM in 2018 than in past years, but there were some surprising new trends (Smith & Anderson, 2018). Two-thirds of adults 18 and older use Facebook, and around half of all adults access it on a daily basis. However, 73% of all adults access YouTube, and 29% of all adults do so several times per day. Younger adults are heavy users of Snapchat and Instagram, and women are more active on social media in general than men. A minority of Americans, 27%, use Twitter, and this is only up 3% since 2014.

BEC has multiple functions, and some functions are more about information than communication. One analysis of SM described seven functions (Kietzmann, Hermkens, McCarthy, & Sivestre, 2011). *Identity* is the extent to which users reveal themselves or construct a role in a particular way. *Sharing* is the extent to which users can exchange, receive, and distribute content. *Presence* is the extent to which users can indicate their availability for connection, either in the digital or non-digital worlds. *Reputation* is the extent to which users can learn the standing of others within the network; this typically occurs through some kind of index reflecting desirable or undesirable activity. *Groups* is the extent to which members can form communities or sub communities within the site. Members created the WELL in the 1980s as one of the first online communities (Rheingold, 1993). *Relationships* refers to the extent users can create multiple but distinct relationships using the SNS (e.g., contacts, friends, direct links or indirect links). The relationships function also means that users exchange different content in different relationships. Finally, *conversation* is the extent to which users exchange messages using BEC. Only the last function is obviously a communication function, but conversation may occur along with other functions. However, simply posting a message does not mean conversation or communication. A sequence of seven Twitter messages from seven unique sources may be about creating or reinforcing an identity, sharing, or improving a reputation.

An additional function is *performance or expression*. Users post messages they would not create in other communication technologies. The message content or style is dramatic and, the users often do not want or care for a response. It is as if they are taking the stage to perform or "top" the performance of someone else. Some have designed sites inviting people to collectively create content and develop a creative community (Atkinson, 2014). Performance can be part of identity and sharing, and it can lead to conversation.

BEC technologies have greater reach than other technologies. On the average, people have over 600 people in their combined communication networks, but most of these links are to acquaintances and professionals (Hampton et al, 2011). Nearly 35% of American adults use at least one SNS, and SNS users tend to have more combined communication network ties generally than non-SNS users (Hampton, et al, 2011). The average number of "friends" among the 721 million users of Facebook is around 200, but 50% have 100 or less (Backstrom, 2011), and people have around 400 outgoing ties and 100 incoming ties on Twitter (Takhteyev, Gruzd, & Wellman, 2012). In other words, many people are creating messages for large audiences.

Table 3.1

Characteristics of Human Communication Technology

De-massification	The extent to which (a) the producer of a message creates different forms of the message to appeal to the diversity of the audience or the producer of a message creates different forms of the same message for each person in an audience attempting to create the perception that the message was personal, (b) the producer of a message designs the message for a separate niche of an audience rather than the commonalities across niches, or (c) the receiver controls access to content rather than producer
Diverse Social Spaces	The extent of social heterogeneity among communicators, such as when one communicator attempts to fashion a message for both the communicator's high school friend and the communicator's supervisor at work.
Face Concerns	The extent to which communicator's may be sensitive to how others view them using a technology.
Interactivity	The extent to which people can develop message sequences such that later messages relate to earlier messages; the extent to which users can develop feedback and coherent episodes with a technology.
Mobility	The extent to which users can communicate in different spaces using a technology.
Para-social Relationships	The extent to which people perceive they are involved in a social relationship with another even though there has been no interaction between those people and the other.
Reach	The number of people who can access and process other people's messages and communication using a technology.
Signal Capacity or Richness	The extent to which people can make various signals available to others to use as cues with a technology.

Social Presence	The extent to which people perceive they are engaged in the interaction with another person or are engaged in interaction with a technology similar to those perceptions of involvement with another person.
Storage and Replicability	The extent to which people can record and reproduce their own communication or the communication of others with a technology.
Synchronicity	The extent to which people can communicate at similar or different times using a technology.

Because of mobility, this also means that many people are carrying their audiences with them. This sensitivity to an audience can influence how people are communicating in other technologies. A person will change the way they will communicate if he/she has alerted their audience to an impending FtF communication and if he/she anticipates reporting on it later. Carrying your audience with you can increase face concerns, something that Chapter 5 will explore more fully.

The audience can strike back. In such a case, one audience member may post something expressing a particularly extreme or critical attitude about the creator of an SNS site, and other audience members may follow by creating similar messages. How can the creator of the site respond, and to whom should he/she respond? Very often, the site creator constructs another public message, and the audience members react or respond again. Bullying or shaming can have tragic consequences such as suicide, and a later chapter will explore competent and incompetent online behaviors more fully.

Instances of bullying or shaming challenge traditional notions of communication, interpersonal communication, and public or mass communication (Polkosky, 2008). If Kim announces her engagement to Juan on her SNS, receives many congratulatory responses, and thanks everyone in a single post for their good wishes, is this communication?

What if she provides more details about the wedding in her second post, and a few people respond? Have she and just those few people been developing an episode and communicating? There is a sequence of her postings to all followed by several comments from others followed by her postings to all, and so on, but is this an episode? From the perspective I described in Chapter 2, these sequences are examples of human communication in a group, but there may be a very large number of members who just observe after their initial message. As noted in the first paragraph, the few people who develop such an episode are more likely to communicate in another way than to continue such an episode using BEC.

Contemporary Information Technologies (CIP)

This category refers to the digitalization of old technologies such as television programming and to the newer technologies associated with the Internet such as websites and YouTube. The primary characteristic of this technology is that users act as consumers, processing the information available to them for a variety of functions. The old models of broadcast technology distinguished between the producer, content, and the audience, but contemporary thinking focuses on the meaning people make of content in their interactions (Anderson & Meyer, 1988; Schoening & Anderson, 1995). Although individuals can process information alone, much of their information processing involves others as part of communication practices.

Traditional definitions of mass communication describe how people attempt to create and distribute messages to large segments of a population. Traditional mass communication hardware includes, newspapers, periodicals, radio, and television. Not only has the technology changed but so has the "mass" audience. National television broadcast networks attempted to reach everyone in a given country who owned a television. Cable television took viewers away from these networks by including channels that appealed to various niche audiences. Broadcast and re-broadcast programming online appeal to an even more limited audience.

Blogs, including personal, news, political, government, and commercial, appeal to more limited viewers who may view them only as needed. Most activity on SM and SNS is the creator of the site updating material for an audience. What was once "mass communication" has gone through a process of *de-massification* (Rogers, 1986). The producers of the content have come to realize they have the same limitations as any communicator. One communicator makes available multiple signals, but others access them as cues and make sense of them.

People tend to personalize their use of information technologies in two distinct ways. *Social presence* is the perception that one's actions are part of interaction with another person even if one's actions do not involve another person (Short, Williams, & Christie, 1976). The idea is that when you process information or engage in some activities on some websites, computer games, computers, or televisions, the interaction has a similar feel as if you were communicating with a person. People can develop psycho-social reactions to features of contemporary technology, and manufacturers and programmers employ designers to improve the human factors elements in their products or services (Reeves & Nass, 1998). Since we tend to anthropomorphize our technology and treat technology as social actors, people's interactions with computers can suggest how people communicate with each other (Nass, 2010). Although people may perceive one technological experience as having more social presence than another, a person could also perceive other people as having more social presence than others.

A *parasocial relationship* is the perception that a person may have a social relationship with another person even though there has been little or no communication between them. What has happened is that one person knows so much about another, the person may feel as if they have a relationship with the other. Initially, this referred to what happens when a person reads several novels about a fictional character or sees so many episodes of a television program, the person has the feeling they have a relationship with the characters or celebrities (Horton & Wohl, 1956). Today, people can have the sense of parasocial relationships with websites, the fans on a fan-site, the other friends on a SNS, and the characters in a computer game (Hartman, 2008). Social presence and parasocial relationships suggest some are substituting technological interaction and textual interaction for social interaction.

Technology Effects

Linear cause-effect approaches dominated the earliest empirical technology research from 1930-1970 (Rogers, 1986). Today, many have challenged the notions that technology could be the direct cause of any "effects". This section explains common psychosocial phenomena research associated with technology or technology use.

The explanations are broad since later chapters provide more details on the factors.

New technology relates to how people *use other technology*. Technologies may complement each other or displace each other (Ruppel & Burke, 2015), but older technologies may re-emerge in surprising ways. Reading something on Facebook (CIT) could lead to more TEL and, in turn to more FtF, an example of complementarity. Using an e-reader or tablet to read is an obvious way new CIP might have displaced print. Sometimes, people discard the older technologies such as taped music or videos. In other cases, people can reify older technologies. Although penmanship is very poor today and most American schools have dropped formal instruction in handwriting from their curriculum, fountain pens have become works of art and collectables as any Fahrney's, Fountain Pen Hospital, or Levenger's catalogs will demonstrate.

The new technologies *decentralize authority and power*. Decentralization is a process of more and more people making more and more decisions on their own. Deregulation of HCT industries should have led to more decentralization, but deregulation has been uneven in reducing the power of a few organizations to control a market sector (Castells, 2010). However, the new technology enables workers in an organization to communicate and coordinate outside the formal chain of command. In politics, the new technologies enable more groups to form independently and bring pressure to their governments. News organizations now rely on ordinary citizens to text, tweet, and capture video about important events. Young people can use technology to work around parental control. Decentralization puts everyone on the same level, and there is greater personal responsibility to act appropriately and effectively. Individual responsibilities and mindfulness are the central themes of this book.

Social evolution involves the development of strong personal relationships and groups with people acting together for common purposes. Technology may encourage tribalism by providing a means for people to screen out different opinions and ideas and associate only with those who reinforce already held beliefs and values (Bishop, 2008). However, technology may provide the means for greater civic engagement. The nature of community has changed (Wellman, 2001), and those with greater Internet use tend to have greater civic engagement than those who use the Internet less (Smith, Lehman, Scholzman, Verba, & Brady, 2009). Those with greater civic engagement also have been wealthier than those with less (Smith et al, 2009).

The digital divide originally referred to the gap between those who had access to the new technologies and those who did not, and many argued that the limited access would amplify already existing *economic inequalities*. One of the earliest studies demonstrated that greater diffusion of news improved the knowledge of those who already knew something about the topic, but not others (Tichenor, Donohue, & Olien, 1970). Those others did not have the economic means to access the increased news. Recent research paints a different picture, however. Differences in knowledge were less about access than about public policy, uses of technologies, and the skills of those using the technologies (Howard, Bush, & Sheets, 2010; Wei & Hindman, 2011).

Deskilling is a process where technologies reduce or eliminate the value of older skills and occupations. In the United States, most workers have had jobs emphasizing HIP or communication skills since the mid 1950s (Porat, 1978). Worldwide, pockets of information and communication skilled workers can connect to compete with more traditional organizations (Castells, 2010). Manual labor has moved to poorer or developing economies. Those with the appropriate information and communication skills have greater social mobility while those without these skills will fall further and further behind. Communication competence and digital literacy are the focus of a later chapter.

The traditional notion of *overload* is that it happens when a system is receiving more information than it can process (Miller, 1978). Input exceeds capacity. For HIP, *overload* means people are enacting and trying to make sense of more data than they can process without error. People may want more information associated with a fear of missing out (FOMO), emotional or health problems, or simply because of their perceptions of a task, and their HIP skills, standards for excellence, or organization of work may limit their capacity. Consistently being overloaded can lead to the death of a system. Stress is one way people perceive overload. Without supportive communication, stress can lead to burnout and severe health problems (Sarason, Sarason, & Pierce, 1990).

Different uses of technology can increase overload but also provide supportive communication. The new technologies allow an increase in the receiver's ability to control access, a sort of "volume control" (Baron, 2008), but many people spend hours just scanning and reviewing messages to catch up (Rainie & Wellman, 2012). Alternatively, the most active SNS members report receiving more social support than others (Hampton et al, 2011).

Privacy is about the ability of individuals to control their personal boundaries, especially information about themselves. Privacy means individuals have control over what others know about them. Hyperconnectivity brings convenience but can challenge privacy. A marketer keeps a record of purchases or "likes" and shares them with other marketers, and soon you receive messages about the availability or sale of similar items or services. You can track where your friends are geographically, SNSs reveal the personal networks of those attached to the site, and you can meet people more conveniently. But, how comfortable are you knowing others are developing a personal profile of you based on your purchases or browsing history? Are you uneasy knowing many others will know where you are at all times? Do you want to be always connected, always on? Expectations and standards for privacy are changing (Rainie & Wellman, 2012).

Personal and psychological development relies on creating and sustaining a network of meaningful personal relationships. The new HCT can connect people as never before, and the technology may allow more hyperpersonal relationships because people could be more thoughtful and direct in an asynchronous environment (Walther, 1996). The new technologies may sacrifice depth of relationships for breadth, and people may become lonely while being more connected. People average just over 20 people in their close personal network with 7 or less within the most intimate network, and people do use the Internet to maintain these relationships (Boase, Horrigan, Wellman & Rainie, 2006). On the other hand, people have lost one very close tie over the period when Internet use skyrocketed (Brahsears, 2011; McPhereson, Smith-Lovin, & Brahsears, 2006). People may use HCT to obtain more social support (Hampton, et al, 2011), but people may also be more alone together (Turkle, 2011).

Explaining the Effects

How does one explain the various effects described above? There are several approaches and each approach comes with different assumptions about technology and humans (Barnes, 2003; Rogers, 1986). More recent approaches consider how humans use technology, and these approaches tend to focus more on process than effects. I will describe six explanations.

Technological determinism explains technology as the basic cause of social impacts. Hot media lead to nationalism and cool media lead to a global village (McLuhan, 1964). People cannot use less rich media to manage conflict well because of the characteristics of the technology that make them less rich (Daft & Lengel, 1986). If there are problems with privacy, then the technology made people do it. Softer versions of this approach claim that technology is a necessary factor to explaining impacts, but that other factors are important as well (Chandler, 1996; Rogers, 1986).

Social determinism explains the relationships between technology and social impacts as more a function of society and culture instead of technology. Humans are naturally social and tribal (Wilson, 2012), and so any sense of tribalism associated with technology is just more of the same. Different cultures will do different things with the same technology. If there are problems, the culture made me do it.

Social construction approaches describe the ways people create their own circumstances, and much of this happens through communication. Technology is not more or less rich, but rather people *perceive* technology as more or less rich. These perceptions come from talking to people in a personal network, and so people match technology to tasks based on the communication around them (Fulk, Schmitz, & Seinfeld, 1990). The fixed features of technology are less important than our use of technology and how we talk about our use. If there are problems, my friends and I created them in our communication.

A *realist approach* focuses on the choices people make about technology. Technology is not good or bad, but the way people choose to use technology may lead to different outcomes. When people are more mindful of their technological choices, they are more likely to choose more effective uses than when they are mindless (Timmerman, 2002). Although various technology may have different qualities and although my communication with others influences my choices and use, ultimately, my choices influence the outcomes more directly than anything else.

A *media ecology* approach recognizes how the interaction of technological, social, and psychological factors creates an environment for nonlinear outcomes (Barnes, 2008). Organizations might adopt a new HCT because they believe it may improve effectiveness. This adoption may lead to short term gains in efficiency but ultimately lead to long-term vulnerabilities in social relationships because the specific HCT weakened communication competence (Salem & Gratz, 1989). People make a Faustian bargain when they adopt technology (Barnes, 2008), and people do not anticipate the undesirable outcomes (Rogers, 1986).

The *complexity of human communication* is an approach that explains changes in technology as changes in the parameters of communication practices. Recall that communication is an iterative, recursive and potentially multiplicative process (Salem, 2013). Communication practices consist of regular behaviors and the rules for their performance. The performance of these practices may lead to the accumulation of small changes that lead to large changes.

When people adopt new technology, they change the circumstances for performing older practices, and they may adapt older practices or develop newer practices. However, there could be catastrophic outcomes. Technology use can act as a *catalyst* speeding current processes and creating multiplier effects. Aiken (2016) refers to the multiplier effect triggered by the newer technologies as the cyber effect. Things could get much better or very worse. Someone who has a healthy self-concept will use HCT to maintain older relationships and develop many diverse new ones, but someone who is afraid of others will use HCT to further isolate himself or herself and communicate only with those who have similar opinions.

The approach I take in this book is a combination of complexity and realist approaches. If there are problems, it is because people have not considered how using HCT with particular practices might lead to these problems. People need to be more mindful of their HCT choices because there is the potential for catalysis that triggers the cyber effect.

References

Aiken, M. (2016) *The cyber effect*. New York: Spiegel & Grau.

Anderson, J, A, & Meyer, T. P. (1988). *Mediated communication: A social action perspective*. Newbury Park, CA: Sage.

Arthur, W. B. (2009). *The nature of technology: What it is and how it evolves*. NY: Free Press.

Atkinson, S. (2014). The performative functions of dramatic communities: Conceptualizing audience engagement in transmedia fiction. *International Journal of Communication, 8*, 2201-2219.

Backstrom, L. (2011). The anatomy of Facebook. *Facebook*. Available at http://www.facebook.com/notes/facebook-data-team/anatomy-of-facebook/10150388519243859.

Barnes, S. B. (2008). Understanding social media from the media ecological perspective. In E. Konijn, S. Utz, M. Tanis, & S. B. Barnes (Eds.), *Mediated interpersonal communication* (pp. 14-33). New York: Routledge.

Baron, N. S. (2008). *Always on: Language in an online and mobile world*. New York: Oxford University Press.

Baym, N. K. (2010). *Personal connections in a digital age*. Malden, MA: Polity Press.

Bishop, B. (2008). *The big sort: Why the clustering of like-minded America is tearing us apart*. Boston: Houghton Mifflin.

Boase, J., Horrigan, J., Wellman, B., & Rainie, L. (2006, July). *The strength of Internet ties*. Report for the Pew Internet and American Life Project, Washington, DC. Retrieved from http://www.pewinternet.org/Reports/2006/The-Strength-of-Internet-Ties.aspx.

Brashears, M. E. (2011). Small networks and high isolation? A reexamination of American discussion groups. *Social Networks, 33*, 331-341.

Breem, J. W., Daily, S. L., Pierce, C. S., & Biffl, D. (2016). What we are talking about when we talk about social media: A framework for study. *Sociology Compass, 10/9*, 768-784.

Burgoon, J. K., Buller, D. B., & Woodall, W. G. (1996). *Nonverbal communication: The unspoken dialogue* (2nd ed.). New York: McGraw-Hill.

Castells, M. (2010). *The rise of the network society* (2nd ed.). Oxford: Wiley-Blackwell.

Daft, R. L., & Lengel, R, H. (1986). Organizational information requirements: Media richness and structural design. *Management Science, 32*, 554-571.

Dance, F. E. X. (1967). Toward a theory of human communication. In F. E. X. Dance (Ed.), *Human communication: Original essays* (pp. 288-309). New York: Holt, Rinehart, & Winston.

Dance, F. E. X., & Larson, C. E. (1972). *Speech communication: Concepts and behavior*. New York: Holt, Rinehart, & Winston.

Davie, W. R. (2012). Telephony. In A. E. Grant & J. E. Meadows (Eds.), *Communication technology update and fundamentals* (13th ed.) (pp. 251-264). New York: Focal Press.

Duran, R. L., Kelly, L., & Rotaru, T. (2011). Mobile phones in romantic relationships and the dialectic of autonomy versus connection. *Communication Quarterly, 59*(1), 19-36.

Fisher, W. R. (1987). *Human communication as narration: Toward a philosophy of reason, value, and action.* Columbia: University of South Carolina Press.

Folger, J. P., Poole, M. S., & Stutman, R. K. (2018). *Working through conflict: Strategies for relationships, groups, and organizations* (8th ed.). Boston, MA: Pearson.

Freeman, J. (2009). *The tyranny of e-mail: The four-thousand year journey to your inbox.* New York: Scribner.

Fulk, J., Schmitz, J., & Steinfeld, C. (1990). A social influence model of technology use. In J. Fulk, & C. Steinfeld, (Eds.). *Organizations and communication technology* (pp. 117-140). Newbury Park, CA: Sage.

Gerbner, G. (1983). The importance of being critical - in one's own fashion. *Journal of Communication, 33.* 355-362.

Goffman, E. (1967). *Interaction ritual: Essays on face-to-face behavior.* Garden City, NJ: Doubleday.

Gurak, L. L. (2001). *Cyberliteracy: Navigating the Internet with awareness.* New Haven, CT: Yale University Press.

Hampton, K. N., Goulet, L. S., Rainie, L., & Purcell, K. (2011). *Social networking and our lives.* Washington, DC: Pew Research Center. Retrieved from http://www.pewinternet.org/Reports/2011/Technology-and-social-networks.aspx.

Hartmann, T (2008). Parasocial interaction and paracommunication with new media characters. In E. A., Konijin, S., Utz, M., Tanis, & S. B. Barnes (Eds.), *Mediated interpersonal communication* (pp. 177-199). New York: Routledge.

Hoag, C. (2012, 24 November). Some states buck the trend and preserve penmanship. *USA Today,* Retrieved at http://www.usatoday.com/story/news/nation/2012/11/24/california-cursive-penmanship-technology/1724263.

Horton, D. R., & Wohl, R. R. (1956). Mass communication and para-social interaction: Observations on intimacy at a distance" *Psychiatry, 19*(3), 215–229.

Howard, P. N., Busch, L., & Sheets, P. (2010). Comparing digital divides: Access and social inequality in Canada and the United States. *Canadian Journal of Communication, 35*, 109-128.

Kelly, L., Keaten, J. A., Becker, B., Cole, J. Littleford, L. & Rothe, B. (2012). "It's the American lifestyle!": An investigation of text messaging by college students. *Qualitative Research Reports in Communication, 13*(1), 1-9.

Kietzmann, J. H., Hermkens, K., McCarthy, I. P., & Silvestre, B. S. (2011). Social media? Get serious! Understanding the functional building blocks of social media. *Business Horizons, 54*, 241-251.

Langellier, K. M., & Peterson, E. E. (2004). *Storytelling in daily life: Performing narrative*. Philadelphia, PA: Temple University Press.

Lengel, R. H., & Daft, R. L. (1988). The selection of communication media as an executive skill. *The Academy of Management Executive, 2*, 225-232.

Lewicki, R. J., Barry, B., & Saunders, D. M. (2010). *Negotiation* (6th ed.). Boston, MA: McGraw Hill Irwin.

McCullagh, D. (2012, December 3). Cops to Congress: We need logs of Americans' text messages. *CNET News*. Available at http://news.cnet.com/8301-13578_3-57556704-38/cops-to-congress-we-need-logs-of-americans-text-messages.

McLuhan, M. (1964). *Understanding media: The extensions of man*. Cambridge, MA: MIT Press.

McPherson, M., Smith-Lovin, L., & Brashears, M. E. (2006). Social isolation in America: Changes in core discussion networks over two decades. *American Sociological Review, 71*, 353-375.

Meyrowitz. J. (1985). *No sense of place: The impact of electronic media on social behavior*. NY: Oxford University Press.

Miller, J. G. (1978). *Living systems*. NY: McGraw Hill.

Naaman, M., Boase, J., & Lai, C. (2010). Is it really about me? Message content in social awareness streams. Is it really about me? *Proceedings of the 2010 Association for Computing Machinery Conference on Computer Supported Cooperative Work*, Savannah, GA, pp 189–192.

Nass, C. I. (2010). *The man who lied to his laptop: What machines teach us about human relationships*. New York: Current.

Nonnecke, B, & Preece, J. (2000). Lurker demographics: Counting the silent. *Proceedings of the Special Interest Group Computer Human Interaction*, 73-80.

Polkosky, M. D. (2008). Machines as mediators: The challenge of technology for interpersonal communication theory and research. In E. A., Konijin, S., Utz, M., Tanis, & S. B. Barnes (Eds.), *Mediated interpersonal communication* (pp. 34-57). New York: Routledge.

Porat, M. U. (1978). Global implications of the information society. *Journal of Communication, 28*, 70-79.

Rafaeli, S., & Sudweeks, F. (1997). Networked interactivity. *Journal of Computer Mediated Communication, 2*(4). Available at http://jcmc.indiana.edu/vol2/issue4/rafaeli.sudweeks.html.

Rainie, L., & Wellman, B. (2012). *Networked: The new social operating system*. Cambridge, MA: MIT Press.

Reeves, B., & Nass, C. (1996). *The media equation: How people treat computers, television, and new media like real people and places*. New York: Cambridge University Press.

Rheingold, H. (1993). *The virtual community: Homesteading on the virtual frontier*. Reading, MA: Addison-Wesley.

Rogers, E. M. 91986). *Communication technology: The new media in society*. New York: The Free Press.

Rubin, J. Z., & Brown, B. (1975). *The social psychology of bargaining and negotiation*. New York: Academic Press.

Ruppel, E. K., & Burke, T. J. (2015). Complementary channel use and the role of social competence. *Journal of Computer-Mediated Communication, 20*, 37-51.

Salem, P. J. (2013). *The complexity of human communication* (2nd ed.). Cresskill, NJ: Hampton Press.

Salem, P. J., & Gratz, R. D. (1989). Computer use and organizational effectiveness: The case of two intervening variables. *Management Communication Quarterly, 2*(3), 409-423.

Sarason, R., Sarason, I. G., & Pierce, G. R. (Eds.) (1990). *Social support: An interactional view*. New York: Wiley.

Schoening, G. T., & Anderson, J. A. (1995). Social action media studies: Foundational arguments and common premises. *Communication Theory, 5*(2), 93-116.

Schuessler, J. (2014, February 18). President Obama writes apology to art historian. *New York Times*. Retrieved from http://artsbeat.blogs.nytimes.com/2014/02/18/president-obama-writes-apology-to-art-historian/?_php=true&_type=blogs&_r=0

Shapiro, T. R., & Voison, S. L. (2013, April 4). Cursive handwriting disappearing from public schools. *The Washington Post*. Retrieved at http://www.washingtonpost.com/local/education/cursive-handwriting-disappearing-from-public-schools/2013/04/04/215862e0-7d23-11e2-a044-676856536b40_story.html.

Shepard, M. (2002). *The art of the handwritten note: A guide to reclaiming civilized communication*. New York: Broadway Books.

Smith, A. (2011). *Americans and text messaging*. Washington, DC: Pew Research Center. Retrieved from http://pewinternet.org/Reports/2011/Cell-Phone-Texting-2011.aspx.

Smith, A., & Anderson, M. (2018). *Social media use in 2018*. Report for the Pew Internet and American Life Project, Washington, DC. Retrieved from http://www.pewinternet.org/2018/03/01/social-media-use-in-2018.

Smith, A., Lehman Scholzman, K., Verba, S., & Brady, H. (2009, September). *The Internet and civic engagement*. Report for the Pew Internet and American Life Project, Washington, DC. Retrieved from http://www.pewinternet.org/Reports/2009/15--The-Internet-and-Civic-Engagement.aspx

Takhteyev, Y., Gruzd, A., & Wellman, B. (2012). Geography of Twitter networks. *Social Networks, 34,* 73-81.

Tichenor, P. J., Donohue, G. A., & Olien, C. N. (1970). Mass Media flow and differential growth in knowledge. *Public Opinion Quarterly, 34*(2), 159-170.

Timmerman, C. E. (2002). The moderating effect of mindlessness/mindfulness upon media richness and social influence explanations of organizational media use. *Communication Monographs, 69*(2), 111-131.

Turkle, S. (2011). *Alone together: Why we expect more of technology and less of each other*. New York: Basic Books.

Walther, J. B. (1996). Computer-mediated communication: Impersonal, interpersonal, and hyperpersonal interaction. *Communication Research, 23,* 3-43.

Watzlawick, P., Beavin, J., & Jackson, D. (1967). *Pragmatics of human communication*. New York: Norton.

Wei, L., & Hindman, D. B. (2011). Does the digital divide matter more? Comparing the effects of the new media and the old media use on education-based knowledge gap. *Mass Communication and Society, 14,* 216-235.

Wellman, B. (2001, October). *The persistence and transformation of community: From neighbourhood groups to social networks*. Report to the Law Commission of Canada. Retrieved from http://www.chass.utoronto.ca/~wellman/publications.

Williams, F. (1987). *Technology and communication behavior*. Belmont, CA: Wadsworth Publishing Co.

Wilson, E. O. (2012). *The social conquest of earth*. New York: Liveright Publishing Company.

Chapter Four: Adoption

The US Patent Office approved the first patent on a mobile phone in 1908. However, Motorola did not create the first walkie-talkie until 1940, and AT&T did not apply for a US patent for a "cellular mobile communication system" until 1972. A year later, on April 3, 1973, Martin Cooper of Motorola made the first handheld cellular call to Joel Engle at the Bell Labs.

By the early 1990s, people were using Short Messages Service (SMS) to text each other. Mobile phones became smartphones and added digital planners, email, and a variety of productivity applications. Today's mobile device includes a host of entertainment and lifestyle applications (apps) as well. One Nokia consultant told me employees began referring to the product as the "thing" in the mid 2000s. The most common estimate is that 85% of American adults (18 and older) and 75% of American teens (12-17 years old) now use mobile phones regularly (Lenhart, 2010; Smith, 2010; Ziclur, 2011).

Apple launched the iPhone in 2007. Apple sold 6.1 million units over the first five quarters (Apple, 2009) and 73.5 million units by the end of fiscal year 2010 – 14.1 million units in the last quarter alone (Kumpark, 2010). The iPhone may be the most successful launch of any technology in history.

Today's technology did not happen overnight. In fact, consumers often rejected earlier variations of these technologies. The first portable computer, the Osborne, failed in 1981, but Toshiba developed and marketed the first truly laptop computers just five years later. Apple's own Newton, one of the first personal digital assistants, never gained acceptance in the early 1990s, but Blackberry did a decade later. The Newton contained "Notes," "Names," and "Dates," and it had a touch screen similar to the iPhone.

Where does technology come from? Why does the public adopt some technologies instead of others? The purpose of this chapter is to explain the evolution of innovations and the innovation adoption process. Communication is central to both processes.

The Evolution of Innovations

The last chapter included a definition of technology as the way humans accomplish tasks and organize their activities. Technology includes using tangible artifacts such as tools, machines, and hardware, but it also includes using specific perceptions in specific ways. Different individuals enact different environments to create different technologies, and different individuals use different technologies to enact different environments to accomplish different tasks. Technology does not become technology until people frame it as technology and use it as technology. One person's technology is another person's junk.

Similarly, an innovation is something people perceive as new (Rogers, 2003). An innovation, just like any technology, can be an object, a practice, or an idea. One person's innovation can be another person's traditional way of doing things.

If the perception of an innovation is so arbitrary, how can one person investigate what another person thought was an innovation? Considering time helps. What has become routine was, at an earlier time, an innovation. What has become routine has become an adopted innovation. How did that innovation come about?

Genes

The evolution of ideas happens much like biological evolution. In biology, genes spur evolution. A gene is a string of chemicals, DNA, and the pattern provides biological information (Dawkins, 1995). A gene provides instructions for the creation of protein. Protein develops cells, cells connect to form organs, and organs connect to form a fully developed biological entity. The fully developed organisms are the carriers of genes, and if the biological forms can survive long enough to replicate their genes in some way, the genes will move onto the next generation.

Genes are *replicators* (Dawkins, 1989). That is, genes can copy themselves. However, they need some help from their hosts. Sexual activity is the primary way genes can replicate themselves, but the replication is often not exact. There is duplication, but there is some variation. All the members of the same family from the same biological parents do not have exactly the same genes.

Recombinations and mutations are ways this variation happens across a given species, but all variations are not helpful. Some variations lead to organisms that can adapt better, other variations develop organisms better fit for specific environments, and still other genes lead to organisms that quickly become extinct. Selection is the term for the winnowing of variations to those that are biologically fit. The species then retains the viable genes by reproducing them again, but with variation, and the variation-selection-retention cycle starts again.

There are three ways genes improve their chances for continued replication (Dawkins, 1989). *Fecundity* means the ability to make many copies, and when there are more copies, there are better chances of copies making it through selection. *Fidelity* refers to the ability of genes to reproduce with little or no variation, and greater fidelity improves the chances of the original genetic patterns. *Longevity* refers to the stability of genes over generations, meaning that the genes have found their way into circumstances that protect them from natural intruders like disease and predators.

One of the important discoveries of the last century was that interaction between organisms was a way to improve fitness and a way to spur transformation. The studies of nonlinear processes described how the intensity of interaction between units can lead to greater stability, transformation, or total dissolution of a system (Holland, 1995, 1998; Kauffman, 1993, 1995; Lorenz, 1996; Prigogine & Stengers, 1984). Small variations of any kind can have large consequences when any things are connected to each other.

Memes and Innovations

Chapter One ends with a description of how humans make information, and this description is consistent with the way genes replicate. Humans enact an environment with many possible explanations for what they have enacted (enactment and variation).

People make sense of this environment by framing it so that it "fits" what they already know (selection), and they integrate that information into their already-existing body of knowledge so they can use it again it (retention). Of course, the next use of this information to frame something new starts the cycle again.

A *meme* is another term for the smallest unit of information humans can create. Blackmore (1999) explained memes as follows:

> When you imitate someone else, something is passed on. This "something" can then be passed on again, and again, and so take on a life of its own. We might call this thing an idea, an instruction, a behavior, a piece of information . . . but if we are going to study it, we shall need to give it a name. Fortunately, there is a name. It is a meme. (p. 4).

She went on to contrast genes with memes. Genes are biological instructions stored in cells and passed on to another generation in reproduction, but memes include instructions for performing behaviors (replication rules), stored in brains, and passed on through imitation (Blackmore, 1999, p. 17). Genes and memes are both units of information, and both involve mapping and replication, but they are about different things, and they map and replicate in different ways.

Humans create memes as part of making sense, and so, humans create memes by framing. The framing involves a mapping what is known onto what is not known. This learning can happen through observation and imitation, but it can also happen through mutual cueing – communication. Coupling several memes together forms memeplexes, and innovations often begin as memeplexes.

Knowledge and innovations can spread throughout a social network similar to the ways a virus can spread, or a species can evolve. A meme can move throughout a culture more rapidly, become viral, today because of ICTs. The current use of meme is for a combination of text with some graphic or figure that goes viral.

There are several histories of major inventions of the last two centuries. Some people might have thought "great" individuals were responsible for these inventions, but historians have discovered that many people had similar ideas at nearly the same time, and all of them used other people's ideas to develop their own (Arthur, 2009; Basalla, 1988; Johnson, 2010). Furthermore, the pattern of development was similar to biological development with periods of variation, selection, and retention.

There were significant differences in how these stages functioned in the "made world" of inventions versus the natural world (Basalla, 1988; Zimm, 2000). However, there are initial periods with many choices of any type of technology, followed by a winnowing of alternatives, and leading to new generations of the surviving technologies. Think of your new computer OS as a product of memetic evolution!

Individuals need time to develop ideas, but they also need communication that helps form ideas and supports developing ideas (Johnson, 2010). There may be several older ideas and competing ideas that lead to the development of an innovation, but people need to be connected to those other ideas to make innovation possible.

Innovations happen in conversations between different people excited about new ideas. This communication can happen over a conference table, online as part of a project, or over coffee between classes. Bill Hewlett and David Packard met each other as students at Stanford in 1936, they communicated with each other after graduation, and two years later they moved into the same apartment to work on electronic equipment – the start of HP.

A small group of Toshiba engineers working together in a separate building developed the first laptop computers (Rogers, 2003). In the same way that the interaction between units is important to genetic evolution, human communication and communication networks are important to the development of innovations.

If a group, organization, or society is afraid of new ideas or ways of thinking, there will be less variety, less information, in their communication networks, and individuals will not be able to connect to others and develop ideas. For example, various US intelligence agencies failed to "connect the dots" about the terrorist plot in September of 2001. Sadly, separate agencies and separate offices in the same agency had some information that suggested the plot, but organizational policies and norms discouraged people from crossing organizational boundaries, and the various agencies had not designed their technologies to share intelligence quickly. Discovery relies on communication.

The Innovation Adoption Process

The innovation adoption process occurs when people learn about something new and then incorporate it into their typical patterns of behavior. Some people learn about an innovation but never adopt it, and still others adopt an innovation but stop using it after a while. Many of us adopt an innovation but upgrade it to something newer. Why are there so many differences?

The continued adoption of an innovation through a social unit generally follows a distinctive pattern. This pattern suggests something is being spread, like a virus. People are copying each other's behaviors but putting their own twist on it. They are buying the same artifacts and hardware but using them in personal ways. There is replication with variation.

Everett Rogers was the pioneer scholar who devoted his life to studying this pattern of successive replication and adoption, and he called this pattern the diffusion of innovations (Rogers, 2003). Explaining this pattern involves careful attention to how people communicate about an innovation over time. How did people come to adopt smartphones and iPhones?

Stages of Adoption

There are five stages to the innovation adoption process (Rogers, 2003). Figure 4.1 depicts those stages.

The first stage is *the knowledge stage*. A person learns there is something new. A person first becomes aware of something new, then how to use it, and the unique principles that govern the use of the innovation (Rogers, 2003, p. 173).

When did you first learn about smartphones or iPhones? Did someone show you how to use one? If you already had a smartphone and then bought an iPhone, how long did it take you to adapt to the unique way the iPhone worked? Your answers to these questions will help you identify the different types of knowledge.

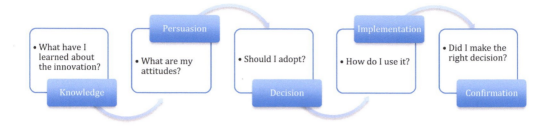

Figure 4.1 Stages of Adoption

Some unanswered questions are about how individual needs relate to knowledge. Sometimes, we go searching for something new because what we have is not working well, but in other cases, we just stumble across something new or see an ad, and then we consider if we can use it. Does awareness come before or after needs? Did you search for your current mobile phone based on some need or did you just become aware of it and then consider your needs? How did you enact the knowledge stage?

Persuasion is the second stage. This stage is about forming attitudes about the innovation. At this stage, you are actively seeking other people's opinions and mentally rehearsing what it would mean to adopt the innovation. You are still gathering information to reduce uncertainty about the innovation, but you also want evaluations. When you considered getting your current mobile phone, whom did you consult? What were the advantages you found? The disadvantages? Was there one moment or instance that moved you more toward the positive attitudes?

In the *decision stage* an individual does things that lead to a choice to adopt or reject the innovation. *Adoption* is a decision to fully use an innovation, and *rejection* is a decision not to adopt an innovation. Sometimes people go through an active and somewhat strategic method to make a decision, but at other times, they never really consider changing their current practices.

One important activity during this stage is to try an innovation on a partial basis. Marketers often send people samples, and companies send trial versions of their software and apps. Sometimes people can try another person's adopted innovation, such as using someone else's handheld device. People also learn from others' trial experiences. If people can more easily try an innovation, they are more likely to adopt it.

What happens when people reject an innovation? (a) They can do nothing and just stick to the way they have been doing things. (b) If they have a serious problem with the way they are currently doing things, they could alter how they are doing those things. The solution might be to do more or less of what they are currently doing or to do it in a different way. A person might just reconfigure his current smartphone instead of buying a new one, for example. (c) People can also revive older ways of doing things. A person might reject a new word processing program but go back to an older, simpler program for some tasks instead of using the current one. (d) Of course, people could just continue searching for something else new. These are typical behaviors when people reject technology for personal use, and these behaviors are also typical when people in organizations reject an innovation (Rogers, 2003).

Implementation is the active use of the innovation after adoption. The process prior to this stage has been primarily a mental exercise leading to the decision to adopt. At one end of the stage, people test the innovation and learn more about a range of applications, advantages, and disadvantages. They may even reinvent the uses. At the other end of the stage, people install the innovation into their normal way of doing things. The innovation becomes routine. People often discover they no longer need earlier technologies. As the sale of handheld devices has increased, so too has the sale and use of land phones and game consoles decreased (Siklur, 2011).

Reinvention occurs when people modify or change an innovation as they adopt and implement it. Sometimes reinvention involves using an innovation for things the originators of the innovation did not intend. Spreadsheet designers thought they were designing a digital way to do financial analysis and not a way to keep up with a person's fantasy baseball team. The designers of the earliest Blackberries thought their smartphones would improve professional telephone and text communication and help people plan, but the Apple team recognized that many people had begun using their handhelds for more personal communication, entertainment, and escape. Most people now text more than make telephone calls on their handhelds (Lenhart, 2010).

Reinvention is a special case of copying with variation. People have their own unique problems to solve and their own unique communication networks. People are more likely to reinvent when an innovation has multiple features and uses. This also means there are even more multiple combinations of use. People will personalize their use by developing their own desktops, program settings, app arrangements, ringtones, etc. If an innovation has greater potential for reinvention, people are more likely to adopt it (Rogers, 2003).

The last stage of the innovation decision process is confirmation. *Confirmation* occurs as people develop more information about the already-adopted innovation. This information is feedback about the use of the innovation, and the feedback may take the form of encouraging or discouraging continued use. A decision to discontinue may lead back to the first stage of the process.

Discontinuance is a decision to reject an innovation after people have adopted it. People may be disenchanted with the innovation. The innovation may not meet needs as well as anticipated or cost more than expected. People may have had a hard time using it or installing it as part of their routines. People may also have learned about something new, and so the confirmation stage about one innovation overlaps with the knowledge stage of another innovation.

These five stages help explain how people make decisions about innovations. However, people don't often proceed from one stage to another in a step-by-step process. They can gather information and form opinions simultaneously, and they can develop opinions that lead to gathering information in different ways. Sometimes people make formal decisions, and at other times, they just act and explain their actions. Communication helps people make sense of innovations, and the decisions about innovations are part of that sense. Specific perceptions and decisions emerge as people make sense of innovations.

Framing Innovations

Rogers (2003) recognized that each innovation has its own unique characteristics or attributes. However, he also knew that the characteristics themselves were less important to explaining adoption than how people perceived these attributes. He identified five categories of perceived attributes, and these categories constituted five clusters of frames for making sense of innovations. When people make sense of an innovation in a favorable way, they will be more likely to adopt the innovation.

Compatibility is the perception that the innovation is consistent with other perceptions. Compatibility is about how easily people can make sense of an innovation. If people can frame an innovation as consistent with something familiar or important, they will be more likely to adopt the innovation. Companies spend much time and money just labeling and marketing a product to demonstrate its compatibility.

Four compatibility frames are (a) how well the innovation meets needs, (b) how well the innovation fits already held beliefs about innovations, (c) how well the innovation fits sociocultural values and beliefs, and (d) how well the innovation fits personal values and beliefs. A person will not buy a professional graphics program if she does not think she needs to draw anything for her job. She sees no problem to solve. A person who has been using an earlier version of a new handheld device is more likely to perceive it as compatible than a person who has been using a different handheld device. An older generation may perceive a particular app as violating a cultural value that a younger generation does not recognize. Different people have different priorities for these frames, and a person may not adopt an innovation because it violates a personal value even though the person perceives that the innovation solves a problem well.

Innovation *complexity* is the perception that an innovation is difficult to use and understand. Some people may perceive an innovation as complex because they don't understand the function of the innovation. Why would anyone really need a smartphone anyway? Others might perceive various features such as the touch screen keyboard as difficult. In some cases, perceptions of complexity accompany perceptions of incompatibility such as the dread people feel with a new OS upgrade. If people perceive an innovation as *less* complex, they are more likely to adopt it.

Relative advantage is the perception that the innovation is better than the technology it supersedes. This is a cost-benefit comparison. Will the innovation cost less to do more? Perceptions of benefits include the various forms of compatibility, but benefits also include monetary rewards for producing a better product or service and social rewards such as status or acceptance. Perceived costs include perceptions associated with complexity, but costs also include economic costs. If people perceive an innovation as having more relative advantage, they will be more likely to adopt it.

Trialability refers to both the degree to which a person might experiment with an innovation on a limited basis and the perception of that degree. Some innovations are more difficult to try than others, but marketers normally make an effort to create the impression that people can try a product easily. If people believe an innovation has greater trialability, they are more likely to adopt an innovation. There is now an expectation, a perception, that digital products will have high trialability, from trial and downloadable versions of software to "free" but limited versions of apps. Today, when people believe that they cannot try a digital product, this violation of expectations becomes an incompatibility perception as well.

Observability is the extent to which people can perceive the results of others adopting an innovation. If the adoption of an innovation led to positive outcomes, there would be greater observability. If the adoption of an innovation led to negative results, there would be less adoption and less observability. Greater observability means that more and more people are adopting the innovation with success. If people have greater observability, they are more likely to adopt.

The five stages help explain how people make decisions about innovations. The various attribute perceptions identify five frame types important to making those decisions. Although these frames seem more important to the persuasion stage, a different set of frames may be more important to some people at one stage and more important to others at a different stage. People make different decisions, and some adopt sooner than others. There is a general pattern to how an innovation spreads throughout a given population.

Patterns of Adoption

The pattern of adoption for a given innovation generally follows an S curve similar to Figure 4.2. The vertical axis represents the percentage of people who have adopted, and the horizontal axis represents periods of time. A few people begin to use a given innovation at the start, and then it catches on. The rate of adoption increases until it reaches the maximum level of adoption. The top of the curve would be only 30-40% of a population for some innovations, but for something like handheld devices, the top of the curve is nearly 100%. Over 85% of Americans now use mobile phones (Zicklur, 2011), but some people have more than one mobile phone, and so, there are more mobile phone subscriptions than there are people in the developed world (International Telecommunication Union, 2011).

There are five categories of adopters, but people will be in different categories depending on the innovation (Rogers, 2003). Some people adopt music much earlier than others, and other people adopt computer technology earlier. The person who is early on one innovation is just as likely to be late on another.

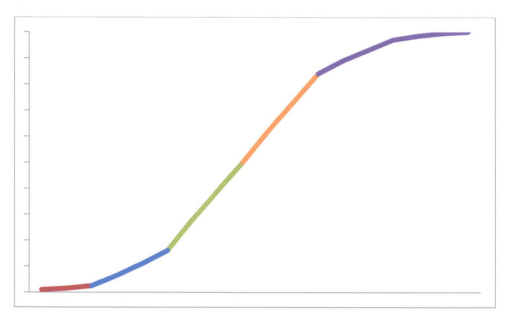

Figure 4.2 The Adoption Curve

Innovators are the first people to adopt an innovation, the first 2.5% noted in red in Figure 4.2. These people are *venturesome*, and they will try anything within a given category of technology. They are on the cutting edge – the bleeding edge for some. Because they are so early, innovators will adopt more innovation than the rest of us, and they will discontinue more as well.

Early adopters are the second group to adopt, the next 13.5% added to the curve in blue. When more and more early adopters begin to use an innovation, the curve will move more sharply. Most us think of these people as experts about particular innovations, and early adopters are careful to earn and maintain our *respect*. An innovator might recommend something because it is the newest thing, but early adopters are more likely to recommend something because they have had success using it.

The *early majority* is the third group to adopt, the next 34% added in green. The members of this group are more *deliberate*, considering several options before they adopt. They are willing to consider new things, but they do not lead in adopting them.

The *late majority* is the fourth group to adopt, the next 34% added in orange. The members of this group are *skeptical* of new things, but economic necessity and peer pressure may push them to adopt. They are cautious and must feel safe in adopting something new.

Laggards are the last people to adopt, the final 16% of a given group of adopters. These people have *traditional* values, and they frame innovations by comparing them to a distant past. They are more than skeptical about innovations; they are suspicious. They may also have economic concerns.

Those who adopt earlier than others are likely to have similar personality traits. They are more likely to be comfortable with abstractions, they tend to be more rational, less dogmatic, and closed-minded, and they tend to have greater empathy for others than the later adopters. They are more comfortable with change and uncertainty and are more willing to try something new than later adopters.

Earlier adopters also share certain socio-economic characteristics as well. They tend to have more formal years of education, generally have higher social status, and have more upward mobility than later adopters. Earlier adopters tend to have more money than later adopters, but there is no age difference between earlier and later adopters of most innovations.

Again, these traits and characteristics may be specific to a specific innovation. The earlier adopters of clothes are similar to the earlier adopters of games. They are both more comfortable with abstractions and more rational about an innovation, but they are interested in different innovations. They may have more formal education, but it may be about different innovations. They may have similar incomes, but they spend more of it on particular innovations.

Older adults have been later adopters of contemporary digital technologies, including handheld devices. Fewer adults over 65 own desktop or laptop computers, mobile phones, music players, or game consoles (ITU, 2011; Smith, 2010). Major considerations for their adoption decisions are functional need and anxiety (compatibility), ease of use (complexity), and price (relative advantage) (Mallenius, Rossi, & Tuunainen, 2007).

Communication and Adoption

Communication is at the center of all facets of the adoption process. Different types of communication are more important at different stages of the process, and different aspects of communication help frame innovations. Communication networks have a special influence on patterns of adoption.

Communication, Making Sense, and Adoption

Rogers (2003) distinguished two general forms of communication: mass communication and interpersonal communication. However, he was sensitive to the emergence of communication as a convergent understanding between people (Rogers & Kincaid, 1981), and he highlighted communication networks through much of his work (Rogers, 2003; Rogers & Argawala-Rogers, 1976; Rogers & Kincaid, 1981). Traditional commercial mass media was more an occasion for making sense and communication than a two-way process of convergence. The last two chapters explained it is difficult to classify much of today's communication technology discretely as either mass communication or interpersonal communication (Bailenson, Yee, Blascovich, & Guadagno, 2008; Polkosky, 2008; Rogers, 1986). The last chapter described mass media as mediated messages sent from a producer to a potentially large audience with no interactivity, and the chapter distinguished any interaction after that message as a separate form of communication. Mass media refers to messages such as magazines, newspapers, videos, music, and most blogs.

Mass media is important for adding potential cues about an innovation to the environment. *Mass media makes its biggest impact in the knowledge stage* when cues help us become aware of a technology, and the earliest adopters process more mass media than later adopters (Rogers, 2003). When people process more diverse mass media, they have greater potential for learning more about an innovation.

Although media might affect persuasion, *interpersonal communication is more important to the persuasion stage.* First, communication with others is more important to making sense about an innovation than the characteristics of the innovation itself. People might match technology to a particular need (Lengel & Daft, 1988), but communicating with others is the primary source for defining the need, learning about the attributes of the technology, and understanding the experiences and attitudes of others (Fulk, Schmitz, & Steinfeld, 1990; Salancik, & Pfeffer, 1978). An individual might enact some form of mass media that assists persuasion, but interaction with others develops accounts and expectations about innovations.

Secondly, communicating with some members of a personal communication network is more important for persuasion than communicating with others. A *personal communication network* is the set of people with whom an individual communicates. Two members of personal networks are important to explaining adoption: change agents and opinion leaders (Rogers, 2003). *Change agents* are members of our network with formal technical expertise in a particular innovation, and they are advocates for innovation. They are professionals such as teachers, consultants, health workers, mechanics, and salespeople. Change agents are more likely to initiate contact with potential clients than clients will initiate contact with them. However, clients will consult with change agents when the need is great enough to get a "professional opinion." *Opinion leaders* are peers and people a person knows for a variety of reasons, but opinion leaders have developed an expertise about an innovation. Since opinion leaders are similar to the other members of a network, people trust them, and opinion leaders are likely to be early adopters of an innovation.

The communication related to persuading you to adopt a new handheld device might have occurred in the following way. You saw a television commercial about the device and happened to also see an attractive ad in several magazines or online. You looked at your old phone and started to reassess what you have. You run into a few friends and ask them about the new product. They think you should call a special friend who everyone recognizes as an expert in such matters - an opinion leader. After talking to that special friend, you decide to visit the telephone company store at the mall and talk to a salesperson –a change agent. You then consult with friends, especially any other opinion leaders, to validate what the change agents said. Change agents will contact you, and you will see more mass media, look for more formal documents about the device, consult with more friends and opinion leaders, and decide about the device. There is typically a mix of some mass media and much interpersonal communication during persuasion.

Interpersonal communication is also important for framing the innovation as people use it and consider whether to continue use. Chapter One described how people develop explanations for themselves about past actions and use these explanations to predict and frame future actions. An *account* is a message containing an explanation of why a person did something. An account might include an explanation of cause, purpose, or clarification (Antaki, 1994), and an account may be a fully developed story or just a fragment of a story (Boje, 2008). What is important to understand is that people develop stories as they are telling them to other people, and that interaction is as important to developing accounts as the experiences related in the stories (Salem, 2013). There may be no need for an account until someone asks about an experience, and the account people tell one person will be different from the account they tell others. People in a personal network will complain about an innovation, or they may become advocates for an innovation. The accounts of using an innovation will influence continued use.

Communication Networks and Adoption

As people communicate with each other, they develop patterns of links to each other. One person develops a personal communication network, and the different personal communication networks interconnect to form larger communication networks. The previous section described the importance of links to particular people, change agents and opinion leaders. This section will describe the overall features of the people in the networks, the nature of the links, or the configuration of the links. These structural characteristics of communication networks are important for the adoption process.

The personal networks of earlier adopters, including opinion leaders, are different from the networks of later adopters. First, earlier adopters have personal networks with links to more people than the networks of later adopters. Secondly, the people in the networks are more diverse or heterogeneous than the people in the networks of later adopters. Earlier adopters communicate with more people with more varied cultural and educational backgrounds than later adopters, and members of their networks represent a wider age range and contain a more balanced mix of males and females than later adopters. Earlier adopters are also linked to more people from different places than later adopters. Third, the people in the networks of earlier adopters are less likely to be connected to each other than the people in the networks of later adopters. The people in the networks of earlier adopters are more likely to represent their own unique source of information than the people in the networks of later adopters.

Rogers (2003) referred to the networks of earlier adopters as cosmopolite networks, and these networks provided so much information they compensated for the lack of exposure to mass media to some communities. Today, a person can use communication technology to develop cosmopolite networks more quickly. People with cosmopolite networks are more likely to adopt an innovation earlier than others.

The pattern of adoption within a network appears to influence those who have not yet adopted. For example, the more friends you have who use iPhones increases the likelihood you will adopt (Birke & Belchamber, 2009). In one two-year study, if you had one friend who used an iPhone, you were three times more likely to adopt, and if you had two friends who adopted, you were five times more likely to adopt than others with no adopters in their networks (Sundsoy, Bjelland, Canright, & Engo-Monsen, 2010). When an innovation enters a large interconnected network, the members begin to communicate and adopt, and the innovation spreads like a virus. It is as if ideas were contagious, and this contagion effect is common in many communication networks (Monge & Contractor, 2003).

The previous two paragraphs may seem contradictory. The earliest adopters have large networks, and the members are not interconnected, but contagion happens in a large network of people who are interconnected. What happens is that the earliest adopters use their networks to gather information and adopt before others. Some earlier adopters are opinion leaders, and others consult these opinion leaders and adopt. The networks of these others are more interconnected than the networks of the opinion leaders. The number of adopters reaches a critical mass (Rogers, 2003) or threshold (Valente, 1995) that triggers rapid diffusion. The early majority starts adopting and the adoption curve is the steepest.

Mindful About Adoption

Both the development of an innovation and the adoption process are instances of making sense. An innovation develops when people frame things in different ways and communicate with others who frame things in different ways (enactment). Further, communication and trial and error testing limit the number of potentially viable technologies (selection). One cycle of the process ends with development of the means of mass production – mass copying - and the adoption by consumers (retention). For the consumer, there are multiple alternatives about a technology such as mobile phones. Consumers learn about the range of potential technologies at the knowledge stage (enactment), they limit the number of alternatives at the persuasion stage (selection), and they decide to adopt or reject (retention). However, a new cycle of making sense starts over at implementation. There is reinvention (enactment) followed by routinization (selection and retention). The final stage of confirmation may end the cycle (more retention) or lead to discontinuance and another knowledge stage (enactment).

Communication is at the center of both processes. Those individuals who have been thinking about new things need to talk about them. Developing an innovation includes thinking, talking, testing, talking, thinking, and more talking. Without the proper connections between people, people don't make the connections between ideas, sometimes with tragic consequences. Consumers often learn about new things through mass media, but their communication with others forms both their beliefs and attitudes. Characteristics of an individual's personal communication networks promote or resist adoption, and some members of those networks are more important than others. Because people communicate with so many other people, an innovation can spread rapidly.

No one can really identify the exact origins of the iPhone any more than one could identify the exact origins of face-to-face communication or mediated communication. However, what is known is that some people at Apple started communicating about the idea of mobile communication, and the development of the product followed a common cycle. For the first several years, AT&T was the only carrier that offered iPhones, and so the diffusion of iPhones was steep but peeked at around 15% of smartphone users. However, since the public has had greater availability and since Apple lowered the cost of its earlier versions of the iPhone, the Apple OS ran 27% of all US smartphones by the first quarter of 2011 (NielsonWire, 2011, June). Furthermore, the development of software for smartphones, apps, has stimulated further growth of smartphones and greater diversity of services. Potential customers will be using more smartphones to communicate more about new smartphones.

References

Antaki, C. (1994). *Explaining and arguing: The social organization of accounts*. London: Sage.

Apple. (2009). *Apple reports first quarter results*. Retrieved from http://www.apple.com/pr/library/2009/01/21results.html.

Arthur, W. B. (2009). *The nature of technology: What it is and how it evolves*. NY: Free Press.

Bailenson, J. N., Yee, N., Blascovich, J. & Guadagno, R. E. (2008). Transformed social interaction. In E. A. Konijin, S. Utz, M. Tanis, & S. B. Barnes (Eds.), *Mediated interpersonal communication* (pp. 77-99). NY: Routledge.

Basalla, G. (1988). *The evolution of technology*. Cambridge: Cambridge University Press.

Birke, D. & Belchamber, J. (2009, March). *New product diffusion over a social network: The iPhone*. Presentation at the International Sunbelt Social Network Conference. San Diego, CA.

Blackmore, S. (1999). *The meme machine*. Oxford: Oxford University Press.

Boje, D. M. (2008). *Storytelling organizations*. Los Angeles: Sage.

Dawkins, R. (1989). *The selfish gene* (rev. ed.). Oxford: Oxford University Press. (Original work published in 1976).

Dawkins, R. (1995). *River out of Eden: A Darwinian view of life*. NY: Basic Books.

Durwin, M. (2011). *Global vs, US statistics: Mobile, social network, PC ownership*. Retrieved from http://www.mdurwin.com/2011/03/global-v-us-statistics-mobile-social-network-pc-ownership.

Fulk, J., Schmitz, J., & Steinfeld, C. W. (1990). A social influence model of technology use. In J. Fulk, & C. W. Steinfield (Eds.), *Organizations and communication technology* (pp. 117-140). Newbury Park, CA: Sage.

Holland, J. (1995). *Hidden order: How adaptation builds complexity*. NY: Free Press.

Holland, J. (1998). *Emergence: From chaos to order*. Cambridge, MA: Perseus Books.

International Telecommunication Union (2011). *Key global telecom indicators for the world telecommunication service sector*. Retrieved from http://www.itu.int/ITU-D/ict/statistics/at_glance/KeyTelecom.html.

Johnson, S. (2010). *Where good ideas come from: The natural history of innovations*. NY: Riverhead Books.

Kauffman, S. (1993). *The origins of order: Self-organization and selection in evolution*. NY: Oxford University Press.

Kauffman, S. (1995). *At home in the universe: The search for the laws of self-organization and complexity*. NY: Oxford University Press.

Kumpark, G. (2010, October 18). Apple sold 14.1 million iPhones last quarter, over 70 million since launch. *MobileCrunch*. Retrieved from http://www.mobilecrunch.com/2010/10/18/apple-sold-14-1-million-iPhones-last-quarter-over-70-million-since-launch.

Lengel, R. H., & Daft, R. L. (1988). The selection of communication media as an executive skill. *Academy of Management Executive, 2*, 225-232.

Lenhart, A. (2010). *Cell phones and American adults: They make just as many calls, but text less often than teens*. Washington, DC: Pew Research Center. Retrieved from http://pewinternet.org/Reports/2010/Cell-Phones-and-American-Adults.aspx.

Lorenz, E. (1996). *The essence of chaos*. Seattle, WA: University of Washington Press.

Mallenius, S., Rossi, M., Tuunainen, V. K. (2007, June). *Factors affecting the adoption and use of mobile devices and services by elderly people*: Results from a pilot study. Proceedings of 6th Annual Global Mobility Roundtable, Los Angeles: University of Southern California Press. Available at http://www.marshall.usc.edu/ctm/Research.

Monge, P. R., & Contractor, N. S. (2003). *Theories of communication networks*. Oxford: Oxford University Press.

NielsonWire (2011). In US, Smartphones now majority of new cellphone purchases: Apple iOS up, Android flat, RIM down among recent acquirers. *NielsonWire*. Retrieved from http://blog.nielsen.com/nielsenwire/online_mobile/in-us-smartphones-now-majority-of-new-cellphone-purchases.

Polkosky, M. D. (2008). Machines as mediators: The challenge of technology for interpersonal communication theory and research. In E. A. Konijin, S., Utz, M., Tanis, & S. B. Barnes (Eds.). *Mediated interpersonal communication* (pp. 34-57). NY: Routledge.

Prigogine, I., & Stengers, I. (1984). *Order out of chaos: Man's new dialogue with nature*. Toronto: Bantam.

Rogers, E, M. (2003). *Diffusion of innovations* (5th ed.). NY: Free Press.

Rogers, E. M. (1986). *Communication technology: The new media in society*. NY: The Free Press.

Rogers, E. M., & Argawala-Rogers, R. (1976). *Communication in organizations*. NY: Free Press.

Rogers, E. M., & Kincaid, L. (1981). *Communication networks: Toward a new paradigm for research*. NY: Free Press.

Salancik, G. R., & Pfeffer, J. (1978). A social information processing approach to job attitudes and task design. *Administrative Science Quarterly, 23*, 224-253.

Salem, P. J. (2013). *The complexity of human communication* (2nd ed.). Cresskill, NJ: Hampton.

Smith, A. (2010). *Americans and their gadgets*. Washington, DC: Pew Research Center. Retrieved from http://pewinternet.org/Reports/2010/Gadgets.aspx

Sundsoy, P. R., Bjelland, J., Canright, G., & Engo-Monsen, K. (2010). Product adoption networks and their growth in a large mobile phone network. In N. Memon & R. Alhajj (Eds.), *Proceedings of the 2010 International Conference on Advances in Social Network Analysis and Data Mining* (pp. 208-216). Odense, Denmark: Institute of Electrical and Electronics Engineers. doi: 10.1109/ASONAM.2010.38.

Valente, T. W. (1995). *Network models of the diffusion of innovations*. Cresskill, NJ: Hampton Press.

Zicklur, K. (2011). *Generations and their gadgets*. Washington, DC: Pew Research Center. Retrieved from http://www.pewinternet.org/Reports/2011/Generations-and-gadgets.aspx.

Zimm, J. (2000). *Technological innovation: An evolutionary process*. Cambridge: Cambridge University Press

Chapter 5: Self

I have always been interested in technology, but my research interest began with my daughter's third birthday party. It was in the late 1970s, what seems like a glacial age ago, and we were celebrating her birthday at a pizza restaurant that featured games and a video arcade. In those days, the arcade was a bank of machines arranged in one large room. It was the first time I had seen a full arcade.

As I entered the arcade room, I bumped into a male in his late teens or early twenties. There was nothing particularly remarkable about him except that he had that stare. When I looked into his eyes as we bumped into each other, he seemed to be in another world. I am sure I have had a similar stare when I have been reading or writing for a long time, and I looked up to talk to someone. I had seen that stare among chess players at a club or during a tournament, among actors getting ready to perform, among athletes just before or during a game, and at nearly any event that demands focused attention. I had also seen that stare when people get lost in their thoughts, when the concentration just evaporates and people just stare. The young man I had encountered entering the arcade had this last type of stare. He seemed lost in another world.

When I looked around the arcade, I saw much familiar behavior. There were couples on a date, parents with children older than my daughter, and just people laughing and enjoying each other as they competed or discovered a new game. I even saw a "hustler", practicing his game, practicing and running up the scores, and looking for a "fish". But I also saw more stares, maybe four or five people among the twenty or so in the arcade. In this case, they reminded me of those people at a casino with buckets of tokens staring at the slots as they fed the machines. Lost.

This chapter is about that stare when it becomes a continuous stare that may evolve into more serious problems. In the first half of this chapter, I will describe self perceptions and how communication constructs our selves. I will include material on how newer HCTs might alter the technology of self. In the second part of this chapter, I will explore the challenges we face constructing viable self perceptions when we are surrounded by the latest HCTs.

Constructing and Negotiating Self

The Nature of Self

Some use "self" to refer to the identifiable style of communication associated with a person, and I will describe communication style in the next chapter. More commonly, self refers to the sense a person makes when reflecting on him/herself. Weick (1995) noted that self, rather than the environment, might be the primary focus of making sense. We make sense of our selves by communicating with others.

Self perceptions are the information and knowledge you create about yourself. Like all perceptions, we construct self perceptions with varying degrees of breadth, depth, and configuration. Self may be more or less complex.

Self-concept is the *organized* set of perceptions an individual has about himself or herself, and so, self-concept is self knowledge. We organize some perceptions into a *self-identity* to create a psychological boundary providing safety but allowing us to adapt and interact with others (Butz, 1997). We create evaluative selves as configurations of self around what we like or don't like about ourselves, and *self-esteem* is our feeling of self worth. We also create configurations around past actions, and this behavioral self is the source of our *self-efficacy*, our perceptions about our ability to perform specific actions to accomplish specific things. Self-identity, self-esteem, and self-efficacy have been common ways of describing self perceptions

(Bandura, 1986; Cushman & Cahn, 1985; Kunda, 1999; Moskowitz, 2004). These three large configurations provide frames for us to make sense of ourselves as we communicate with others and develop communication practices with others.

These three large configurations also intersect with three other large configurations. *Personal self* consists of the idiosyncratic perceptions people have of themselves. Personal self is how people see themselves as different from others. *Relational self* is how people see themselves in particular relationships. In specific relationship such as with a specific friend, people understand how they are similar to and different from each other, but they also develop perceptions about how to communicate with each other that may be similar to or different than the expectations in other relationships. Finally, there is a collective or *social self* consisting of people's perceptions of themselves in groups. People come to associate themselves with groups even though they have not interacted with any members of the group, and they endorse personal standards similar to group members that differentiate themselves from non-group members. Each type of self has identity, esteem, and efficacy dimensions, and a person can be using one aspect of personal self, relational self, or social self when creating one message for one person or group and a different aspect for others. For example, personal or relational self can be important with some communication, and social self can be more important in other instances, (Brewer & Gardner, 1996; Taijfel, 1974).

A *role concept* refers to a specific set of self perceptions we develop when *interacting* with specific others. A role is the part of us we use when we communicate in specific relationships. We can never give all of our perceptions and behaviors to another person in a specific relationship, and so we partially include ourselves in any given specific interaction or series of interactions with particular others (Allport, 1924). We develop recurring patterns for communicating as part of a specific relationship, and others come to expect things from us. Recall the example from Chapter Two of the communication between two sisters. Our role concepts develop and become more complex as our relationships with others and our communication with others become more complex. Our relationship with a parent may be very complex and lead to a complex relational self, but our identification with a group may be based on little or no interaction with group members and so the social identity with the group would be less complex. Developing a role and a role concept is a prerequisite for having a relational self for a specific relationship, but having a social identity with a group without playing a role in the group would mean a person had a shallow and simple social self with that group.

Individuals construct role and self-concepts by framing cues with past knowledge, and there is a tension between similar and different. On the one hand, we may see others as part of a group we identify with, and we may use this similarity to develop a role concept. Conversely, we can have similarities across several relational identities and group others into one social identity. We have high school friends, friends at work, and co-workers. Our social identity helps us develop unique role concepts and also express ourselves to others as a group member. Furthermore, we try to make sense of how one role relates to alternative and previous roles, and we try to reconcile any contradictions between our various presentations (Weinrich & Saunderson, 2003). Learning how we are different from others in various groups and relationships, leads to personal identity.

Consider the twenty or so people you communicate with regularly. You have a sense of your self with each of them - twenty relational selves with their own boundaries, positive and negative senses of worth, and perceptions of effective and appropriate actions. The emerging configuration of those relational selves and your personal self becomes the bedrock for your self-concept, and you may create more general views of your self at the overlaps of role concepts and social identities or at the center of some role concept configurations. Adding your perception of your self with your acquaintances to the periphery of this network can lead to an even more complex self. In some cultures, personal identity is more important than social identity, and in other cultures, social identity with specific groups is most important (Hofstede & Hofstede, 2005).

In some instances, we communicate with others exclusively through newer HCT, such as when people in different countries work on a team for an organization. Our role concept and social identity in this team are tied to how we see ourselves through our use of this technology. Creating a profile and posting on a social network site such as Facebook is creating messages for many others, an audience, and we develop a role concept as a performer and may come to regard our self as one performer in a group of performers. The latest HCT provides the opportunity to communicate with many more people, and so we can develop more role concepts and social identities and change our self-concepts in many ways.

Sustaining Self

Communication is how people create and sustain self. Messages contain potential social cues others use to construct social information about the sender of the message, how the sender sees recipients, and how the sender perceives the relationships between communicators. Responses provide potential feedback about the extent to which communicators endorse these perceptions.

> . . . the young individual must learn to be most himself where he means most to others, to be sure, who have come to be the most to him. The term "identity" expresses such a mutual relation in that it connotes both a persistent sameness within oneself (selfsameness) and a persistent sharing of some kind of essential character with others. (Erikson, 1980, 109).

Communication becomes a self-reinforcing process linking personal self to relational self to social self.

An appreciation of similarities and differences are essential for creating information and knowledge of any kind. This appreciation is vital to our abilities to organize a self-identity, to develop high self-esteem, and to acquire a sense of self-efficacy. Creating a functioning self-concept relies on our abilities to discriminate ourselves from others.

When we first meet someone or begin a conversation with someone we already know, we establish the roles and rules for the conversation. We must be somewhat sensitive to how others respond to our messages in order to mindfully make sense of what is going on. The responses of others help to shape how we present ourselves (Snyder, Tanke, & Berscheid, 1977), but the messages of others become part of an episode. Part of what is going on is how the episode shapes us. We may begin with an ideal sense of who we are to others, but our understanding of the responses of others will tell us whether that ideal is really operating in this conversation or relationship. You might think of yourself as "funny", but you would have learned that specific others would not appreciate your humor. Being funny may be real only in some conversations. The roles you negotiate in some relationships will include being "funny," but your humor will not be part of other roles in other relationships.

When little or no communication can sustain some part of self, that part of self remains only ideal and not real (Cushman & Cahn, 1985). Furthermore, if we are continually unable to present and sustain an aspect of self in communication, we will lose that aspect of self. You might have thought of yourself as humorous, but you would have a hard time holding on to that view if no one laughed at your jokes or if you had no relationships that included joking. If you thought of yourself as a good tennis player, but you have not played tennis for a while, you would become less confident of your tennis prowess.

The challenges to sustaining some part of yourself are not rejection but ambiguities. If you tell a joke and others ridicule the joke, you can be certain you can tell a joke. The others in this situation did not like the telling, but there might be others who will. But, if others respond to your joke by ignoring you or changing the topic, you might start to wonder if you told the joke in the first place. If you sent a text with something funny, and the other person did not comment on the joke or if you posted a joke on your social network site (SNS) and no one indicated whether they liked it, using text driven HCT would at least let you know that you had sent or posted something, but you might wonder whether it was worth doing. Similarly, if you send a text and a second person responds, you can be certain of the exchange, but the second person cannot be certain until you reply.

Doubt about Self

Equivocal social cues are cues we have trouble making social perceptions of. We become uncertain about how others see us, see themselves, or see us together with them. Equivocal social cues are not direct support or rejection of a presentation of self. Rather we make sense of the cues as implicit support or implicit rejection, and the perceived ambiguity challenges our sense that we are even participating in an episode or relationship with another (Dance & Larson, 1976). When we think someone is abruptly changing topics or ignoring us, when someone responds to a question with a comment we think does not fit the question, or when we think someone is interrupting us, we become uncertain about the legitimacy of our performance or our role in the relationship. When someone uses language we don't understand, uses words to refer to themselves that are very general, when some parts of the other's message seem to contradict other parts, or when the verbal and nonverbal parts of the messages seem to contradict, we can have doubts about what the other person is presenting and how the other person is presenting themselves to us. Scholars have studied these ambiguous messages under many labels (Bavalas, Black, Chovil, & Mullet, 1990; Cissna & Sieburg, 1981; Daily, 2006; Haley, 1959; Sieburg, 1973; Williams & Goss, 1975).

We have trouble making sense of cues in two ways. First, there is the ambiguity when we do not have a frame or a connection to the cue. This happens naturally when we meet someone for the first time, especially when s/he is from a different culture. Second, there is the ambiguity when we have too many possible frames and connections to the cues. For example, when we are talking to several people with whom we have different relationships we must decide how to make sense of our relationships together.

These two types of ambiguity present different challenges (Stohl & Redding, 1987; Weick, 1995). In the first instance, we need more cues to make more information, but in the second case, we need more redundancy to choose from the alternatives. When we think someone abruptly changes topics, we might wait for more from the other person while trying to link what they are saying to the original topic or thinking that they will return to the original topic. By contrast, if the other person appears to be contradictory, we are looking for clarification of the alternative frames. The first instance can happen when the message is too short, but the second message can happen when the message is too long.

Most people reading this book know the difficulty trying to construct and interpret messages with different forms of HCT. Emotions and feelings are especially difficult with a text-dominant technology, but just sending a picture also has problems. Different forms of HCT, such as Twitter, seem to be pure expression to a large diverse audience, but there is little reason to continue tweeting if most of your tweets do not lead to some responses.

People trying to make sense of equivocal social cues can easily conclude that their presentations of themselves are not valid and that they are not participating in the conversation or relationship. Rejection leaves the door open for another bid, but equivocal social cues deny any negotiation. A person perceives rejection as "I don't like how you presented yourself or framed our relationship so change the presentation" but perceives an equivocal social cue as "You are not worthy enough to be in a relationship with me" or "You're not here." Rejection might challenge our esteem in a role, but equivocal social cues challenge our relational identity. Persistent equivocal social cues challenge our overall self-identity.

Confirmation is the perception that others have reinforced our presentation of self, and *disconfirmation* is the perception that others have not reinforced our presentation of self. Confirmation is the perception that the other has recognized, acknowledged, and endorsed a person's presentation of self. Confirmation is more about securing our psychological boundaries than it is about feeling good about ourselves or about feeling more confident in what we do. Perceiving continual rejection may lead to disconfirmation, but equivocal social cues lead more directly to disconfirmation and uncertainty about self. Disconfirmation becomes uncertainty, uncertainty becomes anxiety, and, in the worst cases, anxiety becomes depression and then despair.

Responding to Equivocality

There are three common responses to equivocal social cues (Dance & Larson, 1976). *Amplification* refers to the tendency to make the message bigger. One person makes a message, the person perceives the other person's response as equivocal, and the first person re-creates the first message but intensifies or elaborates the first message. The amplified message may be more direct, express more explicit and absolute ideas, use more dramatic language, provide greater detail, or use more nonverbal behaviors. The first message might have been in a conversational tone and normal volume, but the re-sent message has a more urgent tenor and is louder. The first message might have been from one side of the room to another, but the sender moves across the room to face the other to resend the message. The first text might have been in lower case, but the resent message is in all caps and contains emoticons.

Amplification is the more likely choice in close relationships or in relationships that the communicator regards as central to their self-concept. You are communicating something you regard as important or personal about yourself, and the other does not appear to acknowledge the presentation. You think the problem was the message you sent. You did not do it "loud" enough for the other person to hear it. You redo it, but louder. Attempts at getting affection from a romantic partner become flirting with others in front of the romantic partner as the "I am worthy of more affection" message gets bigger. Negotiation over a new contract becomes a strike or lockout as if to say, "We are serious about our position." The communicators become concerned that the other parties do not respect them or their rights – there are face issues. Political demonstrations can become more intense and lead to violence. Amplified messages are all forms of "Pay attention to me" or "I am worthy of your attention and respect."

Re-evaluation happens when the person trying to process equivocal social cues re-assesses and often devalues the source of those cues. Ultimately, the communicator may conclude that the communication and the relationship with the other person are not worth maintaining. If the other person made it difficult to communicate with me or if the other person failed to respect me, I don't need to talk to that person. De-friend!

Re-evaluation is a likely choice when the communicator has high self-esteem. That is, the communicator does not let equivocal social cues or rejection challenge their own sense of self worth or self-identity. However, if a person continues to devalue others, that person's communication network gets smaller as the communicator excludes more and more people. In the end, the network may become so small that sustaining a viable self may become difficult. What happens to you when the few people you rely on to help you define yourself leave or die? Consider what happens when you cannot connect to significant others when your technology fails. The elderly face the realities of shrinking personal networks, but today's HCT provides opportunities to construct alternative networks if they take advantage of those opportunities. A pattern of continuous re-evaluation would use HCT to limit responses to the fewer and fewer people you regard as worthy.

Salvaging happens when people trying to process equivocal social cues re-assesses themselves. It is a reconstruction of a role or self without the features associated with the equivocal social cues. You might have thought you were caring and sensitive, but if no one recognizes your attempts at being supportive, you will drop "caring" as a feature of how you see yourself. As I noted above, you might have thought you were funny, but if no one laughs or even recognizes your attempts at humor, you will drop "funny" as a feature of how you see yourself. Your presentations of yourself will be less caring or funny. Continuous salvaging leads to a narrower view of self and rigid presentations of self.

The Proteus Effect refers to the tendency of individuals to present themselves in a way that conforms to their perceived stereotypes and expectations of a given role (Yee & Bailenson, 2007). That is, an individual comes to a social situation anticipating playing a given role, imagining what others expect in such a performance, and eagerly anticipating the performance and validation reinforcing the correctness of the performance. This happens before any discrimination of how others actually do perceive the performance. Putting on the princess costume and seeing yourself in the mirror with the costume leads to a greater likelihood that you will act more like a princess. Creating an avatar for a game may lead to acting like the avatar outside the game. Creating exaggerated and dramatic messages on social media may lead to expectations that such messages are better in real life. Most of us will change our presentations if others reject or disconfirm, but some of us can become "fairylanders", ignoring the negative responses of others and persisting in a presentation (Miller & Steinberg, 1975).

Salvaging is more likely when we already have some doubts about ourselves. When we begin a conversation or relationship with someone new, we are constantly testing various aspects of ourselves to create the most effective role. Reconstruction becomes salvaging when the adjustments lead to a narrower, shallower, and simpler role. Salvaging becomes a problem when the process occurs frequently across many relationships. Self presentations become stereotypical as the person can only create a limited number of messages others will confirm. Our repertoire of presentations becomes smaller as we may become more dependent on groups of others to define us in a more general way.

The Proteus Effect happens when a person bases their behavior more on what they imagine others are thinking about them regardless of how others react. In some instances, this happens because others may have reinforced the person's behavior in one social situation and the person does not see a difference between the past situation and the present. Similarly, the person may have stereotypes about how she is presenting herself and fail to realize the stereotypes to do not apply to this situation. People have limited themselves to a narrow presentation of themselves because of the rigidity of their beliefs and their failure to discriminate.

Deindividuation refers to any process that encourages or facilitates our losing track of personal differences between our self and others, and between others. Deindividuation could lead to a person losing self awareness and greater uninhibited behavior, and it could accentuate group identity and conformity (Zimbardo, 1969). Alternatively, heightened social identity could provide a clearer boundary for developing personal identity (Reicher, Spears, & Postmes, 1995). Deindividuation could increase the likelihood of the Proteus effect. A combination of amplification and salvaging leads to presenting only those exaggerated and dramatic cues that most others will recognize, and such a combination deindividuates. We could lose the sense of our individuality as we fail to recognize the individuality in others.

Reflecting on Self and Communication

Throughout this volume, I have pointed out that what communicators bring to communication is as important as any other part of the process. All human communication involves information processing inasmuch as it involves making sense of cues. Human communication involves people making sense of themselves besides any other information they may construct.

Table 5.1

The Technology of Self

Self-concept is the organized set of ideas we have about ourselves.

Self-concepts can have greater or lesser breadth, depth, and configuration.

Self-concept includes self-identity, self-esteem, and self-efficacy.

Self-concept includes personal self, relational selves, and social selves.

Humans organize their self-concepts around more specific role concepts.

Our ideal selves become real in the communication we have with others.

We need confirmation from others, and equivocal social cues are a bigger problem to forming our self-concepts than rejection.

When faced with persistent equivocal social cues, we tend to amplify, reevaluate, or salvage.

The Proteus effect, deindividuation, and social anxiety can complicate our efforts to develop and sustain our self-concepts.

Communication is reducing uncertainty about self, but some people are more uncertain than others. Anxiety involves worry and stress over future events, and it generally includes an anticipation of negative consequences. Social anxiety is a fear of the negative evaluation from others (Schry, Roberson-Nay & White, 2012), and communication apprehension is fear or anxiety associated with real or anticipated communication with another person or persons (McCroskey, 2009). Anxious people may need direct assurances and a more positive ratio of support to rejection than the average person to feel safe about themselves. An inability to confirm one's self triggers greater sensemaking (Weick, 1995, pp. 20-23), but anxiety may lead to avoiding communication or greater reliance on others to define self. The latest HCT may help those with high communication apprehension to engage others (Ho & McLeod, 2008; Sanders & Amason, 2011), but communication apprehension may become apprehension about technology and limit the use of technology (Scott & Timmerman, 2005).

Self-concept is an organized set of perceptions we have about our self. Similar to all perceptions, these perceptions have breadth, depth, and configuration. The emergence of self-identity, self-esteem, and self-efficacy happens through a process of negotiating roles in specific relationships, and the complexity of those relationships affects the complexity of our self-concept. Similarly, the complexity of our self-concept affects the complexity of any role and the overall network of relationships.

Sustaining self involves a process of constructing and reconstructing our roles and self-concept through communicating with others. The process becomes more difficult when we have trouble making sense of social cues. We tend to manage most equivocal social cues by finding the aspects of ourselves others can recognize more easily. We all tend to amplify, re-evaluate, and salvage our presentations as we reconstruct ourselves in different relationships. If we are dealing with many equivocal social cues or if we fall into a trap of responding to them in one way, we will have trouble sustaining viable identities. The complexity of self, the complexity of communication, and the complexity of relationships all affect each other. How people use technology can affect these interdependencies. Sometimes, communication technology practices alter these interdependencies in no way at all. In other instances, communication technology practices accelerate and magnify factors already in place because of these interdependencies. Finally, communication technology practices can transform these interdependencies into unique opportunities and challenges.

Technology and Self

Presenting and Negotiating Self Online

People have become increasing aware of the challenges of managing personal information when using the latest HCT. Scholars have developed several ways of analyzing these circumstances, and they suggest many of these difficulties are unique to newer HCT. In this section, I will describe the contemporary difficulties as accelerated and magnified instances of old issues. Communicating online about self is similar to communicating offline about self, but the effects can happen quicker and with greater impact.

Consider all the different ways you present yourself online. Some, such as posting a picture of yourself, supplying information for a biography for a SNS or writing a comment in a discussion forum, seem to be under your control – you decide what goes into the message. Similarly, you choose the words or graphics that are part of an email or text message. "You are what you type" (Slater, 2002, p. 536). That is, your presentation is what you type.

Of course, these messages are just an opportunity for others to make sense of you. How mindful are you of how others might make sense of you as you create a message? How mindful are you of how others see things, of how other people's opinions might be similar to or different from your own? How often do you reflect on how others might make sense of you making sense - of how others might make sense of you based on your style, your graphics, or your language? You will get some answers to these questions as an episode develops, but you won't get these answers if you did not have the questions in the first place. Furthermore, the role identity or self-identity you leave with will be more a function of the episode only if you engage and interact. If you post and leave a forum, you lose any influence on shaping others' perceptions of you.

You present yourself online whenever you are doing anything online. Simply surfing or viewing other people's SNSs provides an opportunity for making sense. There are those autonomous agents – bots – and those cookies that will make sense of your every click (Brown & Duguid, 2000). A website's bot will implant a cookie on your computer to monitor your activity so that it can quickly get the information you want. Indeed, one bot that you commission to do a search for you might send another bot to search your computer and past activity for patterns that might help the search you commissioned. Several bots from several different websites might interact, creating a network of bot activity. Most of us are not very mindful of this activity or the extent of it. It is very easy to create a profile of us based on just surfing the web.

It is very difficult to remain anonymous. The *Oxford English Dictionary* definition of anonymous refers to being "of unknown name". More contemporarily, being anonymous means that personal and distinctive information is unknown. Unknown to whom? How much is not known? Just the name? Every time we do anything online, we are presenting ourselves to others. We are disclosing something about us – providing an opportunity for others to make sense of us. Privacy concerns, presented in Chapter 3, are about how well we can control what others know about us.

Traditionally, *self-disclosure* refers to providing personal information about yourself that others would not be able to obtain in other ways. Genuine self-disclosure is the intentional revealing of personal, private, and risky information to another (Miller & Steinberg, 1975). It is personal to the extent that the sender of the message regards the information as important to their self-concept, and it is private to the extent that the sender has not told many other people. Self-disclosure is a message or series of messages involving truth, sincerity, novelty, and choice (Fisher, 1974). In relational communication literature, episodes involving self-disclosure are necessary for the development of intimacy (Altman & Taylor, 1973; Knapp & Vangelisti, 2009). Self-disclosure seems to be about not being anonymous.

Most of our messages are not strategic efforts at impression management, but all our messages do provide an opportunity for others to make sense of us. Similarly, people do not self disclose often, but they can reveal information about each other with every message. Most uses of newer HCT are asynchronous, and so there would be greater opportunities to strategically present an ideal self and to self disclose (Walther, 2007). However, most research comparing the amounts and intimacy of self-disclosure online to face-to-face (FtF) self-disclosure demonstrates little difference (Kim & Dindia, 2011).

Most online disclosure involves greater reach than FtF disclosure. Online disclosure typically involves multiple persons, and the discloser may not know all the people who are receiving the message (Kim & Dindia, 2011). Posting or sending a message with details of a personal, private, and risky topic to an unknown audience suggests mindless behavior. In a later chapter, I will explain how the old six degrees between people has become four and sending something intended for 20 can quickly reach 62 billion with a reflexive keystroke.

This reach can encourage online bad behavior such as cyberbullying and trolling, and I will discuss these types of messages in the next chapter. The reach of digital HCT means anything you thought was private can quickly become public online. This is a type of catalytic effect. The latest HCT changes the parameters on self-disclosure. Those who already disclosed a lot FtF will find their online disclosures spreading more quickly and having greater impact, and those who disclosed less FtF will find their limited disclosures have become public online.

The experiences of online gamers demonstrate much of the similarities and differences between communicating about self in the digital environment and in the typical face-to-face environment. Gamers select an avatar as an alter ego to play the game. Individuals consciously select the physical appearance and abilities of their character within the restrictions of the game. The character may change because of the successes and failures during the game, or the individual may create a "new and improved" version of the character after they have had failed experiences in earlier attempts at the game.

It would be natural for a person to experience a Proteus Effect when gaming. Just creating an avatar and watching yourself manipulate the avatar would produce this effect. However, the construction of the character is similar to the construction of a role in any given relationship, and the differences between the two instances are the particular technological limitations of the environments. A person may "feel like flying", but only the dragon alter-ego can "fly". A person may want to cry, but the dragon cannot shed tears.

Third parties create the rules and limitations for the game to enhance the gaming experience, and, unlike the typical face-to-face situation, the gamers cannot change the rules for constructing the alter ego or interacting with others. Gamers often create "off line" opportunities to communicate with each other "out of character", and gaming is as much about managing relationships as it is about the game (Klimmt & Hartmann, 2008). Of course, having both an online relationship and an offline relationship with the same person is more complex, but the challenges are similar to being friends with coworkers.

Consider the range of alternative roles that are now possible with the addition of digital HCT. These are the roles that constitute an online or cyber self. First, there are the various roles originally developed through FtF communication, and digital HCT can help sustain and develop these roles. Secondly, there are the roles emerging exclusively through sustained digital HCT use. Often, people choose to limit their interaction to just digital HCT, and these digital relationships provide their own rewards. Thirdly, there are the roles people consciously and strategically create through SNS. Often, these roles are extensions of the earlier roles, but the addition of more people to the audience changes the presentation to construct unique roles. Fourth, there are the roles constructed in a simulated or virtual environment. These relationships can provide stimulation, relaxation, and unique forms of stress in addition to the ones found in other relationships. Problems and opportunities can develop when the boundaries between various forms of relationships become ambiguous, when the roles become unclear, and when self-identity is uncertain.

When Private Becomes Public

A. J Leibling was a giant of sports journalism and a renowned essayist in the last century. In the opening chapter of *The Sweet Science,* his book about boxing, he described his experiences at a boxing match and the joy he experienced being part of the crowd. He analyzed the various members of the audience and the interaction among people attending. He disparaged watching such an occasion on television as a poor substitute for being part of the event itself. He recalled a conversation he had with Thomas Mathews, a former editor of *Time* magazine, describing communication. "What are you going to communicate?" asked Leibling. Mathews answered as follows.

> The most important thing . . . is the man at one end of the circuit saying "My God, I am alive! You are alive" and the fellow on the other end receiving his message, saying "My God, you're right! We are both alive!" (Leibling, 1956, p. 17).

At a live event, there was the opportunity to recognize and confirm each other's existence. At the event, a portion of a crowd can react to a fan's taunts, and even if the crowd rejects the taunts, the reaction validates the presence of the fan. S/he was there and contributed to the event. Although something similar can happen with a small group of friends or family watching an event on television, the reach is greater at the event itself, and the confirmation is that much more valuable.

The fan's confirmation experience is one in which several people react to the performance of the fan. Those several people act as an audience to the fan as a performer. It is similar to the type of confirmation people obtain from SNSs. When people post on a SNS or comment on a blog or news site, they are providing content for an audience and presenting a portion of themselves that is somewhat different from other presentations. The communication practices associated with presenting a public self bring a type of confirmation, but they also involve several ambiguities.

There are several ways communication changes when it is public, and to explore this I will begin by noting some features of communication and technology from earlier chapters. In Chapter 3 I noted how communication might change in diverse social spaces and how newer HCT has challenged earlier distinctions between interpersonal communication and mass communication.

What happens to your messages when you are involved in FtF interaction with more than one person? If you are talking to one person, if a second person enters the scene, and if you now change your message, you have a different relationship with the first person than the second because you changed the message. The new message now accounts for both people. Assume both people are old friends you have known since high school, and you are now talking to "old friends". You chose to change your message to talk to "old friends" instead of the first or second person exclusively because the other person was right there seeing and hearing you talk.

What happens when two new friends enter the scene with the old friends? The social space has become more diverse. You now have four distinctive relationships with four people, you are part of two groups – old friends and new friends, and you are performing for another group – friends. What happens when a co-worker enters the space? A supervisor? A relative? A person you just met? Do you talk to friends while others watch? Do you talk to the others while friends watch? Do you try talking to everyone at once? Do you just talk to the people sitting closest to you? What is your relationship with them? How can you talk to them knowing some others could be watching or overhearing you? Presenting yourself, changing the presentation of yourself in different relationships, and dealing with audiences are common features of any communication (Goffman, 1959).

Three characteristics of dealing with diverse social situations and audiences are worth noting. First, communication is likely to be more dramatic or animated. That is, communicators will use more lively language, tell stories and exaggerate, use grand gestures and facial expressions, or intentionally construct messages in colorful ways. This is common behavior when people know someone is watching, such as during public meetings or when negotiators must face the public. When people are more aware of an audience, a third party, they can become more conscious of making a good impression and saving face (Lewicki, Barry & Sanders, 2010), and their statements seem more polarizing and definitive. All of this is a form of amplification. People are attracting attention to a good impression. The pictures you might post on a SNS will also be dramatic, and you might state your opinions at the extremes. Something more dramatic will get more views.

Secondly, diverse social situations and an audience are likely to lead to a broader presentation to improve your reach. That is, you must use more general language and more general themes. You might be more dramatic about it, but you say less. Before the Internet and cable, television producers faced the challenge of reaching the largest audience. Mass media was about reaching the largest mass. The results were programs that were safe, and there were many programs few objected to, but few really liked. The programs at the start were versions of radio, stage, or film productions, but this quickly moved to situation comedies, westerns, and crime dramas. Networks imitated each other. There were just some basic types of programs that others copied. This is no different from seeing someone post a picture at a party on a SNS and many others posting pictures from their parties. We reinforce our social identity with the audience by saying and doing things that the audience does or that we already know the audience likes. We normally obtain some confirmation for our social identities if we do this for several SNSs. Although knowing your audience and speaking to the audience as a whole are good advice for designing a speech or a marketing campaign (Beebe & Beebe, 2011), continually presenting yourself this way can lead to deindividuation, a way of making sense that loses sight of ourselves as individuals and of others as individuals.

Third, the messages can become equivocal social cues. Although there may be many pictures from an event uploaded to a site from many participants, the pictures can all start to look the same. Most would have a hard time telling who uploaded the pictures or the significance of any of them. Of course, some people upload the pictures as a kind of "insider meaning" for the people in the picture or a few other people who attended the event. If this is so, why post the picture on the site? Why not just share the picture some other way? As people post more and more similar pictures, the differences are lost. When the differences are lost, so is the information.

This blurring of social cues in public has been going on for some time. Fans begin to think they are part of the event. In a later chapter I will explain how even a seasoned reporter can confuse the roles of participants in an event with being a reporter, with being an editorial writer, and with being an entertainer. The various news networks have begun to use comments made on each other's programs as news stories – comments made by the employees of the networks rather than the guests on an interview or a participant of an event at the scene. The drive to create stimulating messages to a wider audience can lead to confusion even for the creator of the messages.

When people have trouble making sense of the social cues in diverse social situations, they can lose sight of how the contours of one relationship are different from another. *Contemporary communication technology practices include a hyperconnectivity that magnifies ambiguity and the number of equivocal social cues.* People can lose their sense of place (Meyrowitz, 1985) and can fail to distinguish the contextual integrity of various communication situations (Nussbaum, 2004). What is private in one relationship can become public in another.

Others can combine data about us, including the selves we presented in the past and across different relationships, to create profiles of us far removed from how we see ourselves in the present (Gerwirtz & Kern, 2013). These challenges have led to several different ways to manage information on SNSs (Angwin, 2013) and an ongoing debate about how to best use SNSs (Hartzog & Selinger, 2013). Clarifying relationships and finding how best to communicate with the people in them is important to maintaining our own sense of self and personal integrity.

The latest HCTs provide many opportunities to develop a richer self. The newer HCTs are electronic and mobile allowing people to develop larger and more diverse personal networks than the past. The latest HCTs accelerated the trend to this networked individualism and away from communicating exclusively in small, densely knit groups like families and small organizations (Rainie & Wellman, 2012). More contacts mean more opportunities to renegotiate roles in more diverse relationships and to develop more aspects of self (Hage & Powers, 1992).

Sustaining closer relationships and developing a richer self involve more mindful communication. Role redefinition requires more frequent, longer, concentrated, and intense communication in which people confront each other as unique contributors to their relationships together (Hage & Powers, 1992, pp. 111-129). But, the stability of any network requires participants to periodically reaffirm connections (Hage & Powers, 1992), and maintaining close contacts involves time and, often, money (Rainie & Wellman, 2012). Too small a network can suffocate, but too large a network spreads a broader self too thin, and the loss of depth can become an ephemeral self. Finding the balance requires reflection.

Internet Addiction Disorder

Concerns about Internet addiction disorder (IAD) exemplify the challenges to maintaining the proper balance. IAD includes addiction to Internet devices (e.g., smartphones), platforms (e.g., Facebook or other social media), content (e.g., online sex), and behaviors (e.g. gaming, shopping). The American Society of Addiction Medicine (2013) identifies very specific criteria to classify any behavior as an addiction, and these criteria include changes in brain functions. The American Psychiatric Association's latest *Diagnostic and Statistical Manual* (2013) reserves a section for "behavioral addiction" and highlights gambling as an example. A more psychological approach points to behavior becoming addictive when a person can receive immediate rewards and cannot control the pursuit of those rewards in the face of harmful life consequences (*Psychology Today*, 2013). Technology researchers have studied these behaviors as addiction, compulsive behaviors, or problem use (Bianchi & Philips, 2005; Griffiths, 2000; Leung, 2008; Yeh, Lin, Tseng, & Hwang, 2012).

Researchers and clinicians have developed a variety of evaluation methods, but it is difficult to make empirically valid conclusions about IAD because of inconsistent classification criteria (Byun, et al, 2009). Estimates for Internet addiction vary from 0.3% to 38% depending on the culture, sample techniques, and the type of addiction - general IAD or a more specific IAD such as gaming (Cash, Rae, Steel & Winkler, 2012). The most reliable estimates classify 12-15% of Americans as having IAD (Aiken, 2016). However, the commonalities across this research demonstrate the necessity for individuals to periodically assess their own technological activities. Exploring this research will lead back to the stare.

Characteristics of IAD include (a) *greater use and* (b) *more varied use.* How much time do you spend online? How many different things do you do? Most compulsive use is (c) *mindless.* and other characteristics of IAD are related to the inability of people to control their activities. Repeated efforts to cut back lead to pain and withdrawal, and it seems as if more and more activity is necessary to achieve the rewards. Part of criteria for any addiction are (d) *feeling out of control,* (e) *withdrawal symptoms, and* (f) *increased tolerance for the addiction* (American Society of Addiction Medicine, 2013), and items about these features are part of most IAD surveys (Cash, Rae, Steel & Winkler, 2012; Yeh, Lin, Tseng, & Hwang, 2012). The mobile phone addict cannot go to bed without the phone (Leung, 2008). There is a whole section of YouTube videos devoted to "gaming freak-outs".

The IAD literature identifies several social and psychological features associated with higher HCT use. Specific HCT uses such as communicating with friends, gaming, or browsing, carry their own rewards, but all HCT use satisfies a human need to be involved in information processing. The need for information processing is part of a biological drive for environmental control. Self-identity emerges as a human achieves this control (Miller & Steinberg, 1975). The drive is such that the organism strives to operate at maximum capacity avoiding both overload and underload (Salem & Gratz, 1983). Some HCT uses can help organize overload, delegate responsibility, or simply avoid the increased load, and other HCT uses can increase complexity the offline world does not provide. A consistent finding in the IAD research is that *high digital HCT users have higher needs for sensation seeking*, and they *use digital HCT more to escape and relieve boredom* than lower digital HCT users (Cash, Rae, Steel & Winkler, 2012; Leung, 2008).

Current HCT engages touch, in addition to sight and sound, and this entry into the somatosensory system means we will use more of our attention to engage (Carr, 2011). This multi-sensory engagement is interactive, and just knowing that our actions bring reactions, feedback, and results is rewarding and would improve self-esteem and self-efficacy.

A person with low self-esteem or self-efficacy would be attracted to more contemporary HCT use, and a people who are nervous about interacting with others could gain some confidence through the interactivity of the technology. Consistent findings in the IAD research is that *high users of digital HCT have lower self-esteem* (Cash, Rae, Steel & Winkler, 2012; Leung, 2008) *and greater social anxiety* (Cash, Rae, Steel & Winkler, 2012).

High digital HCT users can limit their environment to a world dominated by technical cues or one in which they limit their communication to digital methods. There is the potential for social isolation (Gratz & Salem, 1984). Reduced capacity for and limited experiences dealing with social cues lead to diminished relationships and to a less viable self (Gratz & Salem, 1984; Salem & Gratz, 1983). A consensus in the IAD literature is that *digital HCT use becomes problematic or addictive when psychological or relational problems develop with increased digital HCT use.*

People who use greater social media have *less empathy* (Dailey, Howard, Roming, Ceballos, & Grimes, 2018). There are less needs to understand others or exhibit concern for others if there is less personal HCT. Postings on social media may objectify the members of that media. The more we use such HCT the less we care what others think.

Newer HCT use could satisfy interpersonal needs to the point where *digital HCT interactivity could substitute for human communication.* We are first connected to our devices and then to the experiences we create. People have the tendency to treat their technology as if the technology were social actors, and this includes perceiving the technology as the source of information rather than the person or programmer who supplied it (Nass & Reeves, 1996). We can become dependent on the interaction with the devices, and unlike people, the devices are not demanding and do not have their own unique psychological expectations and needs. We feel in control and included. The pull of this interactivity can be so great that it leads to dependence. We become alone together - alone with our devices while feeling we are connected to others (Turkle, 2011).

Nearly all this research is correlational research, meaning the results are not valid evidence to prove HCT practices *cause* these results. Rather, it is just as likely that those with higher social anxiety and other variations of having doubts about themselves and others are more likely to develop IAD. Some have argued that IAD may just be a manifestation of communication addiction disorder (Walther, 1999). Some people may need to communicate with others more than the rest of us and the newer HCTs provide a means of doing so.

Table 5.2

Self and Technology

Maintaining anonymity is difficult with today's HCTs.

Self-disclosure becomes more complicated because of the reach of newer HCTs.

Online gaming demonstrates many of the opportunities and challenges to developing self with newer HCTs.

Protecting your privacy is difficult with today's HCTs.

Communication changes in at least three ways when people are in diverse social spaces such as on social media.

The newer HCTs provide opportunities to develop richer and more complex self-concepts.

Using the latest HCTs leads to periodic overuse and problem use.

Being mindful and reflecting on our uses of HCT can help us develop a deeper sense of self and avoid consistent problem use.

What the literature about social and psychological features suggests is that when people with problems such as self-identity, self-esteem, or self-efficacy, use digital HCT, there is increased potential for IAD. What has happened is that the parameters for the communicators and the technology are at levels that could produce a serious disorder over time. For the rest of us, the research suggests that when we have serious doubts about ourselves or are particularly down on ourselves, we should be careful about our use of newer HCT. In a later chapter, I will describe productive uses for stressful times.

The vast majority of us are not addicted to our digital HCT or to digital HCT uses. However, the previous paragraphs display how normal use can become overuse, overuse can become compulsive use, and compulsive use can become problem use. All of us have had the experience of getting lost in our digital HCT use. It could have happened just browsing, checking out SNSs, shopping online, or playing a game. We are suddenly late for an appointment or behind in our work. We look up, it is dawn, and we have lost a night's sleep. The same thing could have happened watching TV or reading a book. But, the features of newer HCT and how we typically use this HCT increase potential for that stare.

Finding the balance in our HCT use is about maintaining control of how we present and understand ourselves. Our self-concept is a configuration of ideas rooted in and derived from the communication we have with others. Self-concept is a mix of perceived similarities and differences like all information and knowledge. Our sense of our own self worth comes from comparing ourselves to others, and there are tensions between perceived differences and similarities. The more complex and viable self emerges when we can operate within an information processing range that is not so low as to reject the differences in others but not so high as to lose the appreciation for how we are different from others (Weinrich & Saunderson, 2003). An overloaded self is a self saturated with impressions of others (Gergen, 1991). Getting lost in the flow of constantly reconstructing and negotiating ourselves using the newer technologies leads us back to the stare. We need to step back and periodically assess our HCT use.

One way people can assess their use of a given technology is to examine their communication when that technology is not available to them. This can occur naturally and unintended such as when people travel to regions in which access to one or more technologies are impossible or prohibitive. It can also happen as a reaction to being "too connected," and individuals intentionally "detoxify" themselves from technologies (Rufus, 2010).

In one recent study, I asked students to deprive themselves of the use of a technology for one week and report their observations during the week (Salem, 2012). For one week students did not use their telephone, another week they did not use any textual communication (email, texting, IM, etc.), and in another week students avoided any television or television programming. Students became aware they had become dependent on a given technology. One student noted "I believe I have a relationship with my cell phone." The students also became conscious of how they were communicating with the people in their life, and how they were constructing themselves in that environment. In the end, they realized they could adapt. That is, they came to appreciate their own abilities to control and change.

Mindful about Self and HCT

I began this chapter by describing people at a video arcade with a far-off stare. Although we have all had such moments, I began to describe how that stare could be a problem when we mindlessly fall into using HCT. The psychological challenges to using newer HCT are not unique, and so the chapter began with literature about self-concept and moved to how the use of newer HCT might be related.

Self-concept is a perception, and there are many dimensions to self. Similar to other perceptions, self-concepts vary in their complexity, and self-concepts are the source for frames we use to make sense. Self is a configuration of the role concepts a person has made in particular relationships, and so we create, negotiate, and renegotiate aspects of self in our communication with others.

Developing any aspect of self becomes more difficult when a person has difficulty making sense of particular episodes or messages. The social cues are equivocal. We either have too few cues to help us learn what we think might be going on or we have so many cues we have trouble deciding which frames fit the situation. We can become confused about the differences in our relationships, the differences in our roles, and, ultimately, how we are different and similar from others.

The ambiguities in using newer HCT provide opportunities to present and negotiate more and different aspects of self than the older technologies. However, the same increased ambiguities can lead to old problems. How much can we disclose and to whom? How can we control what others know about us online? How careful have we been in how we present ourselves in public digital sites? How do we use technology? Do we overuse it? Have we suspected we have problems with how much we use newer HCT?

The challenges dealing with the ambiguities using the newer HCT are no different from the ones using the older ones. However, the speed and nature of the newer HCT can act as a catalyst to magnify problems related to self, especially for those with more severe psychological problems. For many of us, there is the potential to lose ourselves in our technology and to lose some control over who we are. Our sense of self could become a dreamlike ephemeral and momentary recreation dependent on the instantaneous reactions of others. For most us, we will just have those stares from time to time. Mindful reflection on using newer HCTs can enhance and develop self.

References

Aiken, M. (2016) *The cyber effect*. New York: Spiegel & Grau.

Allport, F. (1924). *Social psychology*. Boston: Houghton Mifflin.

American Society of Addiction Medicine. (2013). Definition of addiction. Retrieved from http://www.asam.org/for-the-public/definition-of-addiction.

Altman, I, & Taylor, D. A. (1973). *Social penetration: The development of interpersonal relationships*. New York: Holt, Rinehart, & Winston.

American Psychiatric Association. (2013). *Diagnostic and statistical manual* (5th ed.). Arlington, VA: American Psychiatric Publishing.

Angwin, J. (2013, February 12). Why I'm unfriending you on Facebook. (Web log post). Retrieved from http://juliaangwin.com/why-im-unfriending-you-on-facebook.

Bandura, A. (1986). *Social foundations of thought and action*. Englewood Cliffs, NJ: Prentice-Hall.

Bavelas, J. B., Black, A., Chovil, N., & Mullett, J. (1990). *Equivocal communication*. Newbury Park, CA: Sage.

Beebe, S. A., & Beebe, S. B. (2011). *Public speaking: An audience centered approach* (8th ed.). Upper Saddle River, NJ: Pearson.

Bianchi, A., & Phillips, J. G. (2005). Psychological predictors of problem mobile phone use. *CyberPsychology and Behavior, 8*(1), 39-51.

Brewer, M.B., & Gardner, W. (1996). Who is this "we"? Levels of collective identity and self representations. *Journal of Personality and Social Psychology, 71*, 83–93.

Brown, J. S., & Duguid, P. (2000). *The social life of information*. Cambridge, MA: Harvard Business School Press.

Butz, M. R. (1997). *Chaos and complexity: Implications for psychological theory and practice*. Washington, DC: Taylor and Francis.

Byum, S., Ruffini, C., Mills, J. E., Douglas, A. C., Niang, M., Stepchenkova, . . . Atallah, M. (2009). Internet addiction: Metasynthesis of 1996-2006 quantitative research. *CyberPsychology & Behavior, 12*(2), 203-207.

Carr, N. (2011). *The shallows: What the Internet is doing to our brains*. New York, NY: Norton & Company.

Cash, H., Rae, C. D., Steel, A. H., & Winkler, A. (2012). Internet addiction: A brief summary of research and practice. *Clinical Psychiatry Review, 8*, 292-298.

Cissna, K. N., & Sieburg, E. (1981). Patterns of interactional confirmation and disconfirmation. In C. Wilder-Mott & J. H. Weakland (Eds.), *Rigor and imagination: Essays from the legacy of Gregory Bateson* (pp. 253 282). NY: Praeger.

Cushman, D. P., & Cahn, D. D. (1985). *Communication in interpersonal relationships*. Albany, NY: State University of New York Press.

Daily, R. M. (2006). Confirmation in parent-adolescent relationships and adolescent openness: Toward extending confirmation theory. *Communication Monographs, 73*, 434-458.

Dailey, S. L., Howard, K. J., Roming, S., Ceballos, N. A., & Grimes, T. (November, 2018). *Playing with fire: Communicative and psychosocial predictors of social media addiction.* Paper presented to the Human Communication and Technology Division of the National Communication Association meeting in Salt Lake City, UT.

Dance, F. E. X., & Larson, C. E. (1976). *The functions of human communication: A theoretical approach.* NY: Holt, Rinehart and Winston.

Erikson, E. (1980). *Identity and the life cycle.* New York: W. W. Norton & Company.

Fisher, D. V. (1984). A conceptual analysis of self-disclosure. *Journal for the Theory of Social Behavior, 14*(3), 277-296.

Gergen, K. (1991). *The saturated self: Dilemmas of identity in contemporary life.* New York: Basic Books.

Gerwirtz, J. B., & Kern, A. B. (2013, July 26). The Internet generation will learn to let go. *The Washington Post.* Retrieved at http://www.washingtonpost.com/opinions/internet-generation-will-learn-to-let-go/2013/07/26/640be4ca-f606-11e2-9434-60440856fadf_print.html.

Goffman, E. (1959). *The presentation of self in everyday life.* Garden City, NY: Doubleday Anchor.

Gratz, R. D., & Salem, P. J. (1984). Technology and the crisis of self. *Communication Quarterly, 32*(2), 98-103.

Griffiths, M. D. (2000). Does Internet and "addiction" exist? Some case study evidence. *CyberPsychology and Behavior, 3*(2), 211-218.

Haley, J. (1959). An interactional description of schizophrenia. *Psychiatry, 22*, 321-332.

Hage, J., & Powers, C, H. (1992). *Post-industrial lives: Roles and relationships in the 21st century*. Newbury Park, CA: Sage.

Hartzog, W., & Selinger, E. (2013, February, 15). Quitters never win: The costs of leaving social media. *The Atlantic*. Retrieved at http://www.theatlantic.com/technology/archive/2013/02/quitters-never-win-the-costs-of-leaving-social-media/273139/

Ho, S. S., & McLeod, D. M. (2008). Social-psychological influences on opinion expression in face-to-face and computer-mediated communication. *Communication Research, 35*(2), 190-207.

Hofstede, G., & Hofstede, G. J. (2005). *Cultures and organizations: Software of the mind*. New York: McGraw-Hill,

Kim, J., & Dindia, K. (2011). Online self-disclosure: A review of research. In K. B. Wright & L. M. Webb (Eds.), *Computer-mediated communication in personal relationships* (pp. 156-180). New York: Peter Lang.

Klimmt, C., & Hartmann, T. (2008). Mediated interpersonal communication in multiplayer video games: Implications for entertainment and relational management. In E. A. Konijin, S. Utz, M. Tanis, & S. B. Barnes (Eds.). *Mediated interpersonal communication* (pp. 309-330). New York: Routledge.

Knapp, M. L., & Vangelisti, A. L (2009). *Interpersonal communication and human relationships* (6th ed.). Boston: Pearson Education.

Kunda, Z. (1999). *Making sense of people*. Cambridge, MA: MIT Press.

Leibling, A. J. (1956). *The sweet science*. New York: Penguin Books.

Leung, L. (2008). Leisure, boredom, sensation seeking, self esteem, and addiction. In E. A. Konijin, S. Utz, M. Tanis, & S. B. Barnes (Eds.). *Mediated interpersonal communication* (pp. 359-381). New York: Routledge.

Lewicki, R. J., Barry, B., & Saunders, D. M. (2010). *Negotiation* (6th ed.). Boston, MA: McGraw Hill Irwin.

McCroskey, J. (2009). Communication apprehension: What we have learned in the last four decades. *Human Communication, 12*(2), 157–171.

Meyrowitz. J. (1985). *No sense of place: The impact of electronic media on social behavior*. NY: Oxford University Press.

Miller, G. R., & M. Steinberg (1975). *Between people: A new analysis of interpersonal communication*. Palo Alto, CA: Science Research Associates.

Moskowitz, G. B. (2004). *Social cognition: Understanding self and other*. NY: Guilford.

Nussbaum, H. (2004). Privacy as contextual integrity. *Washington Law Review, 79*, 119-157.

Psychology Today (2013). Addiction: Compulsive and addictive behavior. Retrieved from http://www.psychologytoday.com/basics/addiction/compulsive-and-addictive-behaviors.

Rainie, L., & Wellman, B. (2012). *Networked: The new social operating system*. Cambridge, MA: MIT Press.

Reeves, B., & Nass, C. (1996). *The media equation*. Stanford, CA: CSLI Publications, Cambridge University Press.

Reicher, S., Spears, R., & Postmes, T. (1995). A social identity model of deindividuation phenomena. *European Review of Social Psychology, 6*, 161–198.

Rufus, A. (2010, April, 21). The dangers of digital detoxing. *The Daily Beast*. Retrieved from http://www.thedailybeast.com.

Salem, P. J. (2012, February). *Personal and interpersonal adaptations to technology deprivation*. Paper presented the annual convention of the Western States Communication Association, Albuquerque, NM.

Salem, P. J., & Gratz, R. D. (1983). High technology and social devolution. In N. Callaos (Ed.), *The 1983 World Conference on Systems*. Caracas, Venezuela: The Foundation for the Investigation and Integration of Systems.

Sanders, W. S., & Amason, P. (2011). Communication competence and apprehension during CMC in online and face-to-face relationships. In K. B. Wright & L. M. Webb (Eds.), *Computer-mediated communication in personal relationships* (pp. 79-97). New York: Peter Lang.

Schry, A. R., Roberson-Nay, R., & White, S. W. (2012). Measuring social anxiety in college students: A comprehensive evaluation of the psychometric properties of the SPAI-23. *Psychological Assessment, 24*(4), 846–854

Scott, C. R., & Timmerman, C. E. (2005). Relating computer, communication, and computer-mediated communication apprehensions to new communication technology use in the workplace. *Communication Research, 32*(6), 683-725.

Sieburg, E. (1973, April) *Interpersonal confirmation: A paradigm for conceptualization and measurement*. Paper presented at the Annual Meeting of the International Communication Association, Montreal, Canada (ERIC Document Reproduction Services No ED 098 634).

Slater, D. (2002). Social relationships and identity online and offline. In L. Lievrouw, & S. Livingstone (Eds.). *Handbook of new media: Social shaping and consequences of ICTs* (pp. 533-546). Thousand Oaks, CA: Sage Publications.

Snyder, M., Tanke, E. D., & Berscheid, E. (1977). Social perception and interpersonal behavior: On the self-fulfilling nature of social stereotypes. *Journal of Personality & Social Psychology, 35,* 656–666.

Stohl C., & Redding, W. C. (1987). Messages and message exchange processes. In F. M. Jablin, L. L. Putnam, K. H. Roberts, & L. W. Porter (Eds.), *Handbook of organizational communication: An interdisciplinary perspective* (pp. 451-496). Newbury Park, CA: Sage.

Turkle, S. (2011). *Alone together: Why we expect more from technology and less from each other.* New York: Basic Books.

Walther, J. B. (1999, August). *Communication addiction disorder: Concern over media, behavior and effects.* Paper presented to the annual meeting of the American Psychological Association, Boston, MA.

Walther, J. B. (2007). Selective self-presentation in computer-mediated communication: Hyperpersonal dimensions of technology, language, and cognition. *Computers in Human Behavior, 23,* 2538-2557.

Weick, K. E. (1995). *Sensemaking in organizations.* Thousand Oaks, CA: Sage.

Weinrich, P., & Saunderson, W. (2003). *Analyzing identity: Cross-cultural, societal, and clinical contexts.* London: Routledge.

Williams, M. L., & Goss, B. (1975). Equivocation: Character insurance. *Human Communication Research, 1,* 265-270.

Yee, N., & Bailenson, J. (2007). The Proteus effect: The effect of transformed self-representation on behavior. *Human Communication Research, 33,* 271-290.

Yeh, Y., Lin, S. S. J., Tseng, Y., & Hwang, F. (2012). The questionnaire of lifestyle change in regard to problematic Internet use: Factor structure and concurrent cross-year predictive utilities. *The Turkish Online Journal of Educational Technology, 11*(4), 315-324.

Zimbardo, P. G. (1969). The human choice: Individuation, reason, and order vs. Deindividuation, impulse and chaos. In W. J. Arnold & D. Levine

(Eds.), *Nebraska symposium on motivation* (Vol. 17, pp. 237–307). Lincoln, NE: University of Nebraska Press.

Chapter Six: Messages

In 2014, Nina Davuluri was a 24-year old native of Fayetteville, New York. Nina earned a degree in brain behavior and cognitive science, and she wanted to be a physician like her father. Her father emigrated to this country from India thirty years ago, and his success and the success of his daughter were another chapter in the big book of the American dream.

Figure 6.1 Miss America 2014

Nina won the 2014 Miss America competition. Although most people online congratulated Nina, there were others who were not flattering. A racist Twitter trickle became a flood and then subsided after 24 hours. The *Daily Mail* reported it as follows:

> Meredith Talley (@MeredithRoanell) said: 'This is Miss America . . . Not Miss Foreign Country.' Her Twitter profile disappeared shortly after her racist tweet, which was shared by numerous people, most were shocked at her comment.

> Kat (@KathrynRyan50), who says on her Twitter profile that she is happily in love with her 'savior Jesus Christ', posted: 'She's

(sic) like not even american and she won miss america.' Kat also later deleted her own comment from her profile.

One girl starts her tweet by saying, 'I'm not a racist...' then goes on to question how Miss Davuluri can represent America 'doing an Indonesian dance'.

A user who calls herself 'FoxxiLiberal' (@FoxxiLiberal) and describes herself as a 'humanist,' and 'prochoice' posted: 'When will a white woman win Miss American? Ever?'

While Matt Haney (@OneProudHonkie) alleged online: 'How can you be Miss AMERICA and look like you should be a gas station clerk or motel owner?'

And Elizabeth (@EJRBuckeye) said: 'Well they just picked a Muslim for Miss America. That must've made Obama happy. Maybe he had a vote.' (Coleman & McCormack, 2013)

Popular Science has been translating scientific articles and stimulating discussion for over 140 years. When the publishers put the magazine online, the editorial board naturally included places for comments on the articles it displayed. No more. The editor wrote, "A politically motivated, decades-long war on expertise has eroded the popular consensus on a wide variety of scientifically validated topics. Everything, from evolution to the origins of climate change, is mistakenly up for grabs again" (LaBarre, 2013). Political, religious, and personal comments had driven out the comments about science, and many comments had become polarizing and abusive. The editor cited a study of how this "nasty factor" can distort how we process the rest of the information (Anderson, Brossard, Scheufele, Xenos, & Ludwig, 2013).

The article announcing the ending of the comments included links to articles and comments demonstrating the problems. One article described a study of what happens to women when they are denied abortions. Rather than discuss the merits of the article or the scientific merits of the study, the first six comments from six different people were as follows (numbers added):

#1 The narrative of this article and the study on which it is based perpetuates the falsehood, in that it assumes pregnancy is not a preventable occurrence.

#2 What happens to the baby when it's denied an abortion?

#3 To piggyback off of MeatForBrains, this article also never explores the possibility of putting the baby of for adoption to a family that will love and look after it's well being, and cover a lot if not all of the mothers medical expenses. Adoption is an option!!

My sister in law is a NICU nurse and has been in a number of different states, and she is baffled when she talks to girls that are considering abortion, all of which indicate that they were never told it was an option to put the child up for adoption. Come on, there are literally hundreds of thousands of people in this country that would do almost anything to have a child, to the point where they will go to Africa for a baby!! I mean when I dont want my dog or cat anymore I dont kill it I give to someone else who will care for it . . . sigh . . . we're doomed.

#4 My mom had 9 kids (quite the opposite from Miss S.) and went through financial collapse and suffered poor health. She didn't ever once consider aborting, if she did neither my brother nor his son would be alive today.

That said, I cannot feel sorry for a woman who hits hard times in spite of her best attempt to kill her child off.

#5 So some women get depressed when they are not allowed to have a government sanctioned murder of a baby. Outstanding . . .

How selfish is humanity that we condone murder of babies
instead of dealing with 9 months of inconvenience,
embarrassment, and adoption . . .

#6 Stop pretending that it wasn't your choice to have a baby. But
I suppose you are selfish and only care about your own
pleasure . . . (Diep, 2013).

Email (EML) and social media sites are not immune to this type of behavior. A small town mayor received threatening EML messages from around the country after local prosecutors decided not to pursue a sexual assault case against an athlete (Eligon, 2013). The family of the alleged victim moved after being harassed on social media. Their former house burned down, and the cause remained unknown.

You might think this sort of bad behavior is about children or adolescents. Wrong. IAC is an Internet based company that manages dozens of websites including the Daily Beast and Match.com. Justine Sacco, 30, was the corporate communications director, and she was traveling to South Africa on a Friday when she tweeted "Going to Africa. Hope I don't get AIDS. Just kidding. I'm white". Several thousand tweets later and before she landed on Saturday, IAC had fired her, and there was no trace of her on their website (Stebner, 2013). The tweets ranged from threats of violence to accusing her of being racist to describing her tweet as a failed joke. Public shaming using social media is now common (Ronson, 2015). It the equivalent of being stoned in the town square, and those throwing the stones are also engaged in bad behavior.

We may all have trouble finding the most effective way to say something in a particular situation, and all of us struggle with texting in the most effective way. The examples above suggest little reflection, and most of us would not find these messages inviting us into a conversation. An author of such messages might be hoping for other messages that confirm the author, and an avalanche of such negative messages can look like "piling on". But very little communication is taking place. In public electronic communication (BEC) a frequent pattern is for one person to run on stage and then run off just as another is running on. Alternatively, any effort to respond to more private text messages like these runs the risk of further amplification and, if there is disagreement, the messages may lead to conflict escalation.

This chapter is about making good and bad messages. The chapter begins by describing good messages. What does it mean to be communicatively competent? Although some aspects of making messages have a nearly universal recognition as competent communication, some messages work better in some situations than others. Are there different forms of communication competence for different types of communication technology? In the second section, I will describe seven types of digital messages people generally recognize as harmful in some way, and when people consistently use these types of messages, others recognize these people as communicatively incompetent. The last section offers explanations for both good and bad digital message behaviors.

Competent Messaging

A *competent communicator* can perform appropriate and effective behaviors necessary to sustain communication. Communication competence is about both perceptions and behaviors, it is about communicating well in various situations, and it is about being flexible and adaptive. There may be some general features to communication competence regardless of the human communication technologies (HCTs), but there are unique challenges and opportunities when using the different forms of HCT.

Messages are symbols in some physical form. They are what one communicator makes available to another to make sense. In a traditional sense, messages are what individuals intentionally create for others, and the individuals assume they share some consensual meaning for those behaviors (Burgoon, Buller, & Woodall, 1996). However, the receiver of a message actively enacts that reception and chooses what will count as cues as s/he makes sense of the array provided by the sender. I presented this review of earlier material to reinforce the limitations for what a sender of a message can control and the importance our roles as human information processors to understanding each other as we communicate. Individuals can only directly control their own behaviors and their own processing of messages. One person makes a message, and others make sense of it.

Describing good or bad messages will always be a matter of perspective because of the technology of communication. There is really no way to say that making a given type of message will always produce a positive result, and determining the success of a particular message is more about the receiver of the message than the sender's intent or performance. Furthermore, a receiver can only make sense of a sender's message as it occurs in an episode and as part of a given relationship the receiver helped create. Making competent messages is about perceptions and behaviors, and it is about the dynamic aspects of individuals communicating together. For example, we might all agree that the harassing or bullying messages noted above are bad messages, but a sequence of such messages from different sources suggests that the people in the sequence might have thought they were doing the right or proper thing to post those messages. My description of making competent messages begins with aspects of human information processing (HIP) to help recognize what generally works and to be sensitive to what generally does not.

Information and Knowledge

HIP proceeds from signals to data to information to knowledge. Knowledge provides the source for the particular frames we use to connect to cues as we make sense. Communication is shared sense making as the participants create and process cues they collectively create in an episode. Competent communicators develop a complex body of knowledge to deal with various circumstances, and they also understand the limitations of HIP.

First, a competent communicator must have information and knowledge of ***the perceptions of others*** involved in communication. Understanding your audience may be the oldest advice for people making a public presentation, and authors have used expressions like "other oriented", decentering, developing an appreciation for the other, and being empathic to describe interpersonal or general communication competence for almost as long (Beebe, Beebe, & Ivy, 2012; Dance & Larson, 1976; Murray, 1937). Although knowing how the members of a large audience are similar to a speaker or to each other are good starting points, perceptions of similarity often degenerate into stereotyping or projecting your own perceptions on others.

Empathy is an ability to accurately understand and appreciate how others are different from you and from each other (Davis, 1983; Salem, 2013), and empathy is an essential part of being competent. What is competent communication to one communicator may be different to others, and understanding how others might frame messages differently will help a person adjust and alter his/her messages. Developing empathy involves being tentative about using past knowledge and creating information about others consistent with how the episode develops.

The use of the newer HCTs highlights an old problem related to empathy – selecting an audience. People don't want to be incompetent or to have others think of them as such, and so I will assume people create messages they believe are competent. But, competent for whom – what audience, what others? Who was the audience for the posts about Miss America? I have highlighted the problems of diverse social spaces several times in this book.

Second, a competent communicator knows what is appropriate. ***Appropriate communication*** is consistent with the rules for communication within a given relationship. A competent communicator knows which ways of creating messages meet the expectations of others and avoids sanctions for communicating inappropriately. Indeed, the rules for communicating and the expectations for how to communicate are often taken for granted assumptions that we fail to recognize until someone violates those assumptions. First meetings, communicating in different cultures, changes of relationships, and first weeks at work have been common times we fail to be appropriate. Also, the knowledge of appropriate communication does not mean the communicator will always seek to comply with what is appropriate since communicators may be seeking to change the rules (Sptizberg, 2000). Scholars have identified appropriateness as a key characteristic of communication competence for some time (Sptizberg & Cupbach, 1984; Wiemann, 1977).

The uses of HCT have changed so fast that it is difficult to know which HCT is appropriate. Should you send a text, call directly on the phone, or send an EML message? Maybe the communication should be face-to-face (FtF)? Approaching HCT choices in a strategic way begins by considering the audience and the purpose of the communication (Linton, 2013). What are the potential social cues when sending a message using a specific HCT? How will the receiver perceive you and your relationship together if you try to call or if you send a text message? What is the appropriate thing to do? Some companies have developed checklists reminding members of their workforce what they regard as appropriate for business communication (Hamilton, Byatt, & Hodgkinson, 2010).

Moving between different HCTs can also be confusing. People tend to use texting as if it were conversation more than as if it were writing, and they tend to regard texting as more informal than formal (Baron, 2010). People also say they regard using EML as more formal, and there are more things to consider (e.g., subject line, salutation) when using EML than texting. Although people seem to have a sense of what is appropriate on one

HCT and not on another, they can lose track of which HCT they have been using and inappropriate content can find its way into a message. Recall from an earlier chapter the example I detailed about how the texting content between my graduate student and her boyfriend became embarrassing SNS postings. Furthermore, people can transfer styles and cues or fail to consider different social cues altogether when dealing with different audiences. The emotional texts between friends or intimates can become an emotional EML response to a coworker. Informal spelling and grammar may be fine for texting, but using the same informal style for EML will make it difficult for a student to get that appointment with the teacher (Stephens, Houser, & Cowan, 2009). You can lose your job because your EML messages had an inappropriate tone (Shipley & Schwable, 2008).

There have always been problems of knowing the right way to say the right thing, but there are unique challenges for knowing what is appropriate for using the current technology. Is it appropriate to scan your mobile phone for texts and alerts while having dinner with someone? Is it even appropriate to place your mobile phone on the table while talking to someone across the table? Should everyone now have a SNS like Facebook? Do people have a responsibility to inform others beyond posting on a SNS? What and with whom should people tweet? Are there limits to tweeting depending on your job? Farhad Manjoo and Emily Yoffe discussed such topics for several years in podcasts for *Slate* magazine.

Inappropriate messages often become cues for potentially damaging social perceptions. That is, when an inappropriate message surprises the receiver of such a message, the receiver must now process more information about the sender and the sender-receiver relationship than the receiver anticipated. Old frames for social cues will not work. At the very least, having the receiver work more to develop social information from the message will distract the receiver from developing technical information. Worse, the receiver might frame the inappropriate message as insulting, disrespectful, or hostile. Ultimately, inappropriate messages have the potential to damage a relationship (Spitzberg, 2006; Spitzberg & Cupbach, 1984).

Third, a competent communicator knows what is *effective*. A message or sequence of messages is effective when the messages accomplish specific functions or goals. Knowing what is effective means the communicator has conscious goals and believes some messages would be most likely to accomplish those goals. Of course, a competent communicator will be sensitive to how effective messages have been, but the senders of messages can only judge the effectiveness as part of an episode they and others help create. A competent communicator has knowledge of effectiveness but processes information about effectiveness as the episode develops.

What were Justine's goals when she tweeted that message? Were the goals of the people who harassed the alleged victim of a sexual assault to have the victim's family move? Did the people who commented on the *Popular Science* articles want the magazine to shut down the opportunity to comment again?

Fourth, a competent communicator has *operational knowledge* about what to do and how to do it well. They know how to construct appropriate and effective messages. They know what types of messages work and can sustain conversation, and they also know how much to do. Operational knowledge also refers to knowing the unique features of different technologies (Sptizberg, 2006). Which technology should you use to accomplish different goals?

Generally, you should select the technology with the greater capacity for messages about more complicated goals. In Chapter 3, I noted that Daft and Lengel had described capacity as richness (Daft & Lengel, 1986; Lengel & Daft, 1988). Richer technology involves more potential cues and could help process more information than leaner technology. Small group and dyadic FtF communication are richer than print or traditional EML. In Chapter 3, I also described how newer technology had the potential to be equivalent to or exceed the richness of FtF.

Table 6.1

Making Competent Technology Choices

	Technology	
Goal	Lean	Rich
Simple	Good choice: Limited message options enhance the chances for simple messages accomplishing the goal.	Poor choice: Many message options that may distract from your focus. Difficulty predicting.
Complicated	Poor choice: Limited message options for dealing with variety related to the goal. Difficulty understanding.	Good choice: Many message options enhancing the chances for accomplishing the goal.

Goals are more complicated or less complicated depending on how many different and interconnected things you have to consider. Goals are more complicated depending on how much relative variety there is to consider. If relative variety looks familiar, it is because I introduced it in Chapter 1, the chapter on information processing. When trying to accomplish a goal with much information to process, use the technology with the greater capacity to process information.

Table 6.1 (adapted from Lengel & Daft, 1988) displays a simplified version of the choices. Failing to match the choices correctly leads to some type of error or ambiguity. I described various types of error and forms of ambiguity in the first and last chapter. When technology is too rich for the goal, there will be an excess of potential cues. Using a leaner technology for a simpler task is better. There is no need to meet someone face-to-face or even to talk to someone on the telephone to check on a meeting time when a text message is available. Similarly, when technology is too lean for the goal, there will be potential for too few cues to process well. Managing conflict with text messages is not a good idea.

People intuitively match technology to the processing demands of the goal, but they choose technology based on what they know about the technology and what they think about the goal. A goal is as simple or as complex as a person has framed it. Technology is as rich or as lean depending on what a person knows about it. Of course, people's experiences and their communication with others have the greatest influence on what people know about technology and various goals (Fulk, Schmitz, & Steinfeld, 1990; Spitzberg, 2006).

Fifth, a competent communicator has knowledge and information about the *social situation* that might alter which appropriateness and effectiveness frames a communicator uses. Social situation refers to different occasions such as at work or at a family gathering. It also refers to the type of relationships communicators might have such as friends, romantic partners, or acquaintances. It also refers to knowing how to change behaviors depending on the situation. That is, knowledge and information about a social situation include knowing how to be flexible and adapt even as the situation may be changing as communication occurs.

Having knowledge of social situations includes understanding the unique circumstances that might occur with today's technology. For example, online gaming provides a unique opportunity to communicate with others, and I noted the potential for the Proteus effect in the last chapter when people do not distinguish their online roles from their offline ones. Similarly, people may meet in a support group or as part of an online dating service, situations I will describe in later chapters, but they may fail to alter their expectations and frames for appropriateness and effectiveness when they meet offline. Consider the potential for confusion when people who meet as part of online dating recognize each other from earlier communication as part of a support group.

Finally, a competent communicator is ***mindful***. When Langer (1989; 1997) described mindfulness, she used expressions like an openness to new things, a willingness to create new categories, alertness to distinctions, being sensitive to different contexts, an awareness of multiple perspectives from different people, and an orientation to the present. Notice the number of times she alluded to differences and novelty. Mindfulness is about active information processing in the here-and-now.

Mindlessness has three distinctive characteristics (Langer, 1989). First, *mindlessness involves an over reliance on old categories*. The people who responded to the new Miss America are a good example of that. They had multiple categories but refused to use them in any novel way such as creating a category for Muslim-American. Second, *mindlessness involves a premature commitment to an interpretation or course of action*. The people who responded to the *Popular Science* article will not consider the value of the article as science since it is about abortion. Since it is about abortion, no other categories are relevant.

Furthermore, the earlier posts might have encouraged the tone in latter posts. Over commitment is about looking at things in a narrow way and then reacting to them within a narrow range of responses. Finally, *mindlessness is about performing overlearned behavior*. People start sequences in a rote way failing to recognize or understand the differences between one situation and another. All those examples above of saying, texting, or posting something without understanding how things were different highlight this feature. Happily, my graduate student married her boyfriend, but Justine is not with her company.

Mindfulness is different from being conscious. Consciousness involves awareness and attention, but mindfulness is about doing something with being aware and attentive (Brown & Ryan, 2003). Mindfulness is about testing new categories and trying new things. Mindfulness is about using consciousness to learn.

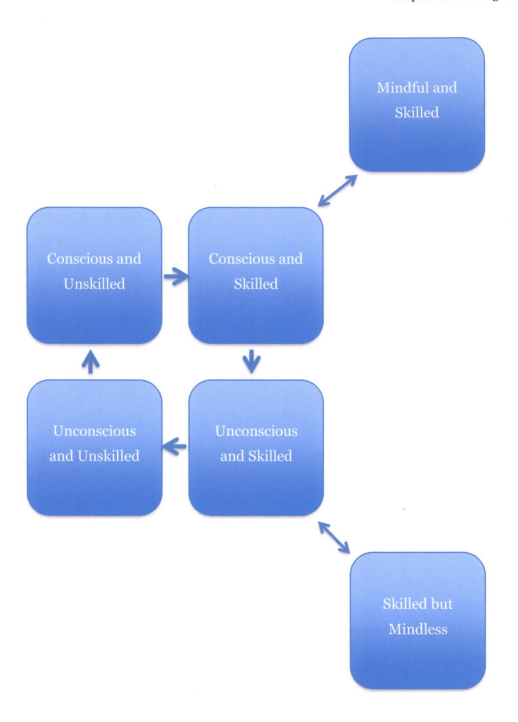

Figure 6.1 Mindfulness and Competence

Figure 6.1 displays an adaptation of a learning model that couples skills and consciousness. In the original 30-year old model, people develop a skill by moving clockwise from being unconscious and unskilled to eventually being unconscious and skilled (Adams, n. d.). Unconsciously unskilled is a state when we don't know that we are doing poorly, but when we recognize that things are not going well, we become consciously unskilled. Being consciously skilled means we make an effort to improve, but we need to think about doing the skill and performing it requires effort. When we are unconsciously competent, performing the skill is natural and easy. The skill has become routine, and we can do it with little thought.

Problems with being unconsciously skilled relate to being on automatic pilot. Without the awareness of situational differences people become very good at doing the things that worked well earlier or with different people, but have unhappy consequences now (Argyris, 1992). People are not testing the skill but performing as if it were perfect. They may be doing things better, but they are not doing better things.

Mindful and skilled means there is a situational awareness focusing on situational differences and the process and outcomes when performing the skill. Competent communicators are aware of situational differences that may lead them to not only change the way they are making messages to be more effective but may change the goals for performing the messages in the first place. Performing well in unexpected and often critical situations happens most often when people are looking for differences (Darwin & Melling, 2011; Weick & Sutcliffe, 2007). Mindful means approaching a situation as an opportunity to test what you know and can do to learn from the experience. It does not mean being self-conscious, but it does mean checking the reactions of others to gage the effect of what you said, recognizing when things are going poorly, and trying something different (Burgoon, Berger, & Waldron, 2000). A mindful communicator will be able and willing to adapt and to be flexible. Flexibility and adaptation have been part of the traditional literature on communication competence and the latest literature on the competent use of the new technologies (Spitzberg, 2006).

A competent communicator uses knowledge and information about others, appropriateness, effectiveness, operational knowledge about performing a skill, and differences in social situations. A competent communicator is mindful and will choose different behaviors from the tool chest of available skills. They will not repeat old skills by rote but will test behaviors and vary skills as they see situations differently. What behaviors do people regard as appropriate and effective in what situations? How does one perform those skills with the newer HCTs?

An Ability to Perform Behaviors

Receivers extract some aspects of messages to make technical information and other aspects of messages to make social information. In face-to-face communication, people have trouble recalling the exact technical and social cues they might have used to make sense. This is especially true about social cues. People are more likely to describe the more general way that the other person communicated with them than a specific set of cues. People can recall specific aspects of messages when pressed to do so or when a particular message seems more meaningful than others, but they are much more likely to give a general impression of the other person's communication behavior.

Table 6.2 displays common terms people use to describe communication, and most scholars use to describe communication style (Norton, 1983) and the skills associated with competent communication (Katt, McCrosky, Sivo, Richmond, & Valencic, 2009; Richmond & McCrosky, 1990; Spitzberg, 2006; Sptizberg & Cupbach, 1984). Other authors might use alternative terms for some of these skills, and I have listed some different terms in parentheses. Also, other ideas about good communication tend to be combinations of the skills in this list.

Table 6.2

Communication Skills

	Face-to-Face Performance
Animated	Frequently varies voice, face, and gestures; nonverbally demonstrates messages
Argumentative	Uses logic and evidence to defend or attack a position (contentious)
Dominant	Commands or directs others; often interrupts; the source for the topics of conversation; fast rate, loud, speaks more often than others (leads, one-up)
Dramatic	Exaggerates, uses stories, anecdotes, jokes, and colorful language
Open	Uses direct language, specific examples, describes feelings, self-discloses (clear, direct, expressive, frank, personal)
Precise	Uses language carefully, uses exact and detailed definitions (clear)
Relaxed	Does not avoid eye-contact, fidget, pause frequently, or stammer (calm, composed, confident, not nervous or apprehensive, peaceful)
Responsive	Gestures to encourage others to talk, paraphrases, asks questions, acknowledges others (attentive, empathic, listens)
Supportive	Compliments, uses intimate language, encourages, validates, and provides needed information or assistance (affectionate, concerned, friendly, warm)

These are behaviors people *could* perform. Some individuals have personalities that predispose them to perform these behaviors more than others (Beatty & McCrosky, 1998). However, competent communicators have knowledge of what they are doing, and consistently performing and adapting these behaviors in an appropriate and effective manner requires operational knowledge of the behaviors.

Being animated is about nonverbal communication, but the rest of the list is more about verbal communication. It would be easy to translate these skills from FtF to other HCT. Using emoticons, pictures, and animations are ways to be animated in a visual technology such as EML, private electronic communication (PEC) such as texting, and public electronic communication (BEC) such as tweeting.

One key skill that involves unique HCT performances is responsiveness. For many of us, responsiveness includes answering a message quickly, and we have developed expectations for what is appropriate response-time for a given situation and relationship. Furthermore, our expectations for response-time vary by technology. We seem to expect a quick response to texts, but we seem to be OK with a longer time between telephone messages. Many of us would prefer a quick text response to voice message instead of a return phone call.

Responsiveness is a critical skill because these behaviors can clarify what we are trying to say to each other, can help develop empathy, and can confirm. My own experiences lead me to conclude that we seldom perform responsive behaviors using the text-centered technologies. Scan your library of text messages or instant messages. How often did someone ask questions about technical information? How about questions or paraphrases about social information? Was there something as simple as "You must be thrilled" or "You sound sad. Are you feeling low about this?"

Trying to be supportive using text-centered technology seems to point to the limitations of the technology, but it is more about how we use the technology. A "like" may not be as supportive as a short message, but several hundred "likes" provide a unique type of support. Furthermore, there is always the possibility of adding an animation to a text-centered message.

The last few paragraphs demonstrate the importance of operational knowledge using various technologies. All technologies have unique features that limit how people could use them, but there are few limits to our imagination. The person with greater operational knowledge can use all the technologies in more novel and competent ways.

The list does not include or suggest how much of any skill is competent. The **level of performance** that is appropriate and effective often varies from one situation to the next. How much of your feelings should you express to your boss? How precise do you need to be effective when ordering your meal at a fast-food restaurant? How dramatic should your language be when you meet your fiancé's parents for the first time? The comments on *Popular Science* were too strident –over the top – for typical readers of the magazine.

The appropriate and effective levels are different in different cultures. Openness includes being clear about your thoughts and feelings. There are different cultural expectations about both how direct you should be about technical information and how expressive you should be about your feelings (Hammer, 2005). Cultural differences include differences between people in different nations, regions, genders, generations, and organizations (Gudykinst & Mody, 2002; Hofstede & Hofstede, 2005). Direct comments in one culture may be rude or offensive in another, especially when people combine dramatic expressions with direct ones.

Were the Twitter comments about Miss America appropriate? Someone thought so, and the performance of these behaviors led to similar comments from others. If the goal were to generate some chatter, these messages were also effective.

What culture or group finds this level of dramatic messages appropriate? Is there a norm for such comments on Twitter? One limited study revealed 65% of Twitter users were under 25 years old, 62% are from the United States, but only 5 % of users accounted for 75% of the activity (Cheng & Evans, 2009). Do 5% of the users respond to a norm associated with younger people? Does the behavior of an American younger generation constitute what is appropriate for this technology? Is this bad? The Miss

America comments may seem hurtful, but is the greater dramatic performance of Twitter messages inherently hurtful?

A competent communicator can **repeat skills with variation**. Since competent communicators are mindful and have empathy and situational knowledge, they will use a basic framework in a way that seems most appropriate and effective in the specific episode they are constructing. For example, being open includes describing feelings when appropriate. One way to do this is to use a word suggesting a feeling (e.g., angry) and another way it to use a metaphor or dramatic language for a feeling (e.g., I feel like hitting something) (Bolton, 1979). Furthermore, the different expressions can vary by level of intensity (e.g., irritated-angry-mad). There are many ways to demonstrate openness by describing feelings, and the competent communicator will not rely on just one way but will test different behaviors. Since a competent communicator is mindful, s/he will adapt the performance as the episode develops, and this repetition of skills with variation also demonstrates flexibility.

Communication involves a process where communicators take turns making messages as part of an episode all are using to develop information. Messages are more or less competent depending on how people performed them and how people made sense of them. Being a consistently competent communicator with today's HCTs begins with information and knowledge about the perceptions of others, about what messages others might find effective and appropriate as well as operational knowledge of a given HCT and the social situation. A communicator can perform competently when they are mindful and can appreciate how things are different. Making competent messages involves selecting a skill and performing it at the varying levels of performance consistent with the situation and the people in it.

Incompetent Digital Messaging

Communication is a complex mix of individual and shared perceptions and behaviors, and an individual message or sequence of messages could be incompetent. Table 6.3 displays some options on the outcomes of your performance (adapted from Morreale, Spitzberg, & Barge, 2007; Nicotera, Steele, Catalini, & Simpson, 2012; Spitzberg, 2000). Sufficing, maximizing, and minimizing are different types of incompetent communication.

All of us have felt incompetent at one time or another. We just can't seem to communicate with that one particular person or in that one particular setting or about that one particular topic. Some of us are better at one HCT than another. Some of us are apprehensive about using our mobile phones for voice calling and would rather text, but those who text more also call more (Lenhart, 2012; Smith, 2011). How competent these messages become depends on the factors mentioned above but also on how competent the communicator could have been using different HCT.

Table 6.3

Competence Grid

Effectiveness	Appropriateness	
	Low	High
High	Maximizing: May meet goals but challenge relationship	Optimizing: May meet goals and sustain relationship
Low	Minimizing: May not meet goals and challenge relationship	Sufficing: May not meet goals but sustain relationship

This section is about making incompetent messages that thwart, disrupt, or end communication. Either by design or accident, these types of messages put a stop to communication. Sometimes, using these messages does not invite a response, and dialogue will not begin or develop. In the most benign instances, using these messages limits the potential for creating sequences of episodes as part of an evolving relationship. These messages are disruptive (Barnes, 2003), unkind or cruel (Lenhart, Madden, *et al.*, 2011), and potentially illegal.

Deception is a deliberate act in which one communicator creates a message that does not contain the truth as that communicator understands it. Communicators may simply create a message they know is untrue, create a message that withholds the truth, or they may equivocate (Burgoon, Buller, Ebesu, & Rockwell, 2009). Online deception includes misrepresenting yourself on a profile, avatar, or other digital format meant to characterize you. The average American tells just over two lies per day, and younger people lie more than older people, but some people, regardless of age group, lie a lot while the rest of us seldom lie (Levine, Serota, Carey, & Messer, 2013). People lie more using the new technology, but they do so more with family and friends than with organizational members (Wise & Rodriguez, 2013; Zimbler & Feldman, 2011). People often misrepresent themselves in profiles and when dating online (Hancock & Toma, 2012; Schmitz, Zillmann, & Blossfeld, 2013).

Gender bending involves presenting yourself as a male when you are female and presenting yourself as a female when you are a male. In the early days of computing, this was a bigger problem than it is today because people have become less wary and because of recent changing attitudes about assuming different gender identities (Barnes, 2003). Some situations such as online games may offer limited choices for avatars, and members of communities such as Second Life may expect each other to "play" with their identities and representations. In 2014, Facebook introduced 18 new categories for gender, and a person can use these categories to identify themselves in 56 different ways (Weber, 2014).

Cyberpredators use contemporary digital HCT to illicit illegal sexual acts. Most uses of this expression or similar expressions refer to adults using deception to prey on children and teens. These acts vary from unwanted exposure to pornography to sexual solicitation. The frequency of most such reported incidents has declined over a ten-year period (Jones, Mitchell, & Finkelhor, 2012).

Trolling refers to creating digital HCT messages, usually after a period of inactivity, designed to provoke others. Trolling is part of BEC, and the idea is to post inciting remarks so many others can see it and respond. Trollers are deceptive, posing as someone with a genuine opinion or something to add, but they are insincere and see their actions as a prank. People can also post their messages out of revenge or just boredom. People who troll frequently also exhibit sadistic tendencies (Buckels, Trapnell, & Paulhaus, 2014).

Flaming is sending or exchanging a stream of dramatic, hostile, and emotional messages using electronic HCT. Flaming involves dramatic displays of hostility such as using all caps or emoticons. Flaming is not one message, but several, and the sequences may appear to be rabid or incessant. A flaming war occurs when two or more people engage in flaming each other. Flaming may be inappropriate for most communication, but it may be the norm in some groups (See Turnage, 2008 for a recent review of research).

Cyberhate involves creating electronic HCT messages that express disgust, revulsion, or animosity to people because of their culture, disability, religion, sex, or sexual orientation. Cyberhate most often occurs as part of online sites where members share a group identity; people direct their messages at outgroups or specific members of outgroups (Perry & Olsson, 2009). Cyberhate messages may be entertaining or reinforcing social identity performances for other group members instead of any attempt to inform or persuade. The comments posted about Miss America are examples of cyberhate.

Cyberbullying involves direct contact with a person and creating intentional and repeated digital HCT messages that are intimidating, hostile, threatening, or harmful to that person. Cyberbullying is similar to other forms of bullying, and bullies normally direct their messages to people they think have less power than themselves. Mobbing happens when former bystanders join in bullying. Most cyberbullies have been the victim of other cyberbullies, and girls are more likely to be cyberbullies than boys, especially when they can use SNS (Gorzig & Olafsson, 2012).

Many people associate cyberbullying with children and use terms such as cyberstalking, cyber harassment, e-harassment, or online harassment to refer to communication between adults. In the workplace, cyberbullying includes incidents of online sexual harassment and also being ordered to do work below your level of competence (Piotrowski, 2012; Privitera & Campbell, 2009). Similar to children and adolescents, adult victims of workplace cyberbullying also report face-to-face bullying.

Cyberostracism refers to using digital HCT to ignore or exclude a person from a group. Cyberostracism includes something as simple as failing to answer an email message to more active exclusion such as removing a person from access to a chat room, discussion group, SNS, or fan site. Exclusion of any sort has negative consequences. Cyberostracism increases negative moods, negative emotions, and loneliness (Williams, Cheung, & Chi, 2000; Zhong & Leonardelli, 2008).

All the bad digital messages are forms of aggressive messages. *Verbal aggression* is a message that attacks the other person's self-concept. By contrast, an *argumentative message* attacks a position or idea, and an *assertive message* is the forceful use of symbols to obtain goals while maintaining or supporting the other's self-concept and self worth.

Generally, assertive and argumentative messages are both constructive types of messages, and verbally aggressive messages are destructive (Infante & Rancer, 1996; Rancer & Avtgis, 2006). Deception is aggressive to the extent that it deprives the other of accurate information and the opportunities to make a reasoned decision. Although the other messages may seem obvious examples of verbal aggression, this may not be the perception of the perpetrators or third parties. At the very least, these verbally aggressive messages risk challenging a relationship for the benefit of a short-term gain, and so these messages may be maximizing for the sender of them. At the worst, the messages lose their effectiveness, and these verbally aggressive messages become minimizing.

A troubling trend is that some groups of users normalize these messages (Aiken, 2016). That is, people now expect aggressive messaging such as trolling to be normal and nothing to worry about. However, although all of us might have been aggressive at one time or another, the persistent use of aggressive messages is related to personality dimensions and may be its own personality trait (Infante & Rancer, 1996; Rancer & Avtgis, 2006). Why do these particular forms of verbal aggression occur? The next section describes several common explanations for digital bad behavior, but these ideas are also explanations for competent digital messages as well.

Explaining Digital Messaging

The most popular explanations of digital messaging suggest technological determinism – the technology is responsible in some way or another for how we construct messages. For example, digital technology allows us to communicate **anonymously**, and so we create messages that are more competent or less competent than if we were communicating FtF. In the last chapter, I noted that some of our HCT gives us the illusion that others will not find out who we are or at least we think that we can remain anonymous in a particular way, for a time, with a particular person or group. Furthermore, we do not know much about the other person beyond what they have already told us, and so they are relatively anonymous. Kathleen Parker, the *New York Times* columnist, believes anonymity liberates hostility and can set off abuse riots (2013).

Digital technologies have been more text based, and they have tended to **limit social cues** (Sproull & Kiesler, 1986). The explanation, first offered to explain flaming and EML, suggests that people have a greater opportunity to disguise themselves since newer HCTs limit nonverbal messages, and the limitation of these cues also makes misunderstanding more likely. Although a communicator could be more careful in their word choice and although people have many more opportunities to consciously add nonverbal cues to their messages today, there is little evidence that many people do this (Baruch, 2005).

Another technological determinism argument is that messages using digital technologies are ephemeral. **Ephemeral** refers to something lasting for a short time. We send the text messages, and it disappears. It is gone. The message is less than real, and the senders feel less ownership and accountability (Sproull & Kiesler, 1991). Surely, a person can lose track of the relative permanence of his/her messages using the new technology.

Those technological determinism explanations seem sound until you examine them more closely. First, these characteristics are not restricted to the newer HCTs. When we meet anyone for the first time using any HCT, we are anonymous, and we have the choice of how much to reveal about ourselves. Any interpersonal communication textbook will have a section on self-disclosure. That same book will describe the problems people have creating and interpreting verbal and nonverbal social cues. What is more ephemeral than the sound of your voice?

Second, these characteristics are just as likely to produce competent messages as bad ones. The sense of anonymity gives us an opportunity to construct a new persona, to discover a new facet of our self, and to increase the complexity of our self-concept (Hage & Powers, 1992). Much of our technology is asynchronous, giving us more time to think about how we are constructing messages. Third, the bad behaviors seem to be more a problem of technology use and of the mindfulness of the person instead of the technology. The communications director lost her job because of her message, but she might have constructed the message because she simply did not consider her audience. "Know your audience" may be the oldest principle of effective communication. Many of us distinguish our online self and our online relationships from those offline, and we can obtain different rewards from different relationships (boyd, 2014; Rainie & Wellman, 2012). Arguing that any features of technology determined the message is a tough sell.

A social determinism explanation focuses on communication rules and appropriateness. On the one hand, the social situations enacted using the new technologies may be so novel that the **lack of rules** encourages experimentation that may lead to bad behavior. At the very least, the lack of rules does not prohibit verbally aggressive behavior. On the other hand, some social situations enacted using the new technologies may have **rules that accept or encourage aggressive behaviors**. The messages gamers send each other during games is an example of this. And so, the rules or the lack of rules made people verbally aggressive; things just got out of hand.

There are several problems with these explanations. First, there is little evidence that verbally aggressive messages are ever appropriate, and people rate such messages as being minimally effective only when they are accompanied by good argument (Nicotera, Steele, Catalini, & Simpson, 2012). A verbally aggressive message is seldom competent. Second, individuals bring differing expectations about what is appropriate as they negotiate their relationship rules. A failure to be mindfully aware of the differences or to be actively engaged in the negotiations is a more likely explanation for many inappropriate behaviors. Teachers perceptions of students were better when they read more formal EML requests from students that met teacher expectations than messages that used casual, short hand expressions found in texting (Stephens, Houser, & Cowan, 2009). Third, having no rules or few rules using the technology is no different than other common social settings such as meeting someone for the first time or trying to communicate with people of different cultures for the first time. These situations do not lead to aggressive behaviors. Fourth, the rules that encourage aggressive behavior are most often directed at outgroup members and not ingroup members, and these rules are not unique to using newer technologies. Hate speech or incessant behaviors such as flaming or bullying become performances for an audience of presumed ingroup members. This is no different than similar behaviors without the technology. Finally, the deterministic character of these explanations denies individual agency. A person still has a choice to participate, and the newer technologies give ample opportunities to change messages. The social determinism explanations do not provide explanations unique to the use of the newer technologies. Communication rules act as a constraint in all communication, and individuals construct those rules together regardless of the technology.

Deindividuation is one explanation that involves technology, psychology, and sociology. In Chapter Five, I noted **deindividuation** refers to any process that encourages or facilitates our losing track of personal differences between our self and others, and between others. The explanation for bad messages is that features and uses of the newer HCTs create circumstances where deindividuation is more likely, and deindividuation leads to polarized attitudes and uninhibited and often aggressive behavior. There has been considerable research inducing deindividuation, there are several underlying psycho-social explanations for how deindividuation occurs and affects a variety of behaviors, and this research has not often involved communication (Lee, 2007). The research involving newer HCTs is just beginning, but there is little to suggest that deindividuation involving using newer HCTs is any different than without HCTs.

Empathy is an ability to understand and appreciate differences, and so empathy is the opposite of deindividuation. Lower empathy has been associated with a greater likelihood of cyberbullying among adolescents (Ang & Goh, 2010). Furthermore, there has been a pattern of decreased empathy among young people over a ten-year period (Konrath, O'Brien, & Hsing, 2011). People using social media more have *less empathy* (Dailey, Howard, Roming, Ceballos, & Grimes, 2018). There are several, often contradictory, correlates to empathy, and technology use is only one of these correlates (Konrath et al, 2011).

Mindlessness seems to be a likely explanation, until one considers the full range of bad messages. Similar to deindividuation, mindlessness could be part of a mobbing incident where a small group of people bully or harass an individual, but prolonged bad behaviors suggest more mindful messages. Similarly, deception and predatory communication suggest strategic communication.

Finally, there is the possibility that a change in HCT becomes a change of parameters for potentially destructive messages. Individuals come with predispositions for constructing such messages or communicators construct relationships with rules that condone or encourage such messages, and **the change in HCT creates a multiplier effect** where the behaviors are more common, intense, and damaging. None of the behaviors noted above is unique to the newer HCTs, but they occur more frequently and can have greater impact with the newer technologies.

Some bad behaviors such as predatory behaviors or the email messages to the small town mayor involve private electronic communication, but much of the displays of verbal aggression involve an audience. Those who displayed their racism regarding Miss America, the people who posted on the *Popular Science* website, and the people who harassed the family of the victim in Ohio, all displayed their verbally aggressive messages on sites in which others watched. They assumed audience members would view these aggressive posts positively. Indeed, Justine Sacco misjudged or forgot who was in her audience. These displays are more reminiscent of the amplified messages described in the last chapter than they are messages that are part of an ongoing episode. The sequence of public posts is more improvisational theater than improvisational conversation. However, all public posts do not involve verbal aggression, and we carry an audience with us through our embeddedness in social networks. Communication technology networks are the focus of the next chapter.

References

Adams, L. (n. d.). *Learning a new skill is easier said than done* (Training material). Gordon Training International. Retrieved from http://www.gordontraining.com/free-workplace-articles/learning-a-new-skill-is-easier-said-than-done.

Aiken, M. (2016) *The cyber effect*. New York: Spiegel & Grau.

Anderson, A. A., Brossard, D., Scheufele, D. A., Xenos, M. A. & Ladwig, P. (2013). The "Nasty Effect:" Online incivility and risk perceptions of emerging technologies. *Journal of Computer-Mediated Communication*. doi: 10.1111/jcc4.12009.

Ang, R. P., & Goh, D. H. (2010). Cyberbullying among adolescents: The role of cognitive and affective empathy, and gender. *Child Psychiatry and Human Development, 41*, 387-397. doi: 10.1007/s10578-010-0176-3.

Argyris, C. (1992). *On organizational learning*. Cambridge, MA: Blackwell.

Baron, N. S. (2008). *Always on: Language in an online and mobile world*. New York: Oxford University Press.

Barnes. S. B. (2003). *Computer-mediated communication*. Boston: Allyn & Bacon.

Baruch, Y. (2005). Bullying on the net: Adverse behavior on e-mail and its impact. *Information & Management, 42,* 361–371.

Beatty, M. C., & McCrosky, J. C. (1998). Interpersonal communication as temperamental expression: A communibiological approach. In J. C. McCrosky, J. A. Daly, M. M. Martin, & M. J. Beatty (Eds.), *Communication and personality: Trait perspectives* (pp. 41-67). Cresskill, NJ: Hampton Press.

Beebe, S. A., Beebe, S. J., & Ivy, D. K. (2012). *Communication: Principles for a lifetime* (5th ed.). New York: Pearson.

Bolton, R. (1979). *People skills.* New York: Touchstone.

boyd, d. (2014). *It's complicated: The social lives of networked teens.* New Haven, CT: Yale University Press.

Brown, K. W., & Ryan, R. M. (2003). The benefits of being present: Mindfulness and its role in psychological well-being. *Journal of Personality and Social Psychology, 84*(4), 822-848.

Buckels, E. E., Trapnell, P. D., & Paulhaus, D. L. (2014). Trolls just want to have fun. *Personality and Individual Differences,* (in press). Retrieved from http://dx.doi.org/10.1016/j.paid.2014.01.016

Burgoon, J. K., Berger, C. R., & Waldron, V. R. (2000). Mindfulness and interpersonal communication. *Journal of Social Issues, 56,* 105-128.

Burgoon, J. K., Buller, D. B., Ebesu, A. S., & Rockwell, P. (2009). Interpersonal deception: Accuracy in deception detection. *Communication Monographs, 61,* 303–325.

Burgoon, J. K., Buller, D. B., & Woodall, W. G. (1996). *Nonverbal communication: The unspoken dialogue* (2nd ed.). New York: McGraw-Hill.

Cheng, A., & Evans, M. (2009). *Inside Twitter: An in depth look inside the Twitter world.* Sysomos Resource Library. http://www.sysomos.com/insidetwitter.

Coleman, A., & McCormack, D. (2013, September 15). Indian-American wins Miss America for first time in its history and brushes off racist Twitter abuse and 'fat' slur to pick up $50,000 medical school scholarship. *The Daily Mail.* Retrieved from http://www.dailymail.co.uk/news/article-2421711/Miss-America-Indian-American-winner-Miss-New-York-Nina-Davuluri-ignores-racist-Twitter-abuse.html#ixzz2nvbvU8cF.

Daft, R. L., & Lengel, R, H. (1986). Organizational information requirements: Media richness and structural design. *Management Science, 32,* 554-571

Dailey, S. L., Howard, K. J., Roming, S., Ceballos, N. A., & Grimes, T. (November, 2018). *Playing with fire: Communicative and psychosocial predictors of social media addiction.* Paper presented to the Human Communication and Technology Division of the National Communication Association meeting in Salt Lake City, UT.

Dance, F. E. X., & Larson, C. E. (1976). *The functions of human communication: A theoretical approach.* New York: Holt, Rinehart and Winston.

Darwin, J., & Melling, J. (2011, June). *Mindfulness and situation awareness.* Paper presented to the 16th International Command and Control Symposium, Quebec City, Quebec, Canada.

Davis, M. H. (1983). Measuring individual differences in empathy: Evidence for a multidimensional approach. *Journal of Personality and Social Psychology, 44*(1), 1113-126.

Diep, F. (2013, June 13). What happens to women when they are denied abortions? *Popular Science.* Retrieved from http://www.popsci.com/science/article/2013-06/first-its-kind-study-tracks-women-who-couldnt-get-abortions-when-they-wanted-them#comments.

Douglas, K. (2008). Antisocial communication in on electronic mail and the internet. In E. A. Konijin, S. Utz, M. Tanis, & S. B. Barnes (Eds.). *Mediated interpersonal communication* (pp. 200-214). New York: Routledge.

Eligon, J. (2013, October 19). High school sexual assault case is revisited, haunting Missouri town. *The New York Times*. Retrieved from http://www.nytimes.com/2013/10/20/us/high-school-sexual-assault-case-is-reopened-haunting-missouri-town.html?pagewanted=1&_r=0&adxnnlx=1387628436-MqBbT/FP82%20IG0y%20lyR2Ew.

Fulk, J., Schmitz, J., & Steinfeld, C. (1990). A social influence model of technology use. In J. Fulk, & C. Steinfeld, (Eds.). *Organizations and communication technology* (pp. 117-140). Newbury Park, CA: Sage.

Gorzig, A., & Olafsson, K. (2012). What makes a cyberbully? Unraveling the characteristics of cyberbullies across twenty-five European countries. *Journal of Children and Media, 7*(1), 9-27.

Gudykinst, W. B., & Mody, B. (2002). (Eds.). *The handbook of international and intercultural communication* (2nd ed.). Thousand Oaks, CA: Sage.

Hage, J., & Powers, C, H. (1992). *Post-industrial lives: Roles and relationships in the 21st century*. Newbury Park, CA: Sage.

Hamilton, G., Byatt, G., & Hodgkinson, J. (2010, December 13). Communication risks within and around a virtual team. *CIO*. Retrieved from http://www.cio.com.au/article/370285/communication_risks_within_around_virtual_team.

Hammer, M. (2005). The Intercultural Conflict Style Inventory: A conceptual framework and measure of intercultural conflict resolution approaches. *International Journal of Intercultural Relations, 29*, 675-695.

Hancock, C. T., & Toma, J. T. (2012). What lies beneath: The linguistic traces of deception in online dating profiles. *Journal of Communication*, *62*(1), 78-97.

Hofstede, G., & Hofstede, G. J. (2005). *Cultures and organizations: Software of the mind* (Rev. 2nd ed.). New York: McGraw-Hill.

Infante, D. A., & Rancer, A. S. (1996). Argumentativeness and verbal aggression: A review of recent theory and research. In B. Burleson (Ed.), *Communication yearbook* (Vol. 19) (pp. 319-351). Thousand Oaks, CA: Sage.

Jones, L. M., Mitchell, K. J., & Finkelhor, D. (2012). Trends in youth Internet victimization: Findings from three youth Internet safety surveys 2000-2010. *Journal of Adolescent Health*, *50*, 179-186.

Katt, J. A., McCrosky, J. C., Sivo, S. A., Richmond, V. P., & Valencic, K. M. (2009). A structural equation modeling evaluation of the general model of instructional communication. *Communication Quarterly*, *57* (3), 239-258.

Konrath, S. H., O'Brien, E. H., & Hsing, C. (2011). Changes in dispositional empathy in American college students over time: A meta-analysis. *Personality and Social Psychology Review*, *15*(2), 180-198. doi: 10.1177/1088868310377395.

LaBarre, S. (2013, September 24). Why we're shutting off our comments. *Popular Science*. Retrieved from http://www.popsci.com/science/article/2013-09/why-were-shutting-our-comments?dom=PSC&loc=topstories&con=why-were-shutting-off-our-comments-

Langer, E. L.(1989). *Mindfulness*. Cambridge, MA: De Capo Books.

Langer, E. J. (1999). *The power of mindful learning*. Cambridge, MA: Perseus Books.

Lee, E. (2007). Deindividuation effects on group polarization in computer-mediated communication: The role of group identification, public-self-awareness, and perceived argument quality. *Journal of Communication, 57*, 385-403.

Lengel, R. H., & Daft, R. L. (1988). The selection of communication media as an executive skill. *The Academy of management Executive, 2*, 225-232.

Lenhart, A. (2012). *Teens, smartphones, and texting*. Washington, DC: Pew Research Center. Retrieved from http://www.pewinternet.org/Reports/2012/Teens-and-smartphones.aspx.

Lenhart, A., Madden, M., Smith, A., Purcell, K., Zikuhr, K., & Rainie, L. (2011). *Teens, kindness and cruelty on social network sites*. Washington, DC: Pew Research Center. Retrieved from http://pewinternet.org/Reports/2011/Teens-and-social-media.aspx.

Levine, T. R., Serota, K. B., Carey, F., & Messer, D. (2013). Teenagers lie a lot: A further investigation into the prevalence of lying. *Communication Research Reports, 30*(3), 211-220.

Linton, I. (2013). How to determine the appropriate communication channel. *Houston Chronicle*. Retrieved from http://smallbusiness.chron.com/determine-appropriate-communication-channel-24098.html.

Morreale, S. P., Spitzberg, B. H., & Barge, J. K. (2007). *Human communication: Motivation, knowledge, and skills*. Belmont, CA: Thomson.

Manjoo, F., & Yoffe, E. (n. d.). Manners for the digital age. *Slate*. Retrieved from http://www.slate.com/articles/podcasts/manners_for_the_digital_age.html.

Murray, E. (1937). *The speech personality*. New York: J. B. Lippincott Company.

Nicotera, A. M., Steele, J., Catalini, A., & Simpson, N. (2012). Conceptualization and test of an aggression competence model. *Communication Research Reports, 29*(1), 12-25.

Norton, R. W. (1983). *Communicator style.* Beverly Hills, CA: Sage.

Parker, K. (2013, December 27). Thanks for the memories. *The Washington Post.* Retrieved from http://www.washingtonpost.com/opinions/kathleen-parker-thanks-for-the-memories-2013/2013/12/27/f186f77c-6f37-11e3-a523-fe73f0ff6b8d_story.html.

Patchin, J. W. & Hinduja, S. (2006). Bullies move beyond the schoolyard: A preliminary look at cyberbullying. *Youth Violence and Juvenile Justice, 4*(2), 148-169.

Perry, B., & Olsson, P. (2009). Cyberhate: The globalization of hate. *Information and Communication Technology Law, 18*(2), 185-199.

Piotrowski, C. (2012). From workplace bullying to cyberbullying: The enigma of e-harassment in modern organizations. *Organizational Development Journal, 30*(4), 44-53.

Privitera, C., & Campbell, M. A. (2009). Cyberbullying: The new face of workplace bullying? *Cyberpsychology & Behavior, 12*(4), 395-400.

Rainie, L., & Wellman, B. (2012). *Networked: The new social operating system.* Cambridge, MA: MIT Press.

Rancer, A. S., & Avtgis, T. A. (2006). *Argumentative and aggressive communication: Theory research, and application.* Thousand Oaks, CA: Sage.

Richmond, V. P., & McCrosky, J. C. (1990). Reliability and separation of factors on the Assertiveness-Responsiveness measure. *Psychology Reports, 67,* 449-450.

Ronson, J. (2015). *So you've been publicly shamed.* London: Picador.

Salem, P. J. (2013). *The complexity of human communication* (2nd ed.). Cresskill, NJ; Hampton Press.

Schmitz, A., Zillmann, D., & Blossfeld, H. (2013). Do women pick up lies before men? The association between gender, deception patterns, and detection modes in online dating. *Online Journal of Communication and Media Technologies*, 3(3). Retrieved from http://www.ojcmt.net/articles/33/334.pdf.

Shipley, D., & Schwable, W. (2008). *Send: Why people email so badly and how to do it better*. New York: Alfred A. Knopf.

Smith, A. (2011). *Americans and text messaging*. Washington, DC: Pew Research Center. Retrieved from http://www.pewinternet.org/Reports/2011/Cell-Phone-Texting-2011.aspx.

Smith, P. K., Mahdavi, J., Carvalho, M., Fisher, S., Russell, S., & Tippet, N. (2008). Cyberbullying: Its nature and impact in secondary school pupils. *Journal of Child Psychology and Psychiatry*, 49(4), 376–385.

Spitzberg, B. H. (2000). What is good communication? *Journal of the Association for Communication Administration*, 29, 103-119.

Spitzberg, B. H. (2006). Preliminary development of a model and measure of computer mediated communication (CMC) competence. *Journal of Computer–mediated Communication*, 11(2), 629–666.

Spitzberg, B. H., & Cupach, W. R. (1984). *Interpersonal communication competence*. Newbury Park, CA: Sage.

Sproull, L., & Kiesler, S. (1986). Reducing social context cues: Electronic mail in organizational communication. *Management Science*, 32, 1492-1512.

Sproull, L., & Kiesler, S. (1991). *Connections: New ways of working in the networked organization*. Cambridge, MA: MIT Press.

Stebner, B. (2013). IAC fires PR exec Justine Sacco over 'racist' tweet over AIDS. *The Daily News*. Retrieved from http://www.nydailynews.com/news/national/pr-exec-justine-sacco-tweet-sparks-aids-donations-article-1.1554932#ixzz2oCfRCZLK

Stephens, K. K., Houser, M. L., & Cowan, R. L. (2009). R U able to meat me: The impact of students' overly casual email messages to instructors. *Communication Education, 58* (3), 303-326.

Timmerman, C. E. (2002). The moderating effect of mindlessness/mindfulness upon media richness and social influence explanations of organizational media use. *Communication Monographs, 69*(2), 111-131.

Turnage, A. K. (2008). Email flaming behaviors and organizational conflict. *Journal of Computer-Mediated Communication, 13,* 43-59.

Vanden Abeele, M, & de Cock (2013). Cyberbullying by mobile phone among adolescents: The role of gender and peer group status. *Communications: The European Journal of Communication Research, 38*(1), 107-118.

Weber, P. (2014, February 14). Facebook offers users 56 new gender options: Here's what they mean. *The Week*. Retrieved from http://theweek.com/article/index/256474/facebook-offers-users-56-new-gender-options-heres-what-they-mean#.

Weick, K. E., & Sutcliffe, K. M. (2007). *Managing the unexpected*. San Francisco, CA: Jossey-Bass.

Wiemann, J. M. (1977). Explication and test of a model of communicative competence. *Human Communication Research, 3,* 195–213.

Williams, K. D., Cheung, C. T. K., & Choi, W. (200). Cyberostracism: Effects of being ignored over the Internet. *Journal of Personality and Social Psychology, 79*(5), 748-762.

Wise, M., & Rodriguez, D. (2013). Detecting deceptive communication through computer-mediated technology: Applying Interpersonal Deception Theory to texting behavior. *Communication Research Reports, 30*(4), 342-346.

Writing Center, University of North Carolina (2013). *Effective email communication*. http://writingcenter.unc.edu/handouts/effective-e-mail-communication

Zhong, C., & Leonardelli, G. J. (2008). Cold and lonely: Does social exclusion literally feel cold? *Psychological Science, 19*(9), 838-842.

Zimbardo, P. G. (1969). The human choice: Individuation, reason, and order vs. Deindividuation, impulse and chaos. In W. J. Arnold & D. Levine (Eds.), *Nebraska symposium on motivation* (Vol. 17, pp. 237–307). Lincoln, NE: University of Nebraska Press.

Zimbler, M., & Feldman, R. S. (2011). Liar, liar, hard drive on fire: How media context affects lying behavior. *Journal of Applied Social Psychology, 14*(10), 2492-2507.

Chapter Seven: Networks

I asked my son, Noah, for a recommendation for a home repairman, and he said, "Crystal's brother's friend's uncle would be good." His answer was the long version of "I know a guy". We all know a lot of people, but we don't often reflect on the web of relationships we create that surrounds us. "It's not what you know but who you know" is a common piece of advice. Some people have "pull", an ability to use their networks to gain some sort of advantage.

On the other hand, when a video goes "viral" on the Internet, the video has spread throughout many networks. It is similar to when a rumor spreads through a friendship network. Networks influence individual members.

We create these relational networks by communicating with each other, and today we have many ways to communicate with each other. A recent article in my local newspaper featured reminiscences about Austin in the 1960s when "anybody could know everybody " (Barnes, 2014). At that time, the primary communication technologies were face-to-face communication (FtF) and telephone (TEL), and the population was around 200,000. With the advent of digital technologies and the enormous reach of those technologies, it may now be possible for everybody to know anybody. But what does "know" mean? How are our relationships and networks created through email (EML), private electronic communication (PEC), and public electronic communication (BEC) such as social network sites (SNS) similar and different from relationships and networks created with more traditional technologies?

In this chapter I will describe basic ways to think about relationships, networks, and communication technology. The next section includes a review and extension of material about relationships presented in Chapter

2, and the second section explains some key features of relational networks, especially personal networks. The last section begins with comparisons of the networks we create with different technologies and then focuses specifically about SNS and the networks we create using them. Communication technology networks can provide unique resources, and these networks are related to loneliness, but I will deal with these issues in later chapters.

Relationship Foundations

Relationships are the set of shared or aligned perceptions we have about each other with each other. Individuals approach communication with ideas about what might be expected of each other and about how to create episodes together. As the communicators continue to create messages, the differences in these social perceptions become apparent, the communicators adjust, and people converge around a set of rules for continuing the episode. In some relationships and in some episodes, this convergence happens more quickly than in others.

Closeness is a perception of attachment or connectedness to others as part of a relationship. We communicate more with those whom we regard as closer, we talk to them about important things, and we can rely on them when we need them. Other words associated with feeling close to others are cohesive, interdependent, identify, included, intimate, mutual and shared interests, and trust (Baxter & Montgomery, 1996; Johnson, Becker, Wigley, Wittenberg, & Haigh, 2008; Simmons & de Ridder, 2004).

Flexibility is the extent to which the members of a relationship can change or alter their relationship. Some relationships are rigid with many rules that are difficult to change and few exceptions to the rules, but relationships can be chaotic with few changeable rules with many exceptions (Olson, Sprenkle, & Russell, 1979). Some associate rigidity with being too close and chaotic relationships with being too distant, but relationships are more varied than that (Baxter & Montgomery, 1996; Olson, Sprenkle, & Russell, 1979). Friendships, for example, can be very close but more flexible than family relationships (Johnson & Becker, 2011).

Relationship *functions* are what the relationship provides for the participants. Different types of relationships may have different and even unique functions such as the nurturing function of families. Alternately, both family relationships and friendships can provide emotional support. Furthermore, *social resources* are resources available just from being connected in a particular network. *Social capital* are the social resources people can use to create more resources (Monge & Contractor, 2003).

Relationships are dynamic, and it is possible to have too much of a good thing. Relationships move between the extremes of very close and very far and between very flexible and very inflexible (Baxter & Montgomery, 1996). People can be too close and lose their abilities to act alone (Olson, Sprenkle, & Russell, 1979). Some friendships serve completely different functions at different times. Weak links, relationships with people we feel less close, can become important for supplying just the right resource when we need it (Granovetter, 1973).

Communication varies with differing relationships and at different times. Greater openness, especially self-disclosure, should lead to greater satisfaction in our closest relationships, but we go through periods when being closed is better, and we don't communicate openly about particular topics (Baxter & Montgomery, 1996). Positivity, a combination of responsive and supportive messages, should dominate the communication between partners in order to sustain a marriage (Gottman, 1994; Gottman, Murray, Swanson, Tyson, & Swanson, 2002). Being as open and as positive as you are in close personal relationships may be inappropriate at work. In the last chapter, I noted the importance of understanding the appropriateness of messages to becoming a competent communicator.

Every type of relationship and specific relationships within a type develop arch typical messages, communication styles, and episodes that distinguish relationships from other ones. Workplaces develop a jargon that is unique to an industry, type of organization, or unit. Some conversations can only happen with your closest friends, and others can only happen with a specific family member.

A *parasocial relationship* is the perception that a person has a relationship with someone even though there has been no communication between them. Horton and Wohl (1956) first labeled this phenomenon in reference to the members of an audience feeling as though they had a relationship with the performers. This applies to the viewers of a television series and the characters in the series, fans of a sports team and the players on the team, most followers of a celebrity on Twitter, or even the readers of a series of fiction books featuring the same character. We can come to confuse the performance with the people doing the performing and the dramatic interaction between performers with our own experiences with people. The last chapter deals with some of this confusion, but for now it is enough to know that some of the links we think we might have to people are not personal ties or relationships.

Individuals create relationships together with their communication. Relationships differ in many ways, including the communication that created them. The next chapter includes material on specific types of relationships, but this chapter is about how individuals create a pattern of relationships.

Communication Networks

Network Basics

A *network* is a pattern consisting of a set of connections between things. A *social network* is a network with a set of social connections or connections between social things. For example, a blueprint for a building is a network, but a chart showing how the memberships between corporate boards of directors overlap depicts a social network. A *communication network* is a social network created through communication. A *communication technology network* (CTN) is a communication network created using one or more specific technologies. The communication network consisting of your FtF communication over the last day is one type of CTN, and the communication network consisting of your PEC over the last day is another type of CTN.

There are different levels of networks such as group networks, organizational networks, and international networks. A *personal network* is the social or communication network of an individual person. The pattern that emerges from the communication between members of sorority over the last day is an organizational communication network, but the pattern Noah created communicating with people is Noah's personal communication network.

When analyzing a personal network, *ego* is the term for the focal person at the center of the network, and *alters* are the persons directly connected to the ego (Borgatti, Everett, & Johnson, 2013). When analyzing Noah's communication over the last week, Noah is the ego, and Crystal is an alter. Crystal's brother is one of Crystal's alters, but Crystal's brother is not part of Noah's personal network since Noah does not communicate with him.

Actor Attributes

The characteristics of the participants in a network are important. These actor attributes include age, sex, and education, but they also include physical characteristics, beliefs, attitudes, and intentions. People are more likely to be obese if their communication network partners are also obese (Christakis & Fowler, 2009), and people (e.g., Noah) tend to be happier if their communication network partners (e.g., Crystal) are happy and happier still if the partners of their partners (e.g., Crystal's brother, Crystal's brother's friend) are happy (Fowler & Christakis, 2008).

Network diversity is the extent to which the members of a network are different from each other, and *network heterogeneity* is the extent to which the alters in a personal network are different from the ego. *Network homogeneity* is the just the opposite of heterogeneity and refers to the extent of similarity. Noah is in his early thirties, and if we measured the age heterogeneity of his alters, we could find out exactly how different the ages of his alters were from him.

Tie Dimensions

A *link, degree, or tie* refers to the connection between people. In this book, the tie refers to the nature of the relationship people have between each other. A *strong tie* means people communicate frequently or are close to each other while a *weak tie* means less frequency or greater emotional distance.

Core ties refers to the people whom we are closest, but it is important to recognize there are people with whom we are somewhat close, *significant ties*, and the *weaker ties* to acquaintances and others who just know us by name (Blau & Fingerman, 2009; Granovetter, 1973; Wellman, Hogan, Berg, Boase, Carrosco, Cote, Kayahara, Kennedy, & Tran, 2006). The *core network* consists of the closest contacts in your personal network, and your *active network* adds significant ties, those who are somewhat close. Your entire personal network would include acquaintances.

The *distance* between people in a network is the number of ties connecting people to each other with the geodesic distance being the shortest path (Borgatti, Everett, & Johnson, 2013). In a personal network, the distance is one for every connection between the ego and the alters since the ego is directly connected to the others. However, a friendship network consists of the connections between many people similar to a group or organizational network. Noah has a distance of one link between himself and Crystal, a distance of two degrees between himself and Crystal's brother since he does not directly communicate with him, a distance of three degrees between himself and Crystal's brother's friend, and a distance of four between himself and Crystal's brother's friend's uncle. Noah is directly connected to Crystal, but he does not know and does not communicate directly with the other members of this chain. Note also that although Noah's distance to Crystal's brother's friend's uncle is four, there are three "degrees of separation", three people between Noah and the uncle (i.e., Crystal, Crystal's brother, and Crystal's brother's friend).

Six degrees of Kevin Bacon is a popular game sensitive to the idea of distance. The idea is that Kevin Bacon, the actor, is directly or indirectly connected to everyone who has worked in Hollywood. Go to http://www.thekevinbacongame.com to find how little distance there is between members of the movie industry. Bacon's average distance is less than three, and he does not have the shortest distance (Barabosi, 2002). What is surprising is how little communication distance there is between all of us. More about this below.

Network Structure

Network *size* refers to the number of actors in a network, and in a personal network it refers to the number of alters. How many people are in your entire personal network? How many people are in your core network or your active network? The answers to these questions depend on how you ask the question. Just asking about people with whom you communicate frequently can be difficult. Most people have a difficult time recalling all the people with whom they communicate or whom they feel close. The list of people for this week may be different than last week, and the list for several times a month may be different than the one for at least yearly. Also, the list for FtF communication may be different than the one for PEC such as texting. Estimates of the size of people's *overall* personal networks vary from less than 100 to over 2500, depending on researchers' methods (Kadushin, 2012).

Dunbar (2010) has argued that our cognitive capacity and time limit the size of our personal networks. People can only be concerned about a given number of people, and there is only so much time to communicate with them. Our closest friends and family, the strongest ties, average around five people. When people add other strong ties, those we care about but may not communicate on a daily basis, the core network jumps to around 15. Adding the significant ties enlarges the active network to 50. When people add those they communicate with around once a year, the network size is around 150. This is Dunbar's number, the number of relationships people can maintain. The numbers noted above are averages or the center of a range. Online patterns appear to be similar to the FtF 5, 15, 50, and 150 pattern (Dunbar, Arnaboldi, Conti, & Passarella, 2015).

How big is your personal network?

(1) Jot down the first names of the people with whom you generally communicate with at least several times a month. Think about family members, friends, people with whom you work or with whom you see at school, and people you see often. *This is a list of people with whom you communicate, and that means people with whom you exchange messages several times per month using any technology.*

(2) Add to the list anyone with whom you may have communicated with less than several times per month but are people with whom you might have discussed important matters such as personal matters, work or school matters, financial matters - whatever topics you regard as important.

(3) Add to the list anyone you can count on when you might need them for anything from a recommendation, a ride, or a loan. Obviously, there are some people already on the list you can count on, but this is a check to insure you have not left someone off your list. The result is your core network. Using this method, for most people the size is in the teens to low twenties (Dunbar!), but some can have very large or very small core networks (Boase, Horrigan, Wellman, & Rainie, 2006).

Density is the number of links in a network compared to the maximum number of links (Monge & Contractor, 2003). Getting at density in a personal network means considering the links between alters. Noah's core network of people with whom he communicates at least several times per month or more has 35 people in it. Some of those people are his immediate family, some are friends, and some are the people with whom he works. Each group talks to the members of that group, but there are few links between groups. In the end, his personal network has 200 links between his alters out of a possible 595. The density of his network is 34%, and this is a typical density for a network of strong ties. Do you want everyone you know talking to each other? Do you want all the people in your core network communicating with each other? Does density have advantages?

Network *centrality* is the extent to which activity is concentrated around one or a few members of a network. The easiest way to think about centrality is to think about the extent to which some actors have more links while others have less. Another way to understand centrality is to look at the shortest distance between the network members. If the same few people turn up in nearly everyone's paths between each other, the network is relatively centralized. In a personal network, the ego is the central social actor, but what about the links between the alters? When looking at Noah's network it is easy to identify the alter with the most links to other alters — his wife who directly communicates with all the members of his family, some of his friends, and some of his workers. She also is on the path between most of the other alters. However, the rest of his network is relatively equal with links to others, and most people appear on the path to only a few of the other alters. Noah's core network is relatively decentralized.

Network *constraint* is the extent to which a person's time and energy are concentrated within a single group (Burt, 2010). If much of Noah's communication (i.e., the frequency of communicating regardless of technology in this example) were with his immediate family of his wife and children, if a lot of his family members' communication was with each other, and if many of the other members of Noah's network used a lot of their communication connecting to several of Noah's family members, Noah's network would have high constraint. Constraint will be higher when the network is smaller, denser, and more centralized around a group. As you can see, the idea of constraint combines several of the earlier features of networks. High constraint means you are limiting your communication to people who talk to the same people.

People tend to develop one of two types of networks. Table 7.1 contrasts the network characteristics of brokerage and closure (Burt, 2005). Closure reflects the natural social tendencies of humans to form groups (Burt, 2012). People develop relationships and cluster into groups as the result of interaction opportunities (e.g., work, living near each other, entertainment events) and personal similarities such as age and education. Communication becomes more frequent within than between groups, and the group members develop and reinforce similar ideas. Group members develop their own jargon for things and knowledge becomes more implicit than explicit. Closure improves trust among group members, enhances collaboration, and reinforces group stability.

Table 7.1

Contrasting Brokerage with Closure

Characteristics	Type of Personal Network	
	Brokerage	Closure
Ties	Weaker	Stronger
Heterogeneity	Higher	Lower
Distance Between Alters	Greater	Lesser
Size	Greater	Lesser
Density	Lesser	Greater
Constraint	Lesser	Greater

By contrast, brokerage is more about the individual. Brokers connect groups that have no or few other connections to each other. Brokers get more diverse information, have a greater vision of the entire network, and are more creative. Organizations tend to reward brokers more frequently and with greater rewards than other members of a network, and other network members look to them as opinion leaders. In closure networks, group members protect each other's reputations, but brokers who are not group members must spend more time and energy managing diverse images held by diverse groups. The advantages of one network are the disadvantages of the other.

Although the kinds of networks people construct have distinctive advantages and disadvantages, people help construct their own networks one relationship at a time. Some people may be more motivated or may need the rewards of one type of network than another (Kadushin, 2005). For example, some people may have a high need for the sense of inclusion and security that closure networks bring. The network they help create for work may be different than the one they create for socializing because the needs and functions are different. Also, the advantages and disadvantages of being in a particular network depend on the communication skills of people (Burt, 2010). A person who cannot manage conflict well would have a difficult time in a brokerage network.

What are the features of the overall personal active networks of most people? Chua, Madej, and Wellman (2011) summarized decades of research. Some highlights include the following:

- The alters in their networks are geographically dispersed, and many are several driving hours away.

- The network is not very dense (10-30%).

- The alters tend to fall into specialized groups such as family, friends, or coworkers who perform different functions and provide different types of resources.

- There is little heterogeneity; alters are more similar to the ego than different.

- Social place makes a difference with people of different ages, education, social class, etc. having different networks. For example, younger people tend to have more diverse networks than older people, and more educated people also have more diverse networks than less educated people.

- People in different cultures have different networks.

Most of us have a mix of brokerage and closure in our active networks.

Communication Technology and Networks

People seem to have similar concerns with the introduction of every new communication technology. It should come as no great surprise that people had reservations about the telephone (Fischer, 1992), but, in the nineteenth century, people were concerned that the telegraph would change society in ways people were concerned about the Internet. One article warned of "The Dangers of Wired Love" (Standage, 1998, pp. 136-137). A network of dots and dashes might infect your personal relationships and personal network.

How do communication technology networks compare? Two studies will give us some insight. The first one was about core and active networks using a national survey of Americans conducted in 2004, just before the extensive diffusion of text messages and SNS (Boase, 2008; Boase, et al, 2006). The second study was about core networks only with a smaller sample but in 2010 (Salem, 2012). Both studies found that network size was generally skewed with some people with very large networks but with most people with smaller ones. For example, the first study found that the mean number of people in the core network was 24, but the median, the 50th percentile, was 15.

Table 7.2

Comparing Communication Technology Networks

Network Dimensions	Communication Technology Network					
	FtF	Tel	EML	PEC	BEC	OVR
Heterogeneity						
Education	.53	.54	.44	.47	.35	.54
Cultural	.23	.22	.14	.21	.15	.22
Sex	.43	.43	.29	.41	.28	.43
Age	.52	.50	.43	.43	.27	.51
Degree						
Strong Communication[1] Ties, Mean	13.3	12.1	5.1	11.7	7.9	16.9
Weak Communication Ties, Mean	5.3	4.2	2.0	3.0	1.9	1.8
Overall Ties, Mean[2]	18.6	16.3	7.2	14.2	9.8	18.8
Overall Ties, Median[3]	17.0	15.0	5.0	13.0	9.5	17.0
Density	.34	.20	.35	.21	.39	.32
Constraint	.45	.39	.63	.38	.44	.32

1 = A strong communication tie is one in which people communicated several times a month or more, and a weak communication tie is one in which people communicated less than several times per month. 2 = The mean is the average. 3 = The median is the middle score. 50% had this number or less.

Researchers in the first study asked general questions about networks and technology, but in the second study, I asked more detailed questions about each alter including how often ego communicated with them using various technologies. This produced descriptions of their FtF, TEL, EML, PEC (includes text messages), and BEC (includes social media and SNS) networks with these people. Table 7.2 summarizes the description of the networks in the second study. In the first study, the researchers asked about using landline telephones, but in the second study, I lumped both landline and mobile phone use together since the use of the traditional phones was so infrequent.

The first study found that diversity increases as network size increases, and greater size and diversity generally increase communication activity. FtF, TEL, and EML use increased with greater diversity. Greater EML use was associated with people having more friends, work, and family ties rather than neighbors. People who EML more to their core ties, also communicate more with them with FtF and TEL. Increased density in core networks related to more FtF and TEL. Also, those who communicated the most were in more dense networks. Except for the increased diversity in larger networks, the pattern suggests closure networks in which EML supplements FtF and TEL.

In the second study, the heterogeneity scores demonstrate the students communicated with people who were most similar culturally. Also note that some of the lowest heterogeneity scores are in the BEC networks, meaning we tend to create audiences of people who are like us for our SNS communication. There is a similar pattern for our EML communication, but there is greater diversity in the EML network.

The EML network is the smallest, most dense, and most constrained. Many of the students did not use EML very much to communicate with their core network. Notice that the number of people in the BEC network is also relatively small, meaning we do not use BEC to communicate very much with core network members. What is more likely is that we will see something on SM, and then communicate in some other way. We have the strongest communication ties in FtF, TEL, and PEC networks. We still use the old technology to communicate with core members.

Both studies suggest people use the newer technologies to supplement older ones when communicating to core and active networks. What may be surprising is how infrequently we use BEC to communicate with our active network. BEC could include using telephone, email, or texting to communicate between some people while others watched, but BEC is mostly about using SNS and other forms of social media.

Social Network Sites

The basic SNS has four features: a profile, a list of users (e.g., friends, followers, fans), a view of and the potential to link to other users, and a view of the links of users. Of course, these features vary from one social media to another. Table 7.3 displays the history of SNS (boyd & Ellison, 2008). The first SNS noted was Six Degrees!

Most of our activities on SNSs like Facebook and LinkedIn are expressive rather than communicative. On an average day, 15% of Facebook users update their own status, 22% comment on another's post or status, 20% comment on another user's photos, 26% "like" another user's content, and 10% send another user a private message (Hampton, Goulet, Rainie, & Purcell, 2011). Notice that people are more likely to comment on another's post or update than to update their own content. Some cross comments do lead to BEC, but private messages are PEC. The most popular thing to do is to "like". Although SNS users are getting older, 44% of Facebook users 18-22 "like" their friends' content on a daily basis. Are most SNS activities an electronic version of sharing scrapbooks (Thompson, 2014)?

Table 7.3

Chronology of Social Network Sites (SNS): 1997-2006

Year	SNS	Year	SNS	Year	SNS
1997	Six Degrees	1998	None	1999	Asian Avenue
					Black Planet
					Live Journal
2000	Mi Gente	2001	Cyworld	2002	Fotolog
			Ryze		Friendster
					Skyblog
2003	Couchsurging	2004	aSmallWorld	2005	AsianAvenue
	Last.FM		Care2		Bebo
	LinkedIn		Catster		BlackPlanet
	MySpace		Dodgeball		(relaunch)
	Open BC/Xing		Facebook		Cyworld (China)
	Tribe.net		(Harvard)		Facebook (high
			Flickr		school)
			Hyves		Ning
			Mixi		Yahoo! 360
			Multiply		YouTube
			Piczo		Xang
2006	Cyworld (US)				
	Facebook				
	(corporate,				
	everyone)				
	MyChurch				
	QQ				
	Twitter				
	Windows Live				
	Spaces				

Using newer technology and SNS activity increase the size of the users' overall personal network (Hampton et al, 2011). The average American and the average SNS user have over 630 ties in their overall personal network, cell phone users have over 660 ties, but people who do not use the Internet (21% of Americans) have just over 500 ties. If you use your mobile phone or tablet to access the Internet, the average is over 700 ties.

The average number of ties (i.e., "friends") on Facebook is around 200, but 50% of users have 100 or less (Backstrom, 2011; Backstom, Boldi, Rosa, Ugander, & Vigna, 2012; Hampton et al., 2011). These ties represent 50% of the users' overall network, but some users actually reported more SNS ties than estimates of their overall network (Hampton et al., 2011). An average of 22% of Facebook ties were with friends from high school, 10% were coworkers, 9% were college friends, 8% were immediate family, and 7% were people from voluntary groups, and 2% were neighbors, but only 31% were in these classifications, and users estimated 10% of their ties were people they had never met or met only once (Hampton, et al., 2011). These networks tend to be homogenous with respect to age and country, and relatively dense with 50% density on networks of 20 or less, 20% on networks near 100, and 10% or less with over 200 or ties (Backstrom et al., 2012). *What this suggests is two groups of users: one group that restricts their SNS network to their active personal network and a few acquaintances and a second group whose network is expansive.*

A constant challenge to using any SNS is diverse social spaces. Posting anything through SNS risks unintended interpretations by some members of the network. Teens, for example, face the normal challenges of finding a place to meet friends without adult supervision while trying to provide assurances to parents that they are safe. They want autonomy and security at the same time. Should they allow parents or other family members access to their SNS? What about postings read by prospective employers that were initially posted to high school friends? Changing the privacy settings might be one way to solve these problems, deactivating and reactivating accounts is another way, but most teens see all of this as a bother (boyd, 2014). *Most teens have an imagined audience that does not account for the diverse social spaces.*

These challenges get magnified when one considers the short distances between network members. In the famous original study of our small world, researchers asked subjects to use the mail to contact people they did not know, targets, by using people they did know (Milgram, 1967; Travers & Miligram, 1969). And so, if the target lived in Boston, the subject contacted a person in Boston they did know. If this first knew the target, then they contacted the target, but if they did not know the target, they contacted someone they thought might know the target. And this continued until the chain was complete. The project started with nearly 300 subjects, but they only completed 64 chains. The average distance between the original person and the target was just under seven, meaning there were six degrees (people) in between the subject and the target. An analysis of the Microsoft Messenger network of 180 million users and 1.3 billion links produced similar results (Lescovic & Horvitz, 2008), but an analysis of over 721 million Facebook users with over 69 billion friendship links demonstrated that the average distance shrinks to under five steps or four degrees of separation and to under four steps or three degrees of separation for networks within country (Backstrom et al., 2012).

How is this possible? How can a Facebook user with the average 200 "friends" be only three "friends" away, on average, from any one of the remaining 721+ million users? For this example, assume the 200 links are unique, the network has 0% density, and all the "friends" are just like the original user with similar networks. One step away, the user has 200 ties, but since his ties also have 200 unique ties, the user is connected to 40,000 "friends of friends" (200 multiplied by 200). Such a network gets to be over 1.6 billion (200x200x200x200) just four steps away of the original user.

Facebook could double the number of users and the distance would still be very small.

Of course, everyone does not have the same number of unique "friends", and over half the Facebook users have 100 or less. As an environment becomes stable, systems become more specialized and centralized (Salem, 2013). What this means for the material in this chapter is that as people become more and more familiar with using different technology, they make choices to restrict the use of technologies in different ways to meet different functions. Some people were a little more strategic at the start of using a particular technology (see Chapter 4). Some people are more popular than others, and so some groups or individuals have more links to others than most people do. The result is many separate groups connected by brokers, a few very popular individuals, or a few groups that seem important to all the groups – specialized and centralized. This kind of process occurs naturally and occurs as personal networks develop regardless of technology. All it takes is for a person to have a tie to someone who is popular, and the whole network can know what each other is doing. Consider what this means for distance on Twitter. In 2010, Twitter had over 175 million users spreading 65 million tweets per day, but less than 1% had over 1000 tweets (Gruzd, Wellman, & Takhteyev, 2011). One analysis of an individual's Twitter network of 56 ties revealed that the number of second degree links (i.e., friends of friends) varied from 256 to 23,110 (Gruzd et al., 2011). Even if you do not use social media to follow or to be a fan of celebrities, and if you only use this technology to maintain an already existing typical active network, you are only a short distance from everyone else in the world.

Using social media reduces relational distance and increases reach. On the one hand, this means that speed and magnitude of positive responses to a post can be exhilarating, but on the other hand, the speed and magnitude of the negative responses can be devastating. It takes extra steps to make messages, posts, and communication private. *Using social media is entering a world where being in public is the default position and being private takes effort* (boyd, 2014). Robin Williams, a comedian and actor, recently committed suicide. His daughter, Zelda, disconnected from social media after she was deluged with cruel comments and tweets (Rosenbloom, 2014). Many bad behaviors described in the last chapter existed prior to social media, but increased reach means they have greater impact.

Personal Networks Changes

This chapter began by describing my son's recommendation for a repairman and quickly moved to considering how people embed themselves in the configuration of relationships they create. People create their own networks, but the network also influences the individuals who created it. In addition to any immediate effects to an individual, there are the cumulative effects from communicating with those direct contacts, and there are the effects from the indirect contacts, those "friends of friends". Noah recommended a person he had never met because he trusted Crystal, and we contacted his recommendation because we trusted Noah.

People naturally develop an active personal network of around 50 contacts featuring a dense core of 20 or so family, friends, and fellow students or workers. Most people use a variety of the newer HCTs to reinforce and extend already existing active relationships and add more acquaintances to their personal network. People use different HCTs to communicate with different groups in their personal network.

Has technology changed our core networks? There have been some changes in the makeup of our personal networks over the last forty years (Fischer, 2011). We are less likely to be married or living with a significant other, and this means there are fewer relatives and more friends in our networks. Of course, we use technology to sustain relationships to overcome time and space limitations such as communicating with people in other countries, and this keeps them in our network. Much of the changes that did occur over the last forty years could be explained by other factors such as lower birthrates, economic upheaval, wives in the workplace, delaying marriage, and extended lifespans (Fischer, 2011). What the data in the last section also suggests is that there are disproportionate changes such as a few people with much greater ties using SNSs and most people with the number of ties similar to the traditional data on personal networks. The way we organize our personal networks does not appear to have changed, but the newer HCTs have shrunk the distance between us and increased the reach of our messages.

None of this suggests technological determinism. The technology did not make us do anything. The changes in society that accompanied the changes in HCTs may have interacted with the increased availability of the newer HCTs, and this type of interaction would support arguments for social determinism. However, this argument is difficult to make without demonstrating that different cultures had different changes in their networks. We certainly have changed the way we talk about and use these technologies, suggesting a social construction explanation, and the disproportionate uses also suggest a realist explanation. There are unique positive and negative features of how we use our new mix of HCTs. Using SNS to trigger later FtF or TEL would not have happened 20 years ago, nor would using a text message to coordinate a FtF meeting. This suggests a media ecology explanation. However, we seem to be resilient of the changes in HCTs, and most of us seem to be able to sustain our personal networks very well. The positive and negative features and impacts on personal networks do not appear to be new, but rather a type of catalytic or multiplier effect. The good and bad messages by some SNS users have always been with us, but those messages have less relational distance to travel, and they travel more quickly. What is happening to our personal networks as we use the newer HCTs appears to be part of the complexity of human communication.

What does it mean to carry around, in your pocket, a social media audience of 50 or more with the ability to reach everyone? Are we always on, meaning "always switched on", or always on as in "always on stage"? How does our communication change when we are performing? Are we more dramatic in our FtF communication when we have the world watching? Does having the potential for all these connections mean people are less lonely? Have technology changes corresponded to changing the functions of relationships? Does this increased connectivity mean we are more a part of a community? Are we more engaged in our communities? Some answers to these questions are in later chapters.

References

Backstrom, L. (2011). The anatomy of Facebook. Unpublished manuscript. Facebook. Available at http://www.facebook.com/notes/facebook-data-team/anatomy-of-facebook/10150388519243859.

Backstrom, L., Boldi, P., Rosa, M., Ugander, J., & Vigna, S. (2012, June). *Four degrees of separation*. Paper presented at the 4th ACM International Conference on Web Science, Evanston IL.

Barbabsi, A. (2002). *Linked: The new science of networks*. Cambridge, MA: Perseus Publishing.

Barnes, M. (2014, July17). A time in Austin when anybody could know everybody. *Austin American Statesman*, pp. D1, D10.

Baxter, L. A., & Montgomery, B. M. (1996). *Relating: Dialogues and dialectics*. NY: Guilford.

Blau, M., & Fingerman, K. L. (2009). *Consequential strangers: The power of people who don't seem to matter . . . but really do*. New York: W. W. Norton and Company.

Boase, J. (2008). Personal networks and the personal communication system: Using multiple media to connect. *Information, Communication, and Society, 11*(4), 490-508.

Boase, J., Horrigan, J., Wellman, B., & Raine, L. (2006, July). *The strength of Internet ties*. Report for the Pew Internet and American Life Project, Washington, DC. Retrieved from http://www.pewinternet.org/Reports/2006/The-Strength-of-Internet-Ties.aspx.

Borgatti, S. P., Everett, M. G., & Johnson, J. C. (2013). *Analyzing social networks*. Los Angeles, CA: Sage.

boyd, d. m. (2014). *It's complicated: The social lives of networked teens*. New Haven, CT: Yale University Press.

boyd, d., m., & Ellison, N. B. (2008). Social network sites: Definition, history, and scholarship. *Journal of Computer-Mediated Communication, 13*, 210-230.

Burt, R. S. (2005). *Brokerage and closure: An introduction to social capital*. Oxford: Oxford University Press.

Burt, R. S. (2010). *Neighbor networks: Competitive advantage local and personal*. Oxford: Oxford University Press.

Christakis, N. A., & Fowler, J. H. (2009). *Connected: The surprising power of our social networks and how they shape our lives*. New York: Little Brown and Company.

Chua, V., Madej, J., & Wellman, B. (2011). Personal communities: The world according to me. In P. Carrington & J. Scott (Eds.), *The handbook of social network analysis* (pp. 101-115). Thousand Oaks, CA: Sage

Dunbar, R. I. M. (2010). *How many friends does one person need? Dunbar's number and other evolutionary quirks*. Cambridge, MA: Harvard University Press.

Dunbar, R, I. M. Arnaboldi, V., Conti, M., & Passarella, A, (2015). The structure of online social networks mirrors those in the offline world. *Social Networks, 15*, 39-47.

Fischer, C. (1992). *America calling: A social history of the telephone*. Berkley, CA: University of California Press.

Fischer, C. (2011). *Still connected: Family and friends in America since 1970*. New York: Russell Sage Foundation.

Fowler, J. H., & Christakis, N. A. (2008). The dynamic spread of happiness in a large social network: Longitudinal analysis of the Farmington Heart Study social network. *British Medical Journal, 338*(7658), 23-27.

Gottman, J. M. (1994). *What predicts divorce? The relationship between marital processes and marital outcomes*. Hillside, NJ: Erlbaum.

Gottman, J. M., Murray, J. D., Swanson, C. C, Tyson, R., & Swanson, K. R. (2002). *The mathematics of marriage: Dynamic nonlinear models*. Cambridge, MA: MIT Press.

Granovetter, M. (1973). The strength of weak ties. *American Journal of Sociology, 78*, 1360-1380.

Hampton, K. N., Goulet, L. S., Rainie, L., & Purcell, K. (2011). *Social networking and our lives*. Washington, DC: Pew Research Center. Retrieved from http://www.pewinternet.org/Reports/2011/Technology-and-social-networks.aspx.

Horton, D., & Wohl, R. R. (1956). Mass communication and para-social interaction: Observations on intimacy at a distance. *Psychiatry, 19*, 185-206.

Johnson A., & Becker J. (2011). CMC and the conceptualization of "friendship": How friendships have changed with the advent of new methods of interpersonal communication. In K. B. Wright & L. M. Webb (Eds.), *Computer-mediated communication in personal relationships* (pp. 225-243). New York: Peter Lang.

Johnson A., Becker J., Wigley S., Wittenberg E., & Haigh M. (2008, November). *What geographic distance can illustrate about relational closeness: Close long-distance friendships*. Paper presented at the meeting of the National Communication Association, San Diego CA.

Kadushin, C. (2012). *Understanding social networks: Theories, concepts, and findings*. Oxford: Oxford University Press.

Miligram, S. (1967). The small world problem. *Psychology Today*, *2*(1), 60-67.

Monge, P. R., & Contractor, N. S. (2003). *Theories of communication networks*. Oxford: Oxford University Press.

Olson, D. H. L., Sprenkle, D. H., & Russell, C. S. (1979). Circumplex model of marital and family systems: Cohesion and adaptability dimensions, family types, and clinical applications. *Family Process*, *18*, 3-28.

Rosenbloom, S. (2014, August 24). Dealing with digital cruelty. *New York Times*, SR1.

Simmons, M. E., & de Ridder, J. A. (2004). Renewing connections and changing relations: Use of information and communication technology and cohesion in organizational groups. *Communications*, *29*(4), 159-177.

Salem, P. J. (2013). *The complexity of human communication* (2nd ed.). Cresskill, NJ: Hampton Press.

Salem, P. J. (2012). Civic engagement and communication technology networks. In M. H. Safar, & K. A. Mahdi (Eds.), *Social networking and community behavior modeling: Qualitative and quantitative measures* (pp. 51-66). Hersey, PA: IGI Global.

Standage, T. (1998). *The Victorian Internet: The remarkable story of the telegraph and the nineteenth century's online pioneers*. New York: Walker & Company.

Thompson, C. (2014, July/August). When copy and paste reigned in the age of scrapbooking: Today's obsession with posting material to Pinterest, Facebook and Twitter has a very American history. *Smithsonian*, Retrieved from http://www.smithsonianmag.com/history/when-copy-and-paste-reigned-age-scrapbooking-180951844/?all

Travers, J., & Miligram, S. (1969). An experimental study of the small world problem. *Soicometry*, *32*(4), 425-443.

Ugander, J., Karrer, B., Backstrom, L., & Marlow, C. (2011). *The anatomy of the Facebook social graph*. Unpublished manuscript. Cornel University Library. Retrieved from http://arxiv.org/abs/1111.4503,

Wellman, B., Hogan, B., Berg, K., Boase, J., Carrasco, J.A., Coté, R., Kayahara, J., Kennedy T., & Tran P. (2006), Connected Lives: The project. In P. Purcell (Ed.), *The networked neighbourhood* (pp. 157-211). Berlin: Springer.

Chapter Eight:
Close Relationships

There are five prototypical relationships: (a) family or kinships, (b) romantic partners or spouses, (c) friends, (d) formal or work relationships, and (e) acquaintances. The nature of the closeness, functions, and flexibility within and across these categories varies. For example, although people might feel less close generally to acquaintances than kin, a person could feel closer to the server at a favorite restaurant than an uncle who seldom connects. It would seem that newer human communication technology (HCT) affords people different ways to meet, and the different ways to get information about others would improve ways of developing deeper relationships.

This chapter is about developing close relationships online, especially romantic relationships and friendships. This chapter is also about loneliness, the feeling that happens when people do not develop the close relationships they need. The next chapter will be about the resources people can obtain from those relationships.

Over ten years ago, friends introduced me to a couple that married and had met through an online dating service. He had lived in North Dakota and moved to Texas. Similarly, a media specialist in my office met her husband, a minster, through a Christian dating service. Of course, I also have stories about people I know who met online and the FtF dates were a mess. However, traditional *forms* of "courtship" seem to be dead. But, does this mean that courtship is dead (Williams, 2013) or can online relationships be more real than real ones (Roiphe, 2013)? Are most people using the newer forms of HCT to develop and sustain deeper romantic relationships?

David Brooks, *The New York Times* columnist, described the benefits of friendship in an essay (2014). Friendships help people make better judgments since friends can help each other "think through" problems together. Friends bring out better versions of each other since they are more unguarded and fluid with each other. Finally, people generally behave better when they know their friends are watching since they want their friends to admire them. Friendship is about common interests and mutual admiration. Brooks admitted writers tend to romanticize friendship, but, for him, friendships were so important that if he had $500 million to give away, the amount some contributed to political causes, he would spend it helping people develop friendships. "You can go without marriage, or justice, or honor, but friendship is indispensable to life," he wrote.

Friendships are voluntary, and people meet as equals when they are friends. These characteristics make friendships different than kin or formal relationships. Although close friendships are similar to romantic relationships in that both are about sharing emotional and private experiences, people expect that others have many friendships, but one or few simultaneous romantic relationships. One of the trickier features of friendships is negotiating the breadth and depth of disclosure while protecting and guarding confidences and self-identities (Rawlins, 1992, 2009). The tensions associated between open and closed are tensions common to all relationships (Baxter & Montgomery, 1996).

We may have fewer close friends than three decades ago. In 1985, when researchers asked people to list up to five others with whom they had discussed important matters over the last six months, the average number was nearly three people, but twenty years later, the average was just over two (McPherson, Smith-Lovin, & Brashears, 2006). Furthermore, in 1985, 10% said they had discussed important matters with no one, but by 2004, nearly 25% said this. The people listed included family or spouses, but the 1985 lists had one more friend. Researchers have challenged the methods and results of these studies, but they confirm the general pattern (Brashears, 2011).

How can people have lost a friend from part of their core network, but still have 50-200 "friends" online? Jay Baer is a digital marketing consultant, and he is bombarded daily by telephone calls, email messages, and posts of all kinds. A friend of his committed suicide, and he wrote the following:

> **I considered Trey Pennington a friend.** I suspect many of his 100,000+ Twitter followers considered him a friend. Clearly, most of us were not his friends, as his death came as a complete surprise despite the fact that he had a prior suicide attempt earlier this summer and had been discussing his problems with confidants.
>
> But if you'd asked me yesterday morning, I would have said Trey was a friend. **Social media forces upon us a feeling of intimacy and closeness that doesn't actually exist.**
>
> I met Amber Naslund on Twitter and we wrote a book together. But, I've never met her daughter.
>
> Jason Falls is one of my closest colleagues in social media, but he's never been to my home.
>
> Mike Stelzner and I have collaborated on many projects, but we've never had a private meal.
>
> I consider these people (and many, many others) to be friends, and I'm thankful that social media has brought them into my life. But in comparison to my pre-social media friends (many of whom I've known for 30+ years), I know almost nothing about them.
>
> Is that what we want – **spending considerable time building large networks of shallow connections,**

potentially at the expense of deepening a few cherished friendships upon which we can truly rely? (Baer, 2014)
(formatting in the original)

Are the online only relationships equivalent to the ones before social media or are these "pretend friends" with "false intimacy"? Are people developing more shallow relationships? Are these relationships just substitutes to cope with loneliness?

There appears to be little time to be alone. The constant connectivity can prevent us from reflection and the deep thinking that can lead to greater creativity. Time alone can lead to greater appreciation of the present and provide the opportunity to solve problems. Time alone can be very productive (Zomorodi, 2017).

Antone's, the venerable Austin blues club, has seen its share of peculiar customers. In the late 1980s, I spotted a woman who was the fan of one artist, and she always came to his shows dressed in a black semi-formal skirt and blouse and often wore black lace gloves. When I first noticed her standing against a wall, she seemed ominous like Harriett Bird, the character in the movie *The Natural* who shoots the hero, Roy Hobbs. But, the Antone's lady in black simply listened to music and waited for the right song to enter the dance floor to dance alone. She would turn down invitations from others to dance with her, but she danced alone in an area filled with others dancing together. She was in her own world enjoying the music. I told others she was the quintessential person who was "alone in the company of others". Later, I often used the phrase to describe those who seemed lost in their technology even though others were present.

Turkle (2011) described this phenomenon as being "alone together". Watkins (2009) described something similar as "absence-in-presence", a state of emotional or mental detachment while being physically present. Turkle warned that people were substituting connections to technology for connections to people.

Watkins argued that technology allows for "presence-in-absence", a state where we can be emotionally and mentally connected to others even though we are not physically present. Are people substituting technology for people or are they substituting one type of connectivity for another? Are they substituting at all or just developing a mix of different relational experiences?

This chapter is about HCT and close relationships, and it is about the tensions people feel when their social activities do not satisfy their social needs. The next section describes the challenges to disclosing online and developing close relationships. This section includes brief descriptions of how people have developed romantic relationships in the past, and the unique ways people develop them today. The second section explains loneliness and how it is different from being alone. There is controversy over whether or not the newer HCTs reduce or increase loneliness, and I will present those arguments. Finally, the last section contains explanations for the current condition.

Communicating in Close Relationships

Disclosure and Validation

Explaining the initiation, development, and, the termination of relationships is beyond the scope of this book. However, one feature of all relationships is the tension between communicating with people in a specific relationship in a different way than communicating with people outside the relationship. For example, a father and son may naturally develop a unique style for each other, but when they are with other family members, they must communicate in a way common to the entire family. Romantic partners develop their own routines, but they must participate in more general social routines to maintain their group membership when they are with others. In organizational communication, formal communication consists of patterns of communication that conform to organizational rules, and other communication is informal. The extent to which communication is more stylized or is unique is an important feature for explaining communication in intimate relationships (Knapp & Vangelisti, 2009). The tension over how to develop or use unique forms of communication is one of the challenges of dealing with diverse audiences mentioned earlier in this book.

Some unique forms of communication are central to notions of closeness and intimacy. More intimate communication involves more private, personal, and risky content (Altman & Taylor, 1973). *Self-disclosure* is what people verbally reveal about themselves to each other. Disclosure may vary across a range of topics, breath, and disclosure may vary in specificity and detail, depth. When relationships become closer, there is greater depth and breadth of disclosure (Altman & Taylor, 1973; Knapp & Vangelisti, 2009), and the disclosures are about more personal topics that few people know (Archer & Cook, 1986). However, there is a tension between revealing too much or too little, and relationships oscillate between extremes, going through periods with little disclosure and periods of much disclosure (Baxter & Montgomery, 1996).

There are different types of self-disclosure (Culbert, 1967; Miller & Steinberg, 1975). *Self-description* is revealing information that the receiver could easily obtain without communicating with the discloser. It includes disclosures with little risk.

Genuine self-disclosure is the (a) intentional revealing of (b) personal, (c) private, and (d) risky information to another. Personal means the information is important to how the discloser identifies, evaluates, and makes decisions about him/herself. Private means that few people know the information. The information is risky because the discloser is uncertain how the receiver will evaluate the discloser after learning about the information. One way to understand the development of intimacy is that relationship members begin disclosing with self-description and move to genuine self-disclosure. It is possible to develop intimacy in conversations that last less than an hour and involve the reciprocal escalating disclosers answering just 36 questions (Aron, Melinat, Aron, Vallone, & Bator, 1997; Jones, 2015)

Apparent self-disclosure happens when the receiver believes the disclosure is genuine, but the sender knows it is not. The sender may have blurted out something without thinking about it, the information may seem important to others but is really no big deal to the sender, the sender knows lots of people may know the information, or the sender may not care what the receiver thinks. An unscrupulous communicator may use apparent self-disclosure to create a false sense of intimacy or to elicit self-disclosure from the other.

What counts as personal, and how much should a person disclose? These are issues of managing privacy, but unlike the concerns for others invading our personal spaces or discovering information people do not want others to know, managing privacy is about the conscious decisions people make to knowingly tell others about themselves. Although disclosure is important to initiating and developing a relationship, it is also an important part of maintaining close relationships (Canary & Stafford, 1994; Knapp & Vanglisti, 2009). Married couples manage their individual personal boundaries and selectively disclose to their partners even after years of marriage (Petronio, 2002). One of the issues in friendships is how much to keep private with which particular friends and how much of a friendship is more public (Rawlins, 1992, 2009).

Self-disclosure is part of developing close relationships, but self-disclosure is also a means to obtain validation from each other. *Validation* means getting feedback from others about thoughts and feeling and getting this feedback over difficult matters (Derlaga, Metts, Petronio, & Margulis, 1993). *Validation recognizes and confirms the nature of a relationship and the people in it.* Without validation, relationship members are uncertain and anxious about a relationship and their place in it. Without validation people become uncertain and anxious about themselves.

There are three types of validation. *Social validation* reinforces group identity. When someone posts "I just got a raise", the responses, even simple "likes" or "dislikes", reinforce the sender's attachment and membership to the imagined group represented by the network of people linked to the SNS. *Relational validation* refers to reinforcing the roles, rules and boundaries in a relationship. If someone telephoned a close friend to discuss getting or not getting the raise, the feedback from the friends recognizes the unique personal features each person brings to the friendship, and the way they discuss the matter reinforces how those people have chosen to communicate with each other. *Personal validation* comes from interactions that reinforce or highlight the personal characteristics of the people in the communication. All communication can provide personal validation, but the validation comes from sustained interaction between people who regard each other as important for that validation. Jay Baer was receiving social validation from the interactions displayed trough SMS and not the relational or personal validation he may have imagined.

However, some responses to disclosure may not validate. Equivocal messages, those messages that are so ambiguous that do not support or reject, will not validate. As I noted in Chapter Five, equivocal responses jeopardize relationships, role concepts, and self-concepts. Validation is a function of close relationships, and validation is a type of social resource. The study noted at the start of this chapter reported people had lost a friend with whom they "could discuss important matters". What that study was reporting was the loss of a close friend, one who was available for self-disclosure, and one who could validate.

Although social network sites (SNSs) can provide opportunities for disclosure and validation, most young users do not afford themselves of these opportunities. A common explanation for using SNSs is to "hang out with friends", and although the postings on social media contain twice as much personal or relational information as the messages in FtF conversations (Akin, 2016), people are suspicious of these online messages (Mihailidis, 2014). While young people recognize the improved connectivity through SNSs, they spend most of their time checking these sites just to "kill time" (Mihailidis, 2014).

The general patterns of online self-disclosure are similar to the patterns offline. In Chapter Five, I noted the asynchronous nature of the newer HCT provided greater opportunities to strategically present an ideal self and to self-disclose (Walther, 2007), and that most research comparing the amounts and intimacy of self-disclosure online to FtF self-disclosure demonstrates little difference (Kim & Dindia, 2011). There are occasions that people will disclose with greater depth online to strangers than FtF, people report they generally disclose with greater depth to friends, family and strangers FtF than online, and there seems to be little difference between FtF and online breadth of self-disclosure given equivalent time and opportunity (Nguyen, Bin, & Campbell, 2012). Ultimately, the breadth and depth of self-disclosure online depends on the space (e.g., chat, email, SMS) and the audience (Whitty & Johnson, 2009).

Some self-disclosure norms are exactly the same with digital HCT as with FtF. People did restrict what they regarded as most personal to only a few instances in both FtF and online communication, and they revealed the most personal slightly more in FtF than online (Tidwell & Walther, 2002). When one person discloses FtF or online, the receiver tended to reciprocate and disclose as well (Jiang, Bazarova, & Hancock, 2011). People regarded topics disclosed one-on-one or within a small exclusive group through FTF, TEL, or EML as more intimate than if similar disclosure occurred through a wall post or status update (Bazarova, 2012). When someone disclosed something "intimate" in a public way online, others regarded the public display as inappropriate and felt less positive about the discloser (Bazarova, 2012). What this suggests is that people are suspicious of public posts of "private" information or regard them as less genuine and perhaps attempts at apparent self-disclosure.

Some norms for disclosure seem to be changing. What information is so personal that people would limit presentation of it to only people close to them? In an early study, participants thought comments such as "I've considered committing suicide on more than one occasion" and "We got married earlier than we'd planned because I was pregnant" as more personal and less likely to be introduced early in a conversation between strangers (Berger, Gardner, Clatterbuck, & Shulman, 1976). By contrast, researchers confirmed expressions such as "I always think my roommate to be a very distant person" were as intimate in FtF and in online chat as "My parents got divorced two years ago" (Bazarova, 2012). This chapter began with Jay Baer's posting of his thoughts on losing his friend and his re-evaluation of friendship. Was this topic appropriate to post?

While the development of current HCT has increased the breadth of disclosure, people are having a difficult time disclosing the depth of personal information they would like. The most genuine of disclosures involves selecting specific topics to discuss in detail, and these disclosures identify differences between relational partners that could lead to intensifying their relationship or to less communication about safer topics (Knapp & Vangelisti, 2009). The potential gains are also relational and personal validation. With one less friend to discuss these important matters, people lose the opportunity to explore personal topics in depth, lose the chance to develop closer relationships, and lose the possibility of developing greater depth in their self-concepts.

Finding Romantic Partners and Disclosure

Many of the issues about disclosing information as part of developing relationships are central to using dating sites. The profile on a SNS such as Facebook is more for friends and family than it is to attract a romantic partner. Most people use their digital HCT to maintain old relationships and develop a few new ones, but dating sites are about meeting someone new and, hopefully developing a relationship.

Dating is a relatively new phenomenon. Courtship patterns developed and became formal from the late eighteenth century to the early twentieth century as part of and then as an alternative to arranged marriages (Cates & Lloyd, 1992; Zeldin, 1994). In America, the end of World War II was a period when those doing the dating developed courtship expectations challenging parental or institutional norms. The norms have changed as people adjusted to the various social changes in the latter half of the twentieth century and early twenty-first century.

Online dating services usually require a fee, the users construct profiles that typically include photos and may involve videos, and the users search through the system to find other users to contact in a more private way (Whitty & Carr, 2006). The presentation of the user results in a *commodification of the self*. That is, users are advertising and branding themselves, and dating becomes shopping or screening a commodity (Whitty, 2008). The use of digital dating sites and services follows the earlier use of personal ads in newspapers and video dating as methods to initiate relationships. Similar to these previous methods, some form of text available to a public precedes any private communication between likely partners. Users screen through the online service, and then continue to screen the prospective partner through EML, PEC, TEL, and then FtF. Online dating services may be just a new way to speed-up courtship (Fisher, 2016).

Online dating is common (Smith & Duggan, 2013).

- 11% of Internet users (representing 9% of all adults) say that they have personally used an online dating site such as Match.com, eHarmony, or OK Cupid, and 7% of cell phone apps users (representing 3% of all adults) say that they have used a dating app on their cell phone. 11% of all American adults have done one or both of these activities and are classified as "online daters."

- Some 22% of 25-34 year-olds and 17% of 35-44 year-olds are online daters.

- 38% of Americans who are single and actively looking for a partner have used online dating at one point or another.

- 66% of online daters have gone on a date with someone they met through an online dating site or app, up from 43% of online daters who had done so when researchers first asked this question in 2005.

- 23% of online daters say that they themselves have entered into a marriage or long-term relationship with someone they met through a dating site or app, similar to the online daters in 2005.

- 42% of all Americans know an online dater, and 29% know someone who has used online dating to find a spouse or other long-term relationship.

Although people have developed more positive attitudes about online dating, they still hold several negative attitudes (Smith & Duggan, 2013) (note: italics indicate the phrasing on a survey item).

- 59% of all Internet users think *online dating is a good way to meet people*, a 15-point increase from 2005.

- 53% of Internet users think *online dating allows people to find a better match for themselves* because they can get to know a lot more people, a 6-point increase from 2005.

- 21% of Internet users agree that *people who use online dating sites are desperate*, an 8-point decline from 2005.

- 32% of Internet users think *online dating keeps people from settling down because they always have options for people to date*.

- 28% of online daters have been contacted by someone through an online dating site or app in a way that made them feel harassed or uncomfortable.

- 42% of female online daters have experienced this type of contact at one point or another, compared with 17% of men.

Of particular interest are the challenges of how much to disclose when using these services. The most successful approaches online appear to be those that are both attractive but real, BAR (Whitty, 2008a). On the one hand, this provides the opportunity to reveal aspects of an ideal self a user wants to make real. On the other hand, the attempt to be attractive may lead to falsehoods. Just over 54% of online daters have felt someone else seriously misrepresented themselves in their dating profile (Smith & Duggan, 2013). However, many regard these as "exaggerations" rather than lies (Whitty, 2008b). This suggests people detected apparent self-disclosure, but some regard it as benign in online dating.

Finally, the tendency in online dating is to withhold greater detail about topics until the relationship had developed. That is, although users disclose about topics most would think are intimate, the user reveals only enough detail to attract someone or to complete a form or standardized profile (Whitty, 2008a). If the relationship develops, greater detail follows just as in relationships that begin offline.

The commodification presents an ideal self, and some may anticipate meeting the ideal self when the daters meet. Furthermore, the exchange of messages prior to meeting may involve risky disclosures and suggest an unintended intimacy. According to a 2016 UK national crime study, rape incidents associated with online dating increased by six times over the previous five years. Most of these incidents were at someone's residence, and a follow-up study revealed the perpetrators were not known sex-offenders and had no criminal history suggesting these behaviors. Rather, there were false expectations "mutating" into unwanted behaviors (Aiken, 2016).

Some have feared that these sites make it too easy to find temporary relationships. Defining characteristics of traditional romantic relationships are commitment and exclusivity as couples seek to build a life together. People who meet online are more likely to break up after a year, are less likely to marry, and more likely to divorce than people who meet offline (Aditi, 2014). Dan Slater (2013) included comments from executives of dating sites in a recent *Atlantic* article.

> The future will see better relationships but more divorce,"
> predicts Dan Winchester, the founder of a free dating site based

in the U.K. "The older you get as a man, the more experienced you get. You know what to do with women, how to treat them and talk to them. Add to that the effect of online dating." He continued, "I often wonder whether matching you up with great people is getting so efficient, and the process so enjoyable, that marriage will become obsolete."

"Historically," says Greg Blatt, the CEO of Match.com's parent company, "relationships have been billed as 'hard' because, historically, commitment has been the goal. You could say online dating is simply changing people's ideas about whether commitment itself is a life value." Mate scarcity also plays an important role in people's relationship decisions. "Look, if I lived in Iowa, I'd be married with four children by now," says Blatt, a 40-something bachelor in Manhattan. "That's just how it is."

What this suggests is an increase in apparent self-disclosure as people regard the commodification of themselves as just another part of an online game.

An optimistic conclusion would be that more romantic relationships provide the opportunity to find the "right person" and to discover different things about personal self through different relationships. A broader network is one way the newer HCTs provide the potential for a more complex self (Hage & Powers, 1992). Conversely, the increase in breadth could mean an unwillingness to provide genuine self-disclosure because it is too risky. People create a homogeneous network that reinforces a social identity, and there are no relationships with any depth to explore differences. People may become risk aversive and unwilling to discuss anything but the information they have already packaged for consumption (Rophie, 2013).

Several recent films dramatize the misuse of disclosure and the unique risks online. *Catfish* (Jarwecki, Joost, & Shulman, 2010) documents how a bored and lonely person creates false personas to develop a friendship through one persona and a romantic relationship through another persona with the same unsuspecting person. In *Disconnect* (Horburg, Liddell, Monroe, Rubin, & Stern, 2012), two teen bullies use an online site to present themselves as a female adolescent to lure a victim into disclosing and sexting. The bullies then use a SNS to distribute the disclosures and nude pictures, and the distraught victim eventually commits suicide. Some estimates of sending or receiving sexting among teens are as high as 30%, many regard sexting as way to build intimacy, but some collect the nude pictures and share them like sports trading cards, and there have been actual suicides because of distributing nude photos of teens (Lippman & Campbell, 2014; Rosin, 2014).

Self-disclosure is how people develop close relationships. They talk about important things, and the disclosures increase in breadth and depth as relationships become close. Self-disclosure is how people tell each other they are different from each other. Even in the closest of relationships, people monitor their genuine disclosure, and there are periods of great disclosure and other periods where there is little.

People use the newer technologies to supplement older ones to maintain and sustain close relationships. Meeting others and developing relationships through the Internet is common, and disclosure patterns online are similar to the ones offline. However, expectations for the appropriateness of what and how much to disclose are volatile. Furthermore, some services, such as dating sites, encourage apparent self-disclosure as users commodify themselves to attract others. Simple self-descriptions on SNS reach diverse audiences, and even the uniqueness of events is lost. Party pictures on one Facebook look like the rest. Newer HCT used with established relationships can lead to greater disclosure and closeness, but initiating and developing relationships primarily through digital HCT presents its own challenges. People are confused about what is appropriate to disclose and what is the appropriate depth of disclosure. Disclosing with less depth to more people means fewer intimate, deeper, relationships. For many, their uses of these increased opportunities for communication do not meet their social needs.

Loneliness and Technology

Loneliness is a feeling, not a condition of your social circumstances. Loneliness is a feeling that occurs when your current social activity fails to meet your social needs (Cacioppo & Patrick, 2008). People develop a need at a threshold or level, and only when actual social activity fails to meet that threshold will they feel lonely (Russell, Cutrona, McCrae, & Gomez, 2012). People may have one fewer friend than a decade ago, but they may not experience any tension since they still have many friends above their threshold, and they may not feel lonely.

Loneliness, like all feelings, requires some cognitive activity. An emotion is the physiological reaction to a circumstance, but a feeling begins when the brain associates emotions with each other or the circumstances related to the emotion (Damasio, 1999). In the case of loneliness, the feeling begins when the brain relates the emotion to the circumstances and social needs and ends when the brain labels the experience as feeling "lonely". Circumstances are important, but a person must frame her involvement with them as being lonely.

Our needs to be socially connected have genetic roots. Neuroscientists have discovered the regions of the brain humans activate when they engage in communication and think about communication, and these social regions are the default regions of the brain (Lieberman, 2013). This means that when people have nothing else to think about, they think about each other. This individual predisposition to connect allows for the evolution of more complex social structures (Wilson, 2012). Loneliness is related to the underexpression of some genes reducing inflammatory responses and overexpression of other genes increasing pro-inflammatory factors (Cacioppo & Patrick, 2008). That is, there is a genetic predisposition to be more uncomfortable and tense than others. And so, some people's genes assist in developing a greater need to communicate with people than others.

Learning also plays a role in developing social needs. After reviewing past research, Schutz (1958) identified three basic needs: (1) inclusion is a need for belonging, recognition, and contact with others, (2) affection is a need for closeness, warmth, and openness, and (3) control is a need for influence, order, and responsibility. His own data indicated the level or intensity of need fluctuated as children matured, and the intensity of the needs stabilized in the late teens and early twenties. The changes in early childhood and the teen years reflected the family environment and what children had learned from that environment. The combination of genetics and learning are also important to other relational predispositions (e.g., Simpson & Rholes, 1998).

One of the important features of Schutz's work is that his survey to measure these needs asked people to indicate the *frequency* of particular behaviors and the *number of people* involved. For example, one item asked people to indicate how often they liked people to invite them to join in activities and another item asked them to indicate how many people they liked to invite them in activities. The intensity of a particular need was a combination of depth (frequency) and breadth (number of people). Some people need to be with a lot of people, but others could have a need to be with fewer people more frequently. Some might need a lot of affection frequently with a lot of people, but others could have a need for a less frequent affection with fewer people.

There are similar distinctions about loneliness. There are three types of loneliness (Hawkley, Browne, & Cacioppo, 2005). (1) *Social isolation* is a general feeling that you are more detached and withdrawn than others. It is the underlying idea behind most loneliness research. People who feel socially isolated feel they are alone and lack companionship, and they are unhappy about it. (2) *Relational loneliness* is a feeling that you might be disconnected from close personal relationships. People have the sense that there are few people – family, friends, or romantic partners - who really understand them or people with whom they can confide. (3) *Social loneliness* is a feeling of not being connected to larger groups (e.g., males, students, Republicans, celebrity fans). People feel out of touch or radically different from the members of groups. The second type of loneliness is about the lack of affection and inclusion from important relationships, and so it is more about depth. The third type of loneliness is about a lack of inclusion and the breadth of relationships.

For Schutz, if the level of interpersonal activity would fall below or above the needs, people would change their communication to restore equilibrium. Changing behavior in this way is not a strategic act. That is, people do not think to themselves "My needs for affection are not being met, and so I must call my mother." Rather, people feel a tension and then act to reduce that tension. These corrective actions are mindless.

Similarly, everyone feels lonely from time to time, people act to reduce the tension, and these actions are often mindless. *Transient loneliness* is feeling lonely for a short time or in a specific circumstance, but *chronic loneliness* is constantly feeling lonely in most or every circumstance (Cacioppo & Patrick, 2008). People often reduce transient loneliness with mindless actions, but they sometimes must reflect or create a strategy to cope until circumstances change.

When people report loneliness is "a major concern", it is chronic loneliness. Twenty percent of Americans reported loneliness to be a major source of unhappiness in their lives (Cacioppo & Patrick, 2008) and nearly thirty-five percent of older Americans report this (Wilson & Moulton, 2010). However, younger adults reported the highest loneliness scores with Gen Z

(18-22) reporting higher scores than Millennials (23-37) or Gen Xers (38-51) and with Boomers (52-71) lower than the younger groups and the members of the Greatest Generation (72+) the least lonely (Cigna, 2018). Reducing chronic loneliness requires mindfulness and purposeful corrective action.

The people in your network can influence your loneliness. If the direct ties in your network are feeling lonely, you are more likely to feel lonely, but if other people connected to those ties, people with whom you do not communicate and may not know, are feeling lonely, they will influence the people with whom you do communicate. This effect extends to three degrees from you (Cacioppo, Fowler, & Christakis, 2009). Loneliness is catchy.

Loneliness accompanies or leads to a variety of health concerns (Cacioppo, Hawkley, & Bernston, 2003; Cigna, 2018; Wilson & Moulton, 2010). People with greater loneliness are more likely to perceive and feel greater stress, report less social support, are more likely to be obese, and are more likely to have Alzheimer's disease than those who are less lonely. People with greater loneliness spend the same total time in bed compared to less lonely people, but people with greater loneliness spend less time asleep and more time awake after sleep than less lonely individuals. People with greater loneliness are more likely to develop heart problems than those who are less lonely. This is true of both younger and older adults, but the severity of problems is greater with older adults. People with greater loneliness are more likely to commit suicide than those who are less lonely.

Loneliness is about engaging in the disclosure and validation necessary to meet people's needs. Social isolation is a feeling that a person has no one to talk to, and that there are so few relationships he or she has become unsure of himself or herself. Relational loneliness is more specifically about close relationships and a feeling that people cannot disclose about important things to the people that are important to them. Relational loneliness is a sense there is not enough genuine disclosure and the validation that comes from that. Social loneliness is about feeling excluded from groups. A person may not need the common disclosures of others, even if they are self-descriptions, to feel any social identity to groups. Without the minimal needed relationships for disclosures and validation, there is uncertainty and disconfirmation. As I noted in Chapter Five, continued disconfirmation can lead to anxiety, depression, or despair.

How does the use of the newer technologies relate to loneliness? There have been many possibilities, and there has been research that supports nearly every claim. More Internet activity lead to greater loneliness for new users (Kraut et al., 1998), but, over time, the greater loneliness diminished for most personality types (Kraut et al., 2002). Having a better sense of how to use technology reduced the chances for greater loneliness using the Internet (LaRose, Easton, & Gregg, 2001), and, regardless of the technology, those with better communication competence, especially disclosure skills, had less loneliness (Burke, Wozidlo & Segrin, 2012). Although greater Internet use was associated with greater loneliness, lonely people might prefer communicating online while others use a greater variety of HCT (Morahan-Martin & Shumacher, 2003). Older people's greater use of the Internet was associated with less loneliness about romantic relationships, but greater loneliness about friends and family (Sum, Mathews, Hughes, & Campbell, 2008). Although people may have smaller and more homogeneous personal networks, people who use contemporary technology more had bigger and more diverse core networks (Hampton, Sessions, Ja Her, & Raine, 2009). Most research investigated a general feeling of loneliness and how it was related to using the Internet without specifying the technology (e.g., EML, PEC).

Although greater use of social media alone did not predict greater loneliness, the use of social media and reported loneliness was the greatest with Gen Z (Cigna, 2018). More meaningful FtF communication was related to less loneliness (Cigna, 2018). The mix of technologies may be more important than any one type of technology.

Two recent studies investigated the relationships between different kinds of loneliness with newer HCT, and one study compared different types of HCT to loneliness. In a broad survey of communication technology networks (Salem, 2014), college students felt less social isolation and relational loneliness when their core networks members had educational levels similar to themselves (i.e., more homogeneous about education). People felt less social loneliness when they had more contacts across nearly all technology and when the FtF network was less dense. In the technology deprivation study noted in Chapter Five, people felt "lonely", "detached", "disconnected", "left out", "out of the loop", and "isolated", and some felt "sad" or "lost" without their technology (Salem, 2012). These comments were about meaningful relationships with people far away, relational loneliness, and about being disconnected from groups, social loneliness. These two studies demonstrate that when college students used their technology to connect with other college students who are not connected to each other, they developed friendships and acquaintanceships to meet their social needs, and they used the technology to stay connected with groups and with people in important close relationships separated by distance.

There were hints at substituting technology for relationships in the technology deprivation study. One subject commented, "We seem to turn the television 'on' and turn 'off' those who are important to us." Another subject summarized her thoughts as follows:

> My final conclusion is that television plays a big part in my life
> as well as others' (lives). It has always been there for us, unlike
> (our) boyfriends and girlfriends. It never talks back or gets
> angry when you pay no attention to it. It is a one-way ticket to
> entertainment and satisfaction. It hardly ever lets us down and
> can easily be switched on and off. Overall, people could certainly

not do without their televisions. It is their prized possessions. They need it, just about as much as it needs them. One could not operate with(out) the other. And I am just thankful that such a technology is available in our growing and ever changing world. (Salem, 2012, pp. 10-11)

These comments were the exception, however.

When researchers texted participants eight times per day for two weeks about their Facebook and direct contact (i.e., FtF and TEL) with people, there were strong relationships between greater Facebook use and greater loneliness (Kross et al. 2013). Greater loneliness appeared to lead to greater Facebook use, but greater Facebook use did not affect loneliness. More direct contact was related to less loneliness.

Summarily, loneliness is a feeling associated with perceived discrepancies between various needs and current behaviors. Two people may communicate in similar ways, but one feels lonelier than another because of different needs. There are different kinds of needs and different kinds of loneliness, and the discrepancies that define a particular kind of loneliness may reflect differences between the breadth or the depth of current communication when contrasted to the breadth or the depth of social needs. Chronic loneliness can shorten life.

It would seem people are using HCT to increase the breadth of communication as they limit the depth. They are avoiding or limiting the depth that comes with genuine self-disclosure but increasing the breadth while communicating with more people. Having one less friend with whom a person could discuss important matters suggests greater relational loneliness. But, people may be compensating for the loss of one close friend by adding more romantic partners. The need to share self-disclosures in unique ways with specific others could be less for some than others. Furthermore, the gratification with achieving social identities with some groups may compensate for any tensions felt with close relationships.

People appear to be using their technology to connect with many but develop fewer close relationships.

Explaining HCT and Close Relationships

This chapter has been about HCT use and developing close relationships, but it was not about HCT use and deception (in an earlier chapter) or about how people obtain resources from relationships using the newer HCT (the next chapter). People appear to have one less close friend and to have more romantic relationships as they increase the breadth of their communication networks. While people are transferring most of their expectations about self-disclosure from FtF to other HCT, there appear to be more efforts at apparent self-disclosure. People are struggling to discover the appropriate depth of disclosure online. The relationships between these patterns and other HCT relational uses with loneliness are unclear, in part, because researchers have not investigated the various forms of loneliness systematically.

One set of explanations for the less depth in our disclosure and relationships and the wide variances about HCT and loneliness comes from examining the changes in societies. Fischer (2011) noted the following trends in America: economic upheaval, more young people living with parents, lower marriage rates or less living with a significant other, and longer life spans. Moving from job to job, FtF communication with mostly old friends, no sense of a life partner, or a network in which oldest friends are dying would all be good explanations for having fewer close relationships and confusion about depth. Furthermore, in this environment, people may have learned different expectations for depth, and so less depth and more breadth fulfill social needs as well today as earlier patterns did yesterday. The claims lack evidence, and it would be difficult to obtain data to support such claims.

There are few explanations using features of technology alone as an explanation for what is happening to communication and close relationships. Rather, technology features interact with use to create the situation. For example, Walther (1996) suggested that people could use newer technology to form *hyperpersonal relationships*, relationships closer than relationships typically formed through FtF. He noted the *reduced social cues* and the *asynchronous* nature of most computer-mediated communication and suggested these features afforded greater opportunities for *selective self-presentation* and for an *idealized view of the other*.

Social identity-deindividuation (SIDE) theory had explained that people could lose their sense of individuality by stereotyping the members of the group and "self-stereotyping" themselves by focusing on the social identity with the group rather than personal identity, and the resultant deindividuation could explain the bad behaviors noted in Chapter 6 (Reicher, Spears, & Postmes, 1995).

Walther (1996) described a similar process where individuals would over attribute similarities between partners (i.e., project), and these idealized views of the other would include greater liking based on the similarities. Exchanging messages using asynchronous technology with minimal social cues between partners who are making selective presentations and idealized views of others would likely lead to *behavioral confirmation*, a self-reinforcing pattern, and to disclosures that would be unlikely in FtF communication (Walther, 1996).

The hyperpersonal model is more a social construction approach than technological determinism. It may be one way to explain those circumstances when people meet at sites designed to provide support and then later develop close relationships. It does not explain the loss of close friendships or behavior on dating sites where selective self-presentations are the norm.

More realist explanations focus on the choices people make about technology. People may be more willing to risk genuine disclosure with various technologies when they stop to reflect on their communication and make strategic choices. When most of us discover something personally important when viewing Facebook posts, we communicate with our closest friends using more exclusive HCT with limited reach such as EML or some form of PEC. The next chapter will describe those instances when people actively seek particular resources online with great success. However, this requires mindful recognition of a need and mindful use of HCT. When researchers taught older people how to use online methods to communicate, greater online use was related to less social isolation (Cotten, Anderson, & McCullough, 2013).

Individuals may become increasingly lonely by comparing their online selves to their offline selves. Presentations online are often amplified depictions reflecting what people want to be - idealized selves. The idealized selves of the creators and the idealized selves of others may become the standards for evaluating social behavior in real life. The discrepancies become loneliness.

From a media ecology perspective, our HCT environment may have produced *unanticipated* losses of depth and validation. Although we might enjoy the gains in reach and breadth, what is being lost is crucial to developing healthy self-concepts, healthy relationships, and a sustainable society. Being aware of what is happening should stimulate us to a more productive mix of HCT use. However, many may have become so risk aversive and so communicatively incompetent that simply meeting someone FtF is a challenge they wish to avoid (Rophie, 2013).

Explaining the current status of HCT and close relationships from a complexity lens points to the contradictions in the data as evidence of different parameters at work. Although the changes in HCT represent one change of parameters, there are still differences in use and effects linked to the sex, age, personality types, and culture of the users.

These other factors are also parameters, and they have not changed. Explaining broad patterns would come from examining several parameters and the interactions between them. The parameters influence using communication, especially self-disclosure, to develop close relationships that validate.

Several features of popular culture have reflected the desire for validation through using the newer HCT. In one of the final episodes of *The Newsroom* television series, the managing editor confronts the reporter responsible for the social media desk (Sorkin & Motta, 2014). Hallie had tweeted a provocative message as she left at the end of a long day covering responses to the bombing incident at the Boston Marathon. By the time she made it to her apartment, she realized her tweet was inappropriate, and she took it down. Too late – tweets, email messages, and editorials attacked her news organization. The managing editor fired Hallie, but he also asked her why she had posted such an inappropriate message. "Retweets," she said.

The trailer for the film *The Social Network* (Chaffin, Brunetti, Rudin, Da Luca, Fincher, Sorkin, A., & Mezrich, 2010), included a Belgian chorus singing "Creep" (Scala & Kolacny, 2011). The lyrics in the trailer included the following: "I want you to notice. When I'm not around. You are so very special. I wish I was special."

Early in the movie, Mark Zuckerberg, the founder of Facebook, must deal with an investigation into security breaches at his college. At the start of the hearing Zuckerberg asks for recognition from the review board. The stunned chairwoman says she does not understand. "Which part?" says Zuckerberg. Regardless of the outcome of the review, he wants to be recognized for his cleverness.

Our close relationships provide some validation for our sense of ourselves together and for individual self-concepts. When using social media and all forms of BEC, people post and exchange messages in front of an audience. In some instances, such as working in a virtual group or communicating within a restricted group on Facebook, people have some idea about the nature of the relationships represented in the audience. Even in these circumstances, the communicators must adjust their messages to include the audience. In many other instances, people are communicating in front of an imagined audience or as part of an imagined community. Twitter users' descriptions of their audience varied from friends to fans (Marwick, & boyd, 2011). The comments that opened this chapter suggest people can single out the connections they might have made online to develop close relationships and that people may also imagine close relationships.

Validation is one function of close relationships. There are other functions for all relationships, and people use their technology to do other things besides obtain validation. The next chapter describes how people use HCT to obtain a range of social resources.

References

Aron, A., Melinat, E., Aron, E. N., Vallone, R. D., & Bator, R. J. (1997). The experimental generation of interpersonal closeness: A procedure and some preliminary findings. *Personality and Social Psychology Bulletin, 23*(4), 363-377.

Aditi, P. (2014). Is online better than offline for meeting partners? Depends: Are you looking to marry or to date? *Cyberpsychology, Behavior, and Social Networking, 17*(10), 664-667.

Akin, M. (2016) *The cyber effect.* New York: Spiegel & Grau.

Altman, I., & Taylor, D. A. (1973). *Social penetration.* New York: Holt, Rinehart, & Winston.

Archer, R. L., & Cook, C. E. (1986). Personalistic self-disclosure and attraction: Basis for relationship or scarce resource. *Social Psychology Quarterly, 49,* 268–272.

Baer, J. (2014). *Social media, pretend friends, and the lie of false intimacy.* Retrieved February 19, 2014 from https://www.convinceandconvert.com/social-media-tools/social-media-pretend-friends-and-the-lie-of-false-intimacy.

Baxter, L. A., & Montgomery, B. M. (1996). *Relating: Dialogues and dialectics.* NY: Guilford.

Bazarova, N. N. (2012). Public intimacy: Disclosure interpretation and social judgments on Facebook. *Journal of Communication, 62,* 815-832.

Berger, C, R., Gardner, R. R., Clatterbuck, G. W., & Shulman, L. S. (1976). Perceptions of information sequencing in relationship development. *Human Communication Research, 3,* 34-39.

Brashears, M. (2011). Small networks and high isolation? A reexamination of American discussion networks. *Social Networks, 33,* 331-341.

Brooks, D. (2014, September 19). Startling adult friendships: There are social and political benefits to having friends. *The New York Times,* A29. Retrieved at http://nyti.ms/1r47KiV.

Burke, T. J., Wozidlo, A., & Segrin, C. (2012). Social skills, family conflicts, and loneliness in families. *Communication Reports, 25*(2), 75-87.

Cacioppo, J. T., & Patrick, W. (2008). *Loneliness: Human nature and the need for connection.* NY: W. W. Norton & Company.

Cacioppo, J. T., Fowler, J. H., & Christakis, N. A. (2009). Alone in a crowd: The structure and spread of loneliness in a large social network. *Journal of Personality and Social Psychology,* 97(6), 977–991.

Cacioppo, J. T., Hawkley, L. C., & Berntson, G. G. (2003). The anatomy of loneliness. *Current Directions in Psychological Science, 12*(3), 71-74.

Canary, D. J., & Stafford, L. (1994). *Communication and relational maintenance.* New York: Academic Press.

Cates, R., & Lloyd, S. (1992). *Courtship*. Newbury Park, CA: Sage.

Chaffin, C., Brunetti, D., Rudin, S., Da Luca, M., (Producers), Fincher, D., (Director), Sorkin, A., & Mezrich, B. (Writers) (2010). *The social network* (Motion picture). Los Angeles, CA, Boston, MA, & Cambridge MA: Columbia Pictures.

Cigna (2018). *Cigna US loneliness index* (full report). Retrieved at https://www.cigna.com/assets/docs/newsroom/loneliness-survey-2018-full-report.pdf.

Cotten, S. R., Anderson, W. A., & McCullough, B. M. (2013). Impact of Internet use on loneliness and contact with others among older adults: Cross-sectional analysis. *Journal of Medical Internet Research*, *15*(2), 215-227.

Culbert, S. A. (1967). *An interpersonal process of self-disclosure*: *It takes two to see one*. Washington, DC: NTL Institute for Applied Behavioral Sciences.

Damasio, A. (1999). *The feeling of what happens: Body and emotion in the making of consciousness*. San Diego, CA: Harvest Books and Harcourt Inc.

Derlaga, V. J., Metts, S., Petronio, S., & Margulis, S. T. (1993). *Self-disclosure*. Newbury Park, CA: Sage.

Fischer, C. (2011). *Still connected: Family and friends in America since 1970*. New York: Russell Sage Foundation.

Fisher, H. (2016). *Anatomy of love: A natural history of mating, marriage, and why we stray* (Rev.). New York: W. W. Norton & Company.

Hage, J., & Powers, C, H. (1992). *Post-industrial lives: Roles and relationships in the 21st century*. Newbury Park, CA: Sage.

Hampton, K., Sessions, L., Ja Her, E., & Raine, L., (2009, November). *Social isolation and new technology*. Report for the Pew Internet and American Life Project, Washington, DC. Retrieved from http://www.pewinternet.org/Reports/2009/18--Social-Isolation-and-New-Technology.aspx.

Hawkley, L. C., Browne, M. W., & Cacioppo, J. T. (2005). How can I connect with thee? Let me count the ways. *Psychological Science, 16*(10), 798-804.

Horburg, W., Liddell, M., Monroe, J. (Producers), Rubin, H. A. (Director), & Stern, A. (2012). *Disconnect*. USA: LD Entertainment, Liddell Entertainment, Exclusive Media Group, & Wonderful Films.

Jarwecki, A. (Producer), Joost, H. (Producer, Director), & Shulman, A. (Director). (2010). *Catfish*. USA: Supermache', & Hit The Ground Running Films.

Jiang, L. C., Bazarova, N. N., & Hancock, J. T. (2011). From perception to behavior: Disclosure reciprocity and the intensification of intimacy in computer-mediated communication. *Communication Research, 40*(1), 125-143.

Jones, D. (2015, January). The 36 questions that lead to love. *The New York Times*. Available at https://www.nytimes.com/2015/01/11/fashion/no-37-big-wedding-or-small.html.

Kim, J., & Dindia, K. (2011). Online self-disclosure: A review of research. In K. B. Wright & L. M. Webb (Eds.), *Computer-mediated communication in personal relationships* (pp. 156-180). New York: Peter Lang.

Knapp, M. L., & Vangelisti, A. L. (2009). *Interpersonal communication and human relationships* (6th ed.). Boston: Pearson

Kraut, R., Kiesler, S., Boneva, B., Cummings, J. N., Helgeson, V., & Crawford, A. M. (2002). Internet paradox revisited. *Journal of Social Issues, 58*, 49-74.

Kraut, R., Patterson, M., Lundmark, V., Kiesler, S., Mukopadhyay, T., & Scherlies, W. (1998). Internet paradox: A social technology that reduces social involvement and psychological well-being? *American Psychologist, 53*, 1017-1031.

Kross, E., Verduyn, P., Demiralp, E., Park, J., Seungjae, D., Lin, N., . . . Ybarra, Y. (2013). Facebook use predicts declines in subjective well-being in young adults. *PLoS One*, 8(8), e69841. Doi: 10.1371/journl.pone.0069841. Retrieved at http://www.plosone.org/article/info%3Adoi%2F10.1371%2Fjournal.pone.0069841.

LaRose, R., Eastin, M., & Gregg, J. (2001). Reformulating the internet paradox: Social cognitive explanations of internet use and depression. *Journal of Online Behavior*, 1(2). Retrieved November 11, 2014 from the World Wide Web: http://www.behavior.net/JOB/v1n1/paradox.html and http://d3ds4oy7g1wrqq.cloudfront.net/sinergiaymente/myfiles/Depression-Journal.htm.

Leiberman, M. D. (2013). *Social: Why our brains are wired to connect*. New York: Crown Publishers.

Lippman, J. R., & Campbell, S. W. (2014). Damned if you do, damned if you don't . . . if you are a girl: Relational and normative contexts of adolescent sexting in the United States. *Journal of Children and Media*, 8(4), 371-386.

Marwick, A. E., & boyd, d. (2011). I tweet honestly, I tweet passionately: Twitter users, context collapse, and the imagined audience. *New Media and Society*, 13(1), 114-133.

McPherson, M., L. Smith-Lovin, & M.E. Brashears (2006). Social isolation in America: Changes in core discussion networks over two decades. *American Sociological Review, 71* (3), 353-375.

Mihailidis, P. (2014). The civic-social media disconnect: Exploring perceptions of social media for engagement in the daily life of college students. *Information, Communication & Society, 17*(9), 1059-1071.

Miller, G. R., & Steinberg, M. (1975). *Between people: A new analysis of interpersonal communication*. Chicago: Science Research Associates, Inc.

Morahan-Martin, J., & Shumacher, P. (2003). Loneliness and social uses of the Internet. *Computers in Human Behavior, 19*, 659-671.

Nguyen, M., Bin, Y. S., & Campbell, A. (2012). Comparing online and offline self-disclosure: A systematic review. *Cyberpsychology, Behavior, and Social Networking, 15*(2), 103-111.

Parks, M. R., & Floyd, K. (1996). Making friends in cyberspace. *Journal of Communication, 46*, 80-97.

Petronio, S. (2002). *Boundaries of privacy: Dialectics of disclosure*. New York, NY: State University of New York Press.

Rawlins, W. K. (1992). *Friendship matters: Communication dialectics, and the life course*. New York: Aldine De Gruyter.

Rawlins, W. K. (2009). *The compass of friendship: Narratives, identities, and dialogues*. Thousand Oaks, CA: Sage Publications, Inc.

Reicher, S. D., Spears, R., & Postmes, T. (1995). A social identity model of deindividuation phenomena. *European Review of Social Psychology, 6*, 162-198.

Reiner, A. (2014, October 31). Teaching civility: Two daring assignments. *The Washington Post*, Retrieved at http://www.washingtonpost.com/lifestyle/magazine/teaching-civility-two-daring-assignments/2014/10/30/6c71682e-4b3c-11e4-a046-120a8a855cca_story.html.

Rophie, K. (2013, February 1). Can online relationships be more real than real ones? *Slate*, Retrieved at http://www.slate.com/articles/life/roiphe/2013/02/online_dating_is_it_more_real.html.

Rosin, H. (2014, October 14). Why kids sext. *The Atlantic.* Retrieved at http://www.theatlantic.com/magazine/archive/2014/11/why-kids-sext/380798. (This was the cover story on the November issue of the *The Atlantic*).

Russell, D. W., Cutrona, C. E., McCrae, C., & Gomez, M. (2012). Is loneliness the same as being alone?, *The Journal of Psychology: Interdisciplinary and Applied, 146*(1-2), 7-22.

Salem, P. J. (2012, February). *Personal and interpersonal adaptations to technology deprivation.* Paper presented the annual convention of the Western States Communication Association, Albuquerque, NM.

Salem, P. J. (2014). *Loneliness and communication technology networks.* Working paper. Department of Communication Studies, Texas State University, San Marcos, TX.

Schutz, W. (1958). *FIRO: A three dimensional theory of interpersonal behavior.* New York: Rinehart.

Simpson, J. A., & Rholes, W. S. (Eds.) (1998). *Attachment theory and close relationships.* New York: Guilford Press.

Slater, D. (2013, January/February). A million first dates: How online romance is threatening monogamy. *The Atlantic.* Retrieved at http://www.theatlantic.com/magazine/archive/2013/01/a-million-first-dates/309195/1/.

Smith, A., & Duggan, M. (2013). *Online dating and relationships.* Report for the Pew Internet and American Life Project, Washington, DC. Retrieved from http://pewinternet.org/Reports/2013/Online-Dating.aspx

Sorkin, A. (Writer) & Motta, G. (Director). (2014). Run. (Television series episode 21). In Lieberstein, P., Poul, A., Rudin, S., & Sorkin, A. (Executive producers), *The Newsroom.* New York. Home Box Office.

Sum, S., Mathews, R. M., Hughes, I., & Campbell, A. (2008). Internet use and loneliness in older adults. *Cyberpsychology and Behavior, 11*(2), 208-211.

Tidwell, L. C., & Walther, J. B. (2002). Computer-mediated communication effects on disclosure, impressions, and interpersonal evaluations:

Getting to know one another a bit at a time. *Human Communication Research, 28,* 317-348.

Turkle, S. (2011). *Alone together: Why we expect more from technology and less from each other.* NY: Basic Books.

Walther, J. B. (1996). Computer-mediated communication: Impersonal, interpersonal, and hyperpersonal interaction. *Communication Research, 23*(1), 3-43.

Walther, J. B. (2007). Selective self-presentation in computer-mediated communication: Hyperpersonal dimensions of technology, language, and cognition. *Computers in Human Behavior, 23,* 2538-2557.

Watkins, S. C. (2009). *The young and the digital: What the migration to social network sites, games, and anytime, anywhere media means for our future.* Boston, MA: Beacon Press.

Whitty, M. T. (2008a). The joys of online dating. In E. A. Konijin, S. Utz, M. Tanis, & S. B. Barnes (Eds.), *Mediated interpersonal communication* (pp. 234-251). New York: Routledge.

Whitty, M. T. (2008b). Revealing the "real" me, searching for the "actual" you: Presentations of self on an online dating site. *Computers in Human Behavior, 24,* 1707-1723.

Whitty, M. T., & Carr, A. N. (2006). *Cyberspace romance: The psychology of online relationships.* Basingstoke, UK: Palgrave Macmillian.

Whitty, M. T., & Joinson, A. N. (2009). *Truth, lies, and trust on the Internet.* New York: Routledge.

Williams, A. (2013, January 13). Is courtship dead? *New York Times,* ST1. Retrieved from http://www.nytimes.com/2013/01/13/fashion/the-end-of-courtship.html?_r=0.

Wilson, C., & Moulton, B. (2010). *Loneliness among older adults: A national survey of adults 45+.* Washington, DC: AARP.

Wilson, E. O. (2012). *The social conquest of earth.* New York: Liveright Publishing Corporation.

Zamorodi, M. (2017). *Bored and brilliant: How spacing out can unlock your most productive and creative self.* New York: St. Martin Press.

Zeldin, T. (1994). *An intimate history of humanity.* New York: Harper Collins Publishers.

Chapter Nine:
Communication Resources

My friends, Mark and Lauren, bought a home nearly ten years ago. The financing institutions required Mark and Lauren to employ an organization to fulfill a home warranty. A home warranty organization would provide workers to repair any defects my friends might discover in the home during the first year of purchase. My friends paid a fee for the year, and they would only pay a flat fee for each repair if they would need one. My friends soon discovered that most defects were not covered by the warranty, and they could only use workers approved by the organization or risk a larger fee with other repair personnel outside the organization.

One thing that was covered by the warranty was the home air conditioner. When Mark called the home warranty organization, it sent a worker who patched the problems with the AC. Mark had more problems, and he called the home warranty organization again. It sent a worker who patched the problems with the AC again, and Mark and Lauren paid another home visit fee for this repair. The worker told Mark the compressor was defective, and he would need a new one soon. The worker estimated the normal cost at over $10,000, but the worker promised he could do it for around $9,000.

Mark called a friend of his who sent him to Carlos, an AC repairman he trusted. Carlos assessed the situation and estimated the cost at $7,500. Furthermore, Carlos would add a 10-year warranty to guarantee the parts and his service. Mark readily agreed to have Carlos do the work.

Over the years, Carlos has become one of Mark's friends and a visitor to Mark's home. Recently, Carlos called Mark to tell him his 10-year AC warranty would end in April. Carlos thought this would be a good time to inspect the AC. Carlos said he would probably discover the compressor was a mess, Carlos would have to file a report with Carlos's warranty company, and the warranty company would be paying for a new compressor. This was just a favor between friends.

This chapter is about the functions of using human communication technology (HCT). The last chapter described the challenges of using newer HCT to create close relationships and cope with loneliness. Validation is just one resource people can obtain from developing close relationships, and people can use the newer HCT to also obtain resources not associated with close relationships. People can communicate to just have fun in addition to exchanging favors.

This chapter begins with a brief history of research about the various things people can get from communicating and using HCT. The second section will focus on seven specific resources that are common to using contemporary HCT, and the last section will describe how people are using online HCT to obtain those resources and support. Newer HCT provide greater opportunities to obtain the full range of resources.

Understanding Communication Resources

Information processing and communication produce outcomes, and people value these outcomes in some way. Obtaining valued outcomes is important to economic, social, psychological, and physical health. These outcomes accumulate to become a supply of assets people can use. A *resource* is anything a person can use to improve how they function.

An *information resource* is information and knowledge obtained when people make sense and obtaining these resources may or may not involve others since information processing may involve one or many people. *Communication resources* are resources people obtain or make for themselves from communicating with each other. The resources come from episodes we create with others. One communicator offers a message as part of an episode to provide resources for another communicator. The other communicator accesses the message as part of the episode and must make sense of the message as a resource. One person may frame a message as a resource that another did not intend as a resource, and one person may not frame a message as a resource that another person intended as such. Mark and his family may be thinking of moving, and he might not care about his current AC.

Extrinsic resources are something outside a person and something tangible. Carlos was offering to do something for Mark, what Carlos assumed was an extrinsic reward. *Intrinsic resources* are intangible and inside of people. The gratitude Mark felt when Carlos made the offer was an intrinsic reward. One person cannot provide directly an intrinsic resource for another, but one person can improve the conditions for another to obtain those resources. For example, one person cannot provide another person with information but can provide a potential source for information. One person can give another a book, but the other person must read it and process it to get information.

Instrumentality is the extent one resource might contribute to another. Having a steady job might yield the resource of a weekly check, and the check provides some instrumentality for food and shelter. Also, the check might help a person feel secure, and so the extrinsic resource, the check, contributes to an intrinsic reward, feeling secure.

Social capital refers to communication resources people accumulate to invest later (Lin, 2001). The unintended information you learn from just being connected to others is an obvious example. You integrate this information into your body of knowledge not realizing you might be able to use it later. Recall the material in Chapter Seven about brokers. Brokers can intentionally create networks that yield information because they can help others with information as well.

Most social capital research involves studying social networks (Borgatti & Everett, 2013; Monge & Contractor, 2003). In some instances, researchers think of the links between people as social capital without identifying what resources accrue from the links (Lin, 2001). Other researchers think of social capital as the resources available from being part of an active network and community, and this research will be part of the civic engagement material in the next chapter.

In mass communication research, there is a history of studying resources by examining the uses and gratifications of media use. A basic assumption in this research is that consumers of mass media are strategic and use technology to meet specific goals and needs. "Use" is the term for the intended outcomes and "gratifications" is the term for the obtained outcomes, although there has been considerable confusion in how researchers employed these constructs (Ruggiero, 2000).

One impetus for the research was to develop categories to describe uses and gratifications. For radio, television and traditional media, common categories included getting information, solving problems, entertainment, escape, and relieving stress (Rosengren, Wenner, & Palmgreen, 1985). Recent research using this perspective to study the newest HCT including social network sites (SNS), text messaging, and mobile phones includes the following categories: acceptance, affection, task coordination, entertainment, escape, identity creation and maintenance, information, recognition, relationship maintenance, relaxation, socializing, status, and venting feelings (Dunne, Lawlor & Rowley, 2010; Leung, 2013; Raake & Raake, 2008; Wang, Tchernev, Solloway, 2012).

Those studying interpersonal communication developed their own sets of categories based on social or psychological needs and motivations. Chapter Eight included material about Schutz (1958) and his categories of interpersonal needs, for example. Some of the latest research combined interpersonal needs with uses and gratifications (Pausel & Mottet, 2004;

Rubin, Perse, & Barbato, 1988). Affection, control, escape, inclusion, pleasure, and relaxation are the categories of communication motives.

Perhaps the most systematic investigations of communication resources were the social support studies. In the early 1980s, research examined the growing problems of stress and burnout among the helping professions such as counselors, educators, nurses, and social workers (Cohen, Underwood, & Gottlieb, 2000; Miller, 2012), and now this research has extended to examining these problems in a variety of organizational and health settings (Goldsmith, 2004; Miller, 2012). *Social support* is a set of communication resources that promote health and well-being, especially dealing with stress and burnout. Without social support, stress and burnout can lead to psychiatric problems, physical problems, and death (Cohen, Gottlieb, & Underwood, 2000). The most common categories are emotional support, informational support, and instrumental (tangible) support with recent additions being companionship support and validation (Willis & Shinar, 2000).

There are two ways in which social support can promote health and well-being. The *direct effect* happens when a person becomes aware of an issue or is feeling stressed and communicates with others to obtain the support needed to cope with the current situation. The *buffering effect* can happen when a person is obtaining enough support on a regular basis that they feel less stress and are less likely to respond to stress in an unhealthy way than others receiving less support (Cohen, Gottlieb, & Underwood, 2000). A person who is buffered by support does not need to request additional support for a high stress situation since the support is already there. A general pattern is that weak ties in a person's network supply direct support and that strong ties buffer.

Some messages may be intended as supportive but not received that way, and some communication may be negative support. Perceptions of support determine whether or not a message is supportive, not simply the structure of the message (Goldsmith, McDermott, & Alexander, 2000). Some messages and interactions increase stress and can create the perception of a stressful environment (Lincoln, 2000). Phubbing, using your mobile phone while in a FtF conversation with someone, reduces feelings of belongingness (emotional or validation support) and relational satisfaction (Chotpitayasunondh & Douglas, 2018). Just discovering that someone needs direct support through social media and trying to provide support increases the stress of the care giver (Hampton, Rainie, Lu, Shin, & Purcell, 2015).

There have been a variety of research traditions exploring the value of communication and the resources people can obtain by communicating. Each research tradition uses its own terms, and researchers within a tradition use the same terms differently (Lackey & Cohen, 2000). However, it is still possible to describe a limited list of resources that will allow for an integration of these research traditions. Especially important is the social support literature since the most research about contemporary HCT and communication resources has been about support.

Seven Resources

This section will detail the seven common resource categories investigated in the literature noted above. In the past, some used these terms as motives, gratifications, or needs. Here, these terms refer to intrinsic resources or to extrinsic resources obtained by any messages or episodes created to assist in that. There will be an explanation of each resource category, common forms of it, and common sources for it. Additionally, there will be special attention to how people use contemporary HCT to obtain these resources.

Inclusion refers to feelings of attachment, belonging, closeness, and intimacy. Various researchers have investigated inclusion as feeling connected in some way and feeling included reduces loneliness. As noted in the previous chapter, communication with strong ties reduces relational loneliness, and communicating with weak ties reduces social loneliness. However, investigations of feelings of inclusion, inclusive messages, or inclusive episodes have not distinguished different types of inclusion comparable to the loneliness research. Social support researchers have regarded inclusion as part of emotional support.

Although inclusion needs are part of all communication, some have argued that there may be unique feelings of inclusion attached to specific HCT. For example, Grieve and her colleagues (2013) discovered feelings of connectedness that were different for FtF and SNS use. It seems natural that SNS users would be more likely to reinforce connections to group membership, socially inclusive messaging, while FtF users would be more likely to reinforce connections to each other as part of more intimate relationships, relational inclusive messaging. There is a need to link the inclusion research more directly to the loneliness research.

Affection refers to feelings of appreciation, approval, caring, liking, or loving. Communication with strong ties such as family, close friends, and romantic partners are the opportunities for affection, but there are also exchanges with weak ties who send cheerful messages and encouragement or who can celebrate a person's success. Any communication people that builds esteem also falls into this category of resources. Communication that provides the opportunities for affection can reduce relational loneliness. Positive attitudes can spread throughout a network (Christakis & Fowler, 2009), and so, if your ties are positive about themselves, you are likely to be positive about yourself as well. Social support researchers include affection as part of emotional support.

Using FtF and TEL as well as exchanging letters have been traditional opportunities for affection. Although many people use email (EML) for more formal or business topics, EML was a way of screening romantic partners noted in the last chapter. What may surprise some is that affection was one of the basic reasons for using both instant messages, a private electronic communication (PEC), and Facebook, a public electronic communication (BEC), but giving and receiving affection was more likely with PEC than BEC (Quan-Haase & Young, 2010).

Validation refers to reinforcement, reassurances, confirmation, or clarification of issues about self. Resources include opportunities for information about self, personal feedback, social comparisons, and feelings of acceptance and recognition. For some, an opportunity for self-expression may be enough to assist in creating validation, but people will have difficulty sustaining any aspect of themselves without the feedback others provide in interaction. Any communication that assists self-concept creation and maintenance falls into this category. Some weak links may serve as constructive critics, counselors, or validation sources about special intimate topics, but validation normally is part of communication with selected strong ties. Traditional social support research had concerns about validation as part of emotional support or informational support, but more recent research has investigated validation as a separate type of support (Willis & Shinar, 2000).

People use the more interactive features of HCT to obtain validation. Self-expression coupled with an interpersonal motive to seek and maintain companionship have been associated with greater use of the interactive features of Facebook (Hunt, Atkin, & Krishnan, 2012). Obtaining greater reassurance was associated with more mobile phone use, and reassurance was also associated with wanting greater inclusion and affection (Auter, 2007). However, people who already felt more socially reassured used newer HCT, including mobile phones, less than others (Pearson, Carmon, Tabola, & Fowler, 2009). What this suggests is that people used newer HCT to obtain validation as direct support when there were doubts.

Information refers to the sense people make of events. Resources include opportunities for technical information about objects, places, and ideas, and social information about self, others, and relationships not part of validation. Most research refers to information in general, suggesting technical information. Technical information generally comes from weak links (recall the parts of Chapter 4 dealing with opinion leaders and change agents) and includes acquaintances, supervisors, coworkers, teachers, financial advisors, and any sort of content expert. Specific social information includes information about prospective romantic partners, about colleagues, and about other people's relationships. Common network sources for these cues are strong ties such as friends, but people can create all types of information in a nonsocial manner such as searching the Internet.

Chapter One described how searching for health information online might lead to further anxiety such as cyberchondria. The continuing challenge to creating information is judging the veracity of the data or the sources of the data. In the United States, 59% of adults have gone online to seek health data, and 35% were looking for data to help diagnose a specific condition (Fox & Duggan, 2013). Clinicians confirmed 41% of the people's online diagnosis, and they rejected or offered a different opinion to 18%, but 35% of people who went online never consulted a clinician (Fox & Duggan, 2013). Although people will gather data such as reviews of drugs and ratings of physicians or hospitals from nonsocial websites such as blogs or apps, people also establish links with others using SNS and online groups focused on a disease (Fox, 2011). The interaction between peers is likely to provide opportunities for other resources as well as information.

Tangible resources refer to some valued artifact or behavior. Typical tangible resources include transportation (a ride), money, technical help, assistance moving, and a recommendation. Commerce and e-commerce are about tangible resources. The sources are a mix of strong links such as those people can count on and weak links such as distant relatives, friends of friends, sponsors, technical experts, and personal advocates or public relations specialists. The importance of weak ties for supplying this kind of support has been documented for at least forty years (Granovetter, 1973). "Networking" workshops are attempts to improve people's abilities to establish such links.

The social support literature has been about the first five resources, and health communication literature also focuses on one or more of these resources. Greater heterogeneity in a personal network has been associated with greater resources along the full range of supportive resources (Uchino, Holt-Lunstad, Smith, & Bloor, 2004). However, some ties are indifferent, ambivalent, and aversive with respect to one or more of these resources, and some ties, even those who historically supply supportive resources, can increase psychological distress (Uchino et al., 2004). The greater connectivity afforded by the newer HCTs can lead to greater support, but it can also lead to more distress.

The May 2014 cover of *Wired* highlighted the "trust" or "sharing" economy. New services provide transportation with drivers using their personal vehicles (e.g., Uber), housing (e.g., Airbnb), and food at the family dinner table (Tanz, 2014). Customers must trust these amateurs or un-vetted service providers, but the providers must also trust the customers. These commercial ventures emerged after the popular eBay and after the not-for-profit communities such as CouchSurfing (Rosen, Lafontaine, & Hendrickson, 2011).

Stimulation occurs when a person feels arousal, pleasure, or engaged. As a resource, stimulation is about likely opportunities for people to feel this way. People often seek stimulation just to kill time – when they are bored. Pleasure can happen through processing content such as watching a you-tube video, but it also involves interacting with people who share common interests or interacting with a specific group of friends.

Relaxation occurs when a person feels less stimulated or less aroused or unwinds, and there is the potential to escape or reenergize. Relaxation is a resource that is the opposite of stimulation. When people feel overloaded, they often choose opportunities to relax, but when they feel underloaded, people seek stimulation and pleasure.

People can use the same technology to achieve stimulation and relaxation. A well-designed computer game can be challenging and so it has the potential for stimulation, but the game has structure, scores, and some finality, and the comparative predictability is an opportunity for relaxation. Adding people and communication to the mix means there are possibilities for even more resources. Other common activities that could provide more or less stimulation are fan sites, hobby groups, and online shopping.

Comparing the motivations for using different electronic technologies demonstrates the mixed nature of the resources people hope to obtain. College students reported the first motive for using mobile phones was social interaction, but entertainment (stimulation) and passing the time (relaxation) were tied for second and third, well ahead of companionship (inclusion and affection) and information (Pearson, Carmon, Tabola, & Fowler, 2009). Entertainment and passing the time were also tied for first and second for motives for using computers and for using television.

I did not include in this list control, companionship, and diversion. Control refers to HCT experiences people use to create a sense of self-efficacy, influence, and responsibility. There has been little research investigating this as a separate resource. Companionship often refers to being with others for the sake of being with others (inclusion), to feel liked (affection), or for assurances (validation), and so it overlaps with other resources. Diversion refers to opportunities to avoid other things, to escape, and to kill time. It overlaps with stimulation and relaxation.

Getting Online Support

Online Support in General

Supportive resources include inclusion, affection, validation, information and tangible resources that could improve health and wellbeing. People have used EML to obtain these resources in the past, and the emergence of the world-wide-web made online communities and sites also available. The most recent developments involve SNSs, especially support group sites.

The pattern for people seeking support for health issues begins by contacting people offline. In a given year, 70% of adults get support from healthcare professionals, 60% from friends and family, and 24% get support from others with similar conditions, and most of this support comes from conversations offline (Fox & Duggan, 2013). Some of this support is in the form of information, especially diagnostic information, but much of this support is encouragement (affection and validation) and bonding with those who have similar experiences (inclusion and validation). Of course, some support comes in the form of treatment and care (tangible resources).

Seeking support online usually begins with a search, and the search may be for information or resources through interaction (Fox & Duggan, 2013). People use EML more for emotional support (inclusion, affection, or validation) than information as a follow-up to searches and as part of the mix of HCT with providers and their active networks (Fox, 2011; Fox & Duggan, 2013). The most effective supportive communication occurs when the resources needed match the opportunities others can provide (Robinson & Turner, 2003). A person needing validation gains little support if others can only provide health diagnostic data.

An analysis of Facebook users reveals all the ways SNS can provide support. Friend requests (inclusion), accepting friend requests (validation), commenting on posts (validation and potentially affection), adding someone to a group (inclusion), and likes (affection) are part of a range of supportive resources. It is not uncommon for offers of help (tangible resources) to follow the posting of a problem or difficulty on Facebook. People generally get the support they need most of the time, but Internet users get more, and Facebook users report they get the most (Hampton, Goulet, Rainie, & Purcell, 2011).

One reason SNS users get more support is because of a network effect. Every network includes some people who are more active than others, and an earlier chapter noted that these people make the distances between people shorter. On Facebook, 20% to 30% are "power users" who perform activities such as making friend requests, tags, or likes on a daily basis while most people perform these activities weekly (Hampton, Goulet, Marlow, & Rainie, 2012). Only 11% were very active on two or more of these activities, but 43% were very active on at least one such activity (Hampton et al., 2012). Being connected to just a few of these power users might lead to a lot of support opportunities, but you also might think other people have more friends than you!

Some have suggested that SNS use can provide support for community college students and lead to greater academic engagement (Center for Community College Student Engagement, 2012). However, greater SNS use has been associated with lower grades (Kirschner, & Karpinski, 2010), but this may be due to the tendencies of some to multitask (Karpinski, Kirschner, Ozer, Mellott, & Ochwo, 2013). SNS use could be more about stimulation or relaxation than support.

Online Support Groups

Support groups consist of people with a common interest or problem who provide resources to improve health or well-being. Support comes in the form of stories, disclosures, and building relationships that validate the health seekers and their concerns, include them in a group and provide a social identity, and demonstrate affection for each other as well as inform and recommend. People will seek greater support through online support groups (OSGs) when they are dissatisfied with their offline support system and develop close relationships within the OSG (Chung, 2013). OSGs are often part of online health communities, blogs, or forums, but people can meet on these sites and form their own OSG.

One feature of OSGs is the relative anonymity of members (Tanis, 2008). Normally, people can participate without revealing their name or use a pseudonym. This feature is especially important to those who may feel some stigma attached to their concerns. People may assume others view negatively their concerns (e.g., a mental or emotional health issue), and they may internalize these assumptions to self-stigmatize. Greater OSG participation reduces the effects of self-stigma as well as provides support (Lawlor & Kirakowski, 2014).

A second important feature of OSGs is a strong social identity with the group (Tanis, 2008). People come to OSGs because of common concerns, and the postings and interactions are about those concerns. People develop a heightened awareness of similarities with other members and a sense of inclusion as a member of the group. This description supports the SIDE theory (Reicher, Spears, & Postmes, 1995) described in the last chapter.

A third feature of OSGs is the selective presentation of self (Tanis, 2008). In an OSG this is about providing more support in the group than one would normally supply offline. People can be friendlier, more empathic, and more affectionate when dealing with others who have similar concerns as themselves.

Fourth, there is a norm for self-disclosure in OSGs (Tanis, 2008). Disclosures may follow a sequence of *naming* a condition, describing the *emotional reaction* to circumstances, *unburdening* by describing details of the condition, and explaining past, current, and expected future *support* for the concern (Moors & Webber, 2012). A systematic review of studies related to online communication and adolescent well-being found little research *focused* on self-disclosure, but the reviewers concluded that most youth prefer to disclose online rather than offline due to the perceived lower risks associated with anonymity (Best, Manktelow, & Taylor, 2014). Over half the posting on 52 OSGs at one university were self-disclosures (Salem, Bogat, & Reid, 1997). On mental health forums, the most common postings, 44%, were self-disclosures, and the two most frequent topics were the patient's social network (family and friends) and symptoms of their condition (Bauer, Bauer, Spiessl, & Kagerbauer , 2013). In a forum, the structure of the site and the group has been major influence on the frequency of disclosures (Salem et al, 1997).

Reducing the risk also reduces the potential for genuine self-disclosure. However, most understand that some risk remains, and there is the potential for abuses such as cyberbullying (Best, Manktelow, & Taylor, 2014). Lurking, just visiting an OSG site and reading posts, will not yield many supportive resources, and overcoming any stigma associated with a specific circumstance will be difficult without active participation (Lawlor & Kirakowski, 2014). A minimal disclosure labeling a condition may be more likely online than off, but disclosers are still very hesitant (Lawlor & Kirakowski, 2014; Salem et al., 1997). If apparent self-disclosure has been the norm on dating sites, then genuine disclosures appear to be the norm in OSGs.

A final feature of OSG sites is a text-only asynchronous environment (Tanis, 2008). This has been the tradition that most OSGs start as forums and move to more interactive but text only forms such as chat. The risks noted above may limit OSGs moving to a more FtF variation such as groupware or Skype.

There are three distinct advantages to developing supportive resources through asynchronous text (Tanis, 2008). First, using text to deal with a stressful condition can improve sensemaking. The text becomes the behavior that a person uses to connect frames to cues. Just trying to create a coherent explanation of what a person is thinking and feeling can reduce the uncertainty a person may have about events, the "problem", and that person's sense of self and self-worth. Overcoming the emotional inhibitions to translating traumatic experiences into language may be necessary to cope effectively with conditions (Shaw, Hawkins, McTavish, Pingree, & Gustafson, 2006).

The second advantage is the asynchronous text gives people time to reflect. Slowing things down may lead to better understanding relationships with other OSG members, but too much reflection can be harmful (Cloven & Roloff, 1991). Finally, OSG members normally focus on the contributions of others and helping others rather than the problems of others. This happens presumably because the reduced social cues encourage greater concern on the data from the text.

The Potential for Resources

Mark discovered Carlos through TEL, and he maintained his relationship with Carlos through a variety of HCT. Mark's reflex is to use FtF or TEL. Mark is a digital immigrant, a person born before 1980, but his daughter, Sarah, is a digital native, a person born into the contemporary HCT (Prensky, 2001). When Sarah wants to know about something or someone, she starts digitally. Indeed, her mobile phone feeds her a limited number of notifications throughout the day.

Gabe, another son, and his wife, Jesse, (also digital natives) jump to the web for housing, automotive, and medical information. If Gabe needed help about his AC, he would have started with an Internet search, then he would have posted something on several SNSs, he would have contacted his close friends through EML, and texted Noah (his brother, the contractor). Then, if all else failed, he might call his parents. Just dealing with his AC could easily yield the full range of resources I noted above. All of us now have the potential to develop these resources very quickly.

Mark uses his technology differently than Sarah or Gabe. Indeed, I, another immigrant, use this technology differently than Mark, and Sarah and Gabe use HCT differently from each other. Some variation of technological determinism would be a poor explanation for the availability of resources through HCT since there is so much variation between us.

Social determinism does not explain much. The reflexes of the natives have been different than the reflexes of the immigrants, but the predilections of generations will not explain the variations in use. My reflexes have changed. Gabe is a musician, and his HCT world is more complicated than any of us, including his fellow natives Jesse and Sarah.

Social construction might be useful, but Mark tolerates digital technology while those around him embrace it in various ways. When he and I talk about anything that involves digital technology, the topic is secondary to something else. For example, we will discuss a recent post by a friend of ours on a website, but it is the content of the post that is more important than the website. I don't spend much time explaining an app, but I do explain how Mark can get what he wants by using it. By contrast, Gabe and I have had several conversations about the viability of streaming video services to deliver the content of traditional television networks.

A realist explanation might be better. People's choices make a difference, and people can choose from different technology. However, a housing problem such as an AC repair, is not new. The parameters for defining the problem, the solutions, and communicating about all of them have changed. It is tempting to argue for complexity (Salem, 2013).

Complexity alone will not account for the differences. The mix of newer HCT appears to be significantly different and generating nonlinear effects. An Internet search will yield more information for me than months in an old library, and the search can be stimulating. The sheer amount of contacts I can have will generate some affection and inclusion, if not validation; conversely, failing to get any interaction would be devastating. I do have more ritualized episodes to maintain. I live in a different world today. And so, the best explanation seems to be a combination of media ecology and complexity.

References

Auter, P. J. (2007). Portable social groups: Willingness to communicate, interpersonal communication gratifications, and cell phone use among adults. *International Journal of Mobile Communications, 5*(2), 139-156.

Bauer, R., Bauer, M., Spiessl, H., & Kagerbauer, T. (2013). Cyber-support: An analysis of online self-help forums (online self-help forums in bipolar disorder). *Nordic Journal of Psychiatry, 67,* 185–190.

Best, P., Manktelow, R., & Taylor, B. (2014). Online communication, social media and adolescent wellbeing: A systematic narrative review. *Children and Youth Services Review, 41,* 27-36.

Borgatti, S. P., & Everett, M. G. (2013). *Analyzing social networks.* Los Angeles, CA: Sage.

Center for Community College Student Engagement. (2012). *A matter of degrees: Promising practices for community college student success: A first look.* Austin, TX: University of Texas at Austin.

Chotpitayasunondh V., & Douglas, K. M. (2018). The effects of "phubbing" on social interaction. *Journal of Applied Social Psychology, 48,* 304-316.

Christakis, N. A., & Fowler, J. H. (2009). *Connected: The surprising power of our social networks and how they shape our lives.* NY: Little Brown & Company.

Chung, J. E. (2013). Social interaction in online support groups: Preference for online social interaction over offline social interaction. *Computers in Human Behavior, 29,* 1408-1414.

Cloven, D. H., & Roloff, M. E. (1991). Sense-making activities and interpersonal conflict: Communicative cures for the mulling blues. *Western Journal of Speech Communication, 55*(2), 134-158.

Cohen, S., Gottlieb B. J., & Underwood, L. G. (2000). Social relationships and health. In S. Cohen, L. G. Underwood, & B. J. Gottlieb (Eds.), *Social support measurement and intervention: A guide for health and social scientists* (pp. 3-25). Oxford: Oxford University Press.

Cohen, S., Underwood, L. G., & Gottlieb B. J. (Eds.) (2000). *Social support measurement and intervention: A guide for health and social scientists.* Oxford: Oxford University Press.

Dunne, A., Lawlor, M., & Rowley, J. (2010). Young people's use of online social networking sites – a uses and gratifications perspective. *Journal of Research in Interactive Marketing, 4*(1), 46-58.

Fox, S. (2011). *The social life of health information, 2011.* Washington, DC: Pew Research Center. Retrieved from http://www.pewinternet.org/Reports/2011/Social-Life-of-Health-Info.aspx.

Fox, S., & Duggan, M. (2013). *Health online, 2013.* Washington, DC: Pew Research Center. Retrieved from http://www.pewinternet.org/Reports/2013/Health-online.aspx.

Goldsmith, D. J. (2004). *Communicating social support.* Cambridge: Cambridge University Press.

Goldsmith, D. J., McDermott, V. M., & Alexander, S. C. (2000). Helpful, supportive and sensitive: Measuring the evaluation of enacted social support in personal relationships. *Journal of Social and Personal Relationships, 17*(3), 369-391.

Granovetter, M. (1973). The strength of weak ties. *American Journal of Sociology, 78*, 1360-1380.

Grieve, R., Indian, M., Whiteveen, K., Tolan, A., & Marrington, J. (2013). Face-to-face of Facebook: Can social connectedness be derived online? *Computers in Human Behavior, 29*, 604-609.

Hampton, K. N., Goulet, L. S., Marlow, C., & Rainie, L. (2012). *Why Facebook users get more than they give.* Washington, DC: Pew Research Center. Retrieved from http://www.pewinternet.org/Reports/2012/Facebook-users.aspx.

Hampton, K. N., Goulet, L. S., Rainie, L., & Purcell, K. (2011). *Social networking and our lives*. Washington, DC: Pew Research Center. Retrieved from http://www.pewinternet.org/Reports/2011/Technology-and-social-networks.aspx.

Hampton, K. N., Rainie, L., Lu, W., Shin, I., & Purcell, K. (2015). Social media and the cost of caring. Washington, DC: Pew Research Center. Retrieved from http://www.pewinternet.org/2015/01/15/social-media-and-stress.

Hunt, D., Atkin, D., & Krishnan, A. (2012). The influence of computer-mediated communication apprehension on Facebook use. *Journal of Broadcasting and Electronic Media, 56*(2), 187-202.

Karpinski, A. C., Kirschner, P. A., Ozer, I., Mellott, J. A., & Ochwo, P. (2013). An exploration of social networking site use, multitasking, and academic performance among United States and European university students. *Computer in Human Behavior, 29*, 1182-1192.

Kirschner, P. A., & Karpinski, A. C. (2010). Facebook and academic performance. *Computers in Human Behavior, 26*, 1237–1245.

Lackey, B., & Cohen, S. (2000). Social support theory and measurement. In S. Cohen, L. G. Underwood, & B. J. Gottlieb (Eds.), *Social support measurement and intervention: A guide for health and social scientists* (pp. 29-52). Oxford: Oxford University Press.

Lawlor, A., & Kirakowski, J. (2014). Online support groups for mental health: A space for challenging self-stigma or a means of social avoidance? *Computers in Human Behavior, 32*, 152-161.

Leung, L. (2013). Generational differences in content generation in social media: The roles of the gratifications sought and of narcissism. *Computers in Human Behavior, 29*(3): 997–1006.

Lin, N. (2001). *Social capital: A theory of social structure and action*. Cambridge: Cambridge University Press.

Lincoln, K. D. (2000). Social support, negative social interactions, and psychological well-being. *Social Service Review, 74*(2), 231-252.

Miller, J. G. (1978). *Living systems.* New York; McGraw-Hill.

Moors, R., & Webber, R. (2013). The dance of disclosure: Online self-disclosure of sexual assault. *Qualitative Social Work, 12*(6), 799-815.

Monge, P. R., & Contractor, N. S. (2003). *Theories of communication networks.* Oxford: Oxford University Press.

Pausel, M. L., & Mottet, T. P. (2004). Interpersonal communication motives: A commmunibiological perspective. *Communication Quarterly, 52*, 182-195.

Pearson, J. C., Carmon, A., Tobola, C., & Fowler, M. (2009). Motives for communication: Why the millennial generation uses electronic devices. *Journal of Communication, Speech and Theatre Association of North Dakota, 22*, 45-55.

Prensky, M. (2001). Digital natives, digital immigrants. *On the Horizon 9*(5), 1–6.

Quan-Haase, A., & Young, A. L. (2010). Uses and gratifications of social media: A comparison of Facebook and instant messaging. *Bulletin of Science Technology and Society, 30*(5), 350-361.

Raake, J., & Bonds-Raacke, J. (2008). MySpace and Facebook: Applying the uses and gratifications theory to exploring friend-networking sites. *CyberPsychology & Behavior, 11*(2), 169-74.

Reicher, S. D., Spears, R., & Postmes, T. (1995). A social identity model of deindividuation phenomena. *European Review of Social Psychology, 6*, 162-198.

Robinson, J. D., & Turner, J. (2003). Impersonal, interpersonal, and hyperpersonal social support: Cancer and older adults. *Health Communication, 15*(2), 227-234.

Rosen, D., Lafontaine, P. R., & Hendrickson, B. (2011). CouchSurfing: Belonging and trust in a globally cooperative online social network. *New Media Society, 13*(6), 981-998.

Rosengren, K. E., Wenner, L. A., & Palmgreen, P. (Eds.). (1985). *Media gratifications research: Current perspectives*. Thousand Oaks, CA: Sage.

Rubin, R. B., Perse, E. M., & Barbato, C. A. (1988). Conceptualization and measurement of interpersonal communication motives. *Human Communication Research, 14,* 602-628.

Ruggiero, T. E. (2000). Uses and gratifications theory in the 21st century. *Mass Communication and Society, 3*(1), 3-37.

Salem, D. A., Bogat, A., & Reid, C. (1997). Mutual help goes on-line. *Journal of Community Psychology, 25*(2), 189–207.

Schutz, W. (1958). *FIRO: A three dimensional theory of interpersonal behavior*. NY: Rinehart.

Shaw, B. R., Hawkins, R., McTavish, F. M., Pingree, S., & Gustafson, D. H. (2006). Effects of insightful disclosure within computer mediated support groups on women with breast cancer. *Health Communication, 19*(2), 133-142.

Tanis, M. (2008). What makes the internet a place to seek social support? In E. A. Konijn, S. Utz, S. Tanis, M., & Barnes, S. B. (Eds.), *Mediated interpersonal communication* (pp. 290.308). New York: Routledge.

Tanz, J. (2014, May). How Airbnb and Lyft finally got Americans to trust each other. *Wired, 22*(5). Retrieved from http://www.wired.com/2014/04/trust-in-the-share-economy.

Uchino, B. N., Holt-Lunstad, J., Smith, T. W., & Bloor, L. (2004). Heterogeneity in social networks: A comparison of different models of linking relationships to psychological outcomes. *Journal of Social and Clinical Psychology, 23*(2), 123-139.

Wang, Z, Tchernev, J. M., Solloway, T. (2012). A dynamic longitudinal examination of social media use, needs, and gratifications among college students. *Computers in Human Behavior, 28*(5): 1829–1839.

Willis, T. A., & Shinar, O. (2000). Measuring perceived and received social support. In S. Cohen, L. G. Underwood, & B. J. Gottlieb (Eds.), *Social support measurement and intervention: A guide for health and social scientists* (pp. 86-135). Oxford: Oxford University Press.

Chapter Ten: Civic Engagement

Demonstrators flooded Tahir Square at the center of Cairo, Egypt in late winter and early spring of 2011 to protest the policies of the regime of Hosni Mubarak.

Mubarak eventually resigned, was replaced briefly by a military regime, followed by the election of Mohamed Morsi and members of the Muslim Brotherhood, followed by more demonstrations, the resignation of the Morsi government, another brief takeover by the military and arrests of members of the Muslim Brotherhood, and in 2014, the election of Abdul Fatah El-Sissi, backed by the military. The Egyptian demonstrations were part of a series of protests triggered by the self-immolation of a man in Tunisia protesting police and government corruption.

In many instances, the protests across the Arab world led to nothing but a government crackdown, but in a few cases there were significant reforms. After three years of changes and demonstrations, the current Egyptian political situation is still fragile. On the fourth anniversary of the first demonstrations, police shot and killed poet Shaimaa el-Sabbagh during a peaceful demonstration, and the government has jailed political opposition and journalists (Abdurraham, Mayer, Riggler, & Sharma, 2015).

Demonstrations erupted in Ferguson, Missouri, USA following a grand jury decision not to indict a police officer in the death of a young black man.

Over two thirds of the population in this St. Louis suburb is African-American, but only three of the 53 officers are black, and the mayor, five of the six city council members, and six of the seven school board members are white. Only 12% of the eligible voters turned out for the 2014 election.

The ASL Association is a group that gives support to victims of amyotrophic lateral sclerosis and their families. In the summer of 2014, the association's Ice Bucket Challenge went viral on social media. The challenge consists of recording dumping a bucket of ice water over someone and posting it online to increase awareness of ALS and encourage donations to the association. Although the challenge had begun earlier in the year, when the challenge went viral, contributions began "pouring" in. According to the association, the challenge led to $115 million in donations (ALS Association, 2014).

These incidents are examples of civic engagement, and in each case social media was important. Why are demonstrations still happening in Egypt, and why is the situation not stable? Why did a predominantly black community participate in demonstrations but fail to participate in an election process that might have prevented an inciting incident? Why were so many willing to post videos and contribute to a charity online while the voter turnout in the election that followed two months later was the lowest in seventy-two years? How was HCT a part of this pattern, and is this pattern any different than the one prior to the use of the newest HCT? None of these questions are easy to answer.

This chapter will analyze the challenges to using HCT for civic engagement. Civic engagement (CE) refers to individual and collective actions designed to identify issues of public concern (American Psychological Association, 2007). The political demonstrations and charitable actions noted above are examples of civic engagement, but some things as simple as voting and putting money in a church collection plate are also examples. The study of civic engagement involves examining both perceptions and behaviors since sustaining civic engagement involves some sense of public concern and how individuals or groups might affect those concerns.

Cultural factors can influence the nature of civic engagement. Individualism-collectivism and uncertainty avoidance are two dimensions that highlight social and political differences related to how citizens organize for their collective wellbeing (Hofstede & Hofstede, 2005). People in the more individualistic cultures such as those in North America and Northern Europe have less CE, and they may be missing out on some social capital.

People in the more collectivist cultures such as those in South America, Southern Europe, and Asia have more CE, but they may feel greater pressures to conform to the values behind the communication practices of a culture. In low uncertainty avoidance cultures, individuals welcome differences of opinion and rely on public discourse and private group formation to engage in CE. In high uncertainty avoidance cultures, people are suspicious of differences and public process, and they rely on many precise but unwritten rules to maintain social order. The political atmosphere within a country includes social and cultural differences since government is a reflection of the extent to which individuals are willing to contribute to the common good and a reflection of how they are willing to contribute to the common good.

Traditional models of civic engagement included three things (1) group involvement, (2) civic activities, and (3) affect or perceptions about civic life, groups, and society. Contemporary models have had four factors: (1) group involvement, (2) traditional civic activities, (3) digital civic activities, and (4) affect or perceptions about civic life, groups, and society. The next section describes contemporary perceptions related to civic engagement. How do we think and feel about our communities and institutions? The second section describes civic activities comparing traditional ones with digital ones. Have the use of contemporary HCT helped or hurt civic activities? The final portion of this chapter explores the nature of groups and especially communities. Have the newest HCT and social media coincided with a greater or lesser sense of community? Without a sense of community, it would be difficult to sustain civic engagement.

Civic Engagement Perceptions

Commitment

Commitment is a necessary but insufficient condition for sustaining civic engagement. *Commitment* is a decision and a desire to begin and continue a behavior or relationship. It is a psychological link between a person and a relationship that makes it less likely the person will voluntarily leave the relationship. In a romantic relationship or friendship, it is an intent to persist in a relationship (Rusbult, Martz, & Agnew, 1998), and in an organization it is about maintaining membership (Allen & Meyer, 1996; Meyer & Allen, 1991), a decision to join and remain (Galbraith, 1977). When the members of civic groups have greater commitment to their organization, they are also more likely to persist in their civic activities (Mannarini & Talo, 2012).

There are three different but related bases for having more or less organizational commitment. *Affective commitment* is commitment based on the extent to which organizational members identify with, feel involved with, and have an emotional attachment to an organization (Allen & Meyer, 1996). Organizational members with a strong affective commitment remain with the organization because they *want* to. *Continuance commitment* derives from the perception that there are costs to leaving an organization (Allen & Meyer, 1996). Members with strong continuance commitment remain with the organization because they *need* to. *Normative commitment* involves a sense of obligation (Allen & Meyer, 1996), and members with strong normative commitment remain with the organization because they *ought* to. High turnover can indicate less commitment, and there are varying turnover rates in volunteer organizations.

Affective commitment is related to the extent to which an individual has developed a social identity with an organization. A social identity with a community improves an appreciation for an individual's personal identity and could contribute to an appreciation of the similarities and differences within a group. A social identity with a community assists in understanding how an individual contributes to and gains from collective action. However, a social identity with a community is similar to any other social identity and could become the dominant factor in a self-concept and could lead to forms of deindividuation.

The members of political groups and activist networks have historically fostered a sense of social identity by highlighting inequalities and the nature of communication between different groups. Categories, labels, and social routines, especially rituals, become part of stories pointing to the boundaries between "us and them" (Tilly, 2005a). Additionally, stories of exploitation and abuse reinforce the boundaries (Tilly, 2005a) and could encourage greater continuance commitment.

Linking these stories to cultural norms can also foster a sense of obligation (Tilly, 2005a) and could foster greater normative commitment. Doing this well improves membership and reduces turnover across a range of civic activities. However, it is possible to do this too well and to foster a sense of deindividuation objectifying those in other groups. Some group processes aim to create deindividuation as a means of improving commitment (Kantor, 1972).

Several types of social network sites (SNSs) provide platforms for improving commitment to various civic causes. "We use Facebook to schedule the protests, Twitter to coordinate, and YouTube to tell the world," one Egyptian activist claimed (Kondker, 2011). Identity, sharing, conversation and forming groups are all functions of SNS (Kietzmann,

Hermkens, McCarthy, & Sivestre, 2011), but how well do SNSs do these things when there are hundreds, thousands, or millions of users attempting these functions? Protest movements face the possibility that those in power could mount their own SNS efforts (Kondker, 2011).

CouchSurfing.com is an online community in which members stay in each other's homes and organize gatherings for each other. The members do things for each other for their own benefit and the benefit of the community of mostly people between 20 and 34 years of age. The million plus members live in over 230 countries and 62,000 cities using 302 languages. The members have a SNS and use the full range of HCT to communicate with each other.

However, members were more likely to respond to personal EML messages for requests to participate in events or requests for accommodations instead of group EML or SNS posts, and the members that had communicated FtF had significantly more affective commitment (a sense of belonging) than those who had not met FtF (Rosen, Lafontaine, & Hendrickson, 2011). Meeting each other FtF and more personal EML or PEC may be more important to fostering a sense of commitment than SNS.

Young people are wary of different information sources for public and political events (Mihailidis, 2014). Although most college students reported their primary sources for news were from SNS or news aggregators associated with those sites, they had doubts about the veracity of those stories. Similarly, these young people relied more on SNS for political information and opinion than traditional news outlets, but they did not regard blogs as a good source. One focus group member noted 'the Internet makes it easier to put lies out into the world just as easily as it is to put truth out there' (Mihailidis, 2014).

Summarily, commitment is important to sustaining civic engagement. Communication that fosters social identity is crucial for increasing commitment, and the newer HCTs can do that. However, shrunken pieces of data at 140 characters a message or the pictures of events are not enough. People must still pull them together as part of a story (Butterworth, 2011). The problem is a lack of trust.

Trust

Trust is an expectation, a prediction, of positive outcomes from another person's or groups' future actions in an interaction characterized by high uncertainty (Bhattacharya, Devinney, & Pillutla, 1998). The perceived uncertainty in the situation implies a sense of vulnerability, and most contemporary definitions of trust include some belief in the positive intentions, behavior, or outcomes of another (Rousseau, Sitkin, Burt, & Camerer, 1998). Traditional notions of distrust involved fear, skepticism, cynicism, and wariness (Lewicki, McAllister, & Bies, 1998). Distrust, then, is the expectation of negative or nonpositive outcomes from the other's future actions in an interaction characterized by uncertainty, and such a framing may induce fear. Mistrust is uncertainty about the direction of the outcomes for interactions with another (Salem, 2013).

Trust means a person risks valued outcomes to others' behavior, and a trust network consists mainly of strong tie relationships in which people put long-term consequences at risk to the behaviors of others (Tilly, 2005b). These networks typically form as a reaction to the failures of "official forms" of social organization (e.g., governments), and these networks form their own boundaries, a name, and communication about mutual obligations (Tilly, 2005b). Volunteer organizations become trust networks when they sustain membership, obligations, and communication, over generations of members - similar to families, trade networks, religious sects, and local communities.

Trust builds as individuals develop predictable patterns of communication. To improve trust, talk similarly to one person as another, talk similarly in all situations, talk similarly today as you did yesterday, talk to others as others talk to you, and talk in the future as you said you would in the past (Salem, 2013). Such a pattern is essential to maintaining trust, but the pattern varies between relationships or groups. That is, a person will talk in a predictable and reciprocal manner that conforms to the expectations and standards for appropriateness in one set of relationships while talking in a different but trustworthy manner in a different set of relationships. Maintaining trust is at the heart of managing the challenges of diverse social spaces on SNSs.

A recent survey of Americans identified the people they trust the most (Smith & Caporimo, 2013). Americans trust people we know more than anyone famous. Americans trust TV personalities and motion picture figures more than political ones. Barack Obama was the highest ranked politician at 65th, but his wife Michelle was 49th. Americans trust doctors especially when they are on TV. Americans trust TV judges more than Supreme Court judges. Individual SNS activity, such as an active Twitter site, did not improve trust. Another poll asked Americans about institutions (Gallup, 2013). The table below displays some results. This poll seems somewhat contradictory. Although people ranked the president in the top 100, less than 50% of the people trusted the presidency as an institution. People rated the police highly, but not the criminal justice system. They rated the Congress as last, but they elect their representatives. The lack of trust in political figures and most political institutions suggests there would be less political involvement. Only 36.4% of eligible voters participated in the 2014 USA election (McDonald, 2014).

Table 10.1

The Percent Who Trust Institutions

Institution	Percent We Trust		
	A Great Deal	Quite a Lot	Total
The Military	43	33	76
Small Business	29	36	65
The Police	26	31	57
The Church or Organized Religion	25	23	48
The Presidency	19	17	36
The Medical System	15	20	35
US Supreme Court	13	21	34
Public Schools	14	18	32
Criminal Justice System	10	18	28
Banks	10	16	26
Television News	11	12	23
Newspapers	9	14	23
Big Business	9	13	22
Organized labor	10	10	20
Health Maintenance Organizations	8	11	19
Congress	5	3	10

At CouchSurfing.com, there were few correlates to trust. Hosting a community event did increase trust somewhat, but the use of other FtF and digital HCT were unrelated (Rosen et al., 2011). Perhaps the relationships between using various HCT to trust depends on the nature of the audience and the particular civic activities. In some cases, people may be interested in limited involvement, and there would be no opportunity to develop a pattern of predictable communication. In other instances, the lack of institutional trust may have evolved over generations and restoring trust will require more than a SNS or a few months of predictable communication (Stiglitz, 2013). In the end, the loss of trust may reach a tipping point and lead to the development of trust networks and the start of a social movement.

Commitment and trust are two important perceptions that accompany civic activities. There appears to be less commitment to and less trust of traditional civic institutions. People can use the newer HCTs and FtF communication to improve these perceptions. There appear to be sporadic outburst of civic activity, but most appear to be difficult to sustain. Have overall civic activities declined? How does using the newer HCTs relate to civic activities?

Civic Engagement Activities

Three Levels of Involvement

There have been several attempts to classify civic activities (Ekman & Amna, 2012), and the classification I am using is a simple variation that provides a way to describe a full range of activities. One type of civic engagement involvement is individual activities. Habitat for Humanity is one of many formal community groups, and this group helps people with housing difficulties. If a person made a charitable contribution to the group or inquired about group activities while avoiding formal membership in the group, that person would be involved in individual activities.

A second type of involvement is through activist network. People of similar interests can learn about each other, connect to each other, inform each other, and in some cases coordinate individual activities. There is no formal group or membership, but there may be periodic coordinated collective activities in support of common interests. Most "groups" involved with Arab Spring protests were activist networks, but so are the "groups" that spring up following some public tragedy such as a hurricane.

Finally, there is involvement in a formal group. Some people become members but only *observe* the activities of others. These members may actually be less involved than those who are performing individual civic engagement. A second type of member *contributes* to the group by providing resources and working with other members to perform group activities. Finally, some members *lead* by assuming roles to provide direction and direct activities for the group.

Individual, network, and group civic engagement may be political or typical community civic engagement. For example, a college student could be involved with a campus group, a business or professional association, a labor union, a sports league, religious organization, a hobby group or club, a community service group, or any organized political group seeking to influence government actions. A recent comparison of the members of political groups, political activist networks, and community groups, found that the members of political groups had greater commitment, but they felt more stress and less support than the members of the other two (Mannarini & Talo, 2012).

Individual activities often lead to network and group activities. Those people who watch the news and make comments to their friends about current affairs are potential participants in some collective actions to change a community or in collective actions to influence those who could change a community situation (e.g., government officials). Some refer to individual activities as a type of "latent civic engagement" since manifest collective action is so central to the idea of civic engagement (Ekman & Amna, 2012).

Changes in Activities

A comparison of civic engagement between 2008 and 2012 demonstrated encouraging trends (Smith, 2013). First, 48% of adults had directly taken part in a civic group or civic activity in 2012, and 35% had recently worked with fellow citizens to solve a problem in their community. General participation in 2012 was equivalent to 2008, but actually working with fellow citizens was lower (28%) in 2008. The remainder of the comparisons focused on political rather than general civic engagement.

Second, many Americans have attempted to influence officials or communicate in a public manner about political matters. These activities included signing a petition, contacting government officials, calling in on a radio or TV show or commenting on a blog, and sending a letter to the editor. As many as 39% of respondents had done one or more of these things offline, and 34% had done these things online.

Third, there has been an increase in the use of SNS to do political or civic activities. As many as 39% had done civic or political activities using SNS, and it was not possible to identify a trend since there was so little political activity with SNS in 2008. 66% of SNS users have engaged is online political activity such as "like" or promote material related to political issues, encourage others to vote, post their own comments about issues, encourage others to take action, and belong to groups involved in political or social issues while only 39% of all adults have done one or more of these things online.

A more recent survey following the 2014 campaign revealed a greater reliance on social media (SM) (Smith, 2014). Subjects revealed they felt closer to candidates by learning about them on SM, and they felt using social media meant they would learn about events before others. Those who trusted traditional news sources less were more likely to use SM more for news.

Alt-right refers to racists and bigots who often use labels such as traditionalist, nationalists, populists, and radical conservatives to make their positions seem more acceptable or natural. There are two types of alt-right individuals:

> . . . garden-variety racists, who complain about mixed-race
> couples, are proud of their Scots-Irish heritage, and use

hashtags such as "#WhiteWomenAreMagic," and violent extremists, who call for genocide against Jews, the killing of Muslims and African-Americans, and even threaten to lynch President Obama. (Morgan, 2016).

During the 2018 campaign, there were 27,000 Twitter accounts associated with the alt-right, and 3,500 of them suggested the second group of users. A distinguishing feature of the Tweets from the extremist was that they used "Jewish" to identify someone they hated rather than a religious group (Morgan, 2016).

Greater use of more "traditional" technology has been associated with group involvement (Smith, 2012). For example, greater FtF and TEL use was related to greater participation in CE groups (Salem, 2012). However, greater use of private electronic communication (PEC) was also associated with greater participation in CE groups, and the personal networks developed through people's EML were more associated with people's civic activities than any other communication technology network (Salem, 2012).

Fourth, people who are active online, especially on SNS, are also active offline. The researchers caution making a causal link (Smith, 2013, p. 36) since the various survey results about activities were correlated to each other, and these studies were not experiments. It is just as likely that those who are politically active offline bring their activism online as the reverse.

Fifth, education is the most consistent demographic variable associated with civic engagement. If you were more educated and wealthy, you were more likely to be involved in political activities, offline or online, than those less educated and wealthy. Also, if you were more educated, you were more likely to be involved in SNS political activities than those who were less educated.

It is also important for people to develop diverse personal networks. Greater age and sex heterogeneity in personal communication technology networks correlated to greater civic engagement (Salem, 2012). And so, more active people are better educated, and have greater resources, but they also maintain networks of men and women from differing generations.

Sixth, discussion of political issues happened more offline than online. More precisely, 76% said they discuss these issues offline with 42% indicting this happened at least once a week or daily. Alternatively, 44% of Americans used texting, email, or SNS to discuss political issues with only 16% indicating this happened at least once a week or more frequently. 50% said they never discuss political issues online.

Political "discussions" are often some form of conflict. There are three types of conflict (Miller & Steinberg, 1975). *Simple conflict* involves argument and competition, and there is often the sense that someone won while another lost. Good argument changes attitudes and informs. There is nothing particularly harmful about this sort of conflict as long as the conflict remains simple and does not include other types. *Pseudo conflict* occurs when misunderstandings are the source of people's differences.

Supplying more information, clarifying, and being more open and responsive are all ways to improve perceptual accuracy and effectively manage this version of conflict. *Ego-defensive conflict* involves saving face and usually includes verbal aggression. In simple conflict, the goal is to win, but in ego-defensive conflict, the goal is to avoid getting hurt and to hurt the other. If the political discussion participants recognized pseudo conflict and cleared up misunderstandings or if the participants brought the best argument while keeping the conflicts simple, people would learn more about issues and gain an appreciation of differences. If these discussions deteriorated into ego-defensiveness, participants would leave doggedly tied to their original positions, have greater identification with those who held similar views, and greater animosity to those with different opinions.

What is the nature of discussions online? Political groups will often use a SNS as a forum for postings and discussions, but the participants often have the same opinions. Researchers analyzed 38,000+ postings about immigration on a Dutch right wing site with the nearly 29,000 postings on the same issues on an immigrant site (Oegema, Kleinnijenhuis, Anderson, & van Hoof, 2008). Patterns in the postings on *both sites* included the following: (1) expressions of *negative emotions* (e.g., disgust, hatred, shame) toward those with opposing views, (2) *polarizing language* emphasizing an "us vs. them" frame, and (3) *flaming*. The specific immigration topics on these sites reflected stories in Dutch newspapers over the period, but the newspaper articles did not have the linguistic features discovered in the forums.

Israeli Jews and Palestinians were part of an online project intended to foster dialogue between the two groups. Twelve 15 and 16 year old students from pairs of Israeli and Palestinian schools communicated about recent violence in the region. The 329 coded messages over a three-week period reflected cultural differences in the types of posted messages, but the most common structure of argument was stunted argument (Ellis & Maoz, 2007). *Stunted argument* is a sequence of only two messages expressing differences in which argument does not develop. People change topics or avoid developing their thoughts. In other words, people avoided developing the conflict. Expressing differences was as far as the members of the project matured.

What was the effect of the audience in these two situations? With the Dutch groups, the audience consisted of like-minded SNS members. With the Israeli-Palestinian student site, the audience consisted of students with similar and different ideas, and the audience also included teachers. There was greater diversity with the Israeli-Palestinian site.

An unanswered question is how communicatively competent were the participants in these sites. More specifically, how skilled were they at argument? A lack of communication competence was part of the explanation for the bad behavior detailed in Chapter Six.

An enduring question is how to sustain civic involvement? Although people reported greater civic and political activity in 2012 than 2008, the voter turnout in the 2014 election continued a downward trend since 1964 in turnout for nonpresidential elections (McDonald, 2014). Politicians may use SNS to communicate directly with voters, use posts to assess the political mood, and to help organize events to directly meet voters and have them meet each other (Davies, 2014). People are more likely to respond and to participate to FtF communication and to personal communication such as a personal TEL call or EML than to a SNS posting or general EML (Rosen et al., 2011; Smith, 2013).

The network created through EML messages has higher predictability for greater civic engagement than other communication technology networks (Kobayashi, Ikeda, & Miyata, 2006; Salem, 2012). The pattern of learning about something through SNS and then following with more personal or offline communication (Smith, 2013) reinforces the notion from Chapter Four that mass communication informs and interpersonal communication persuades. If this is the most effective communication pattern sustaining civic activities, then why don't most people do it?

The newer HCTs provide opportunities for greater civic engagement. People do appear to be gathering more with like-minded people using these technologies. The postings or Tweets seem to encourage division, and people appear to be unwilling to confront differences. Furthermore, people appear to be unwilling to communicate in such a way that improves civic activity and benefits the entire community. Have there been changes in how people understand community or the common good?

Community

Ideas about the nature of community are similar to ideas about groups, organizations, and cultures. A common distinction is that individuals can form communities around a specific geographic area such as a neighborhood, and individuals can form relational communities based on similar values, mutual relational benefits, common goals or concerns, etc. (Gusfeld, 1975; Hershberger, Murray, & Rioux, 2007). Relational communities include fan networks and groups and also virtual communities. The members of a civic engagement group (e.g., charity group, political group) may develop into a relational community, but the group members are performing activities for a larger community.

Communities are about shared and mutual perceptions. A sense of community includes a feeling that members have of belonging, a feeling that members matter to one another and to the group, and a shared faith that members' needs will be met through their commitment to be together (McMillian & Chavis, 1986). And so, the four factors that are part of a sense of community are perceptions of (a) membership, (b) influence, (c) integration and fulfillment of needs, and (d) shared emotional connection. Developing commitment is central to a sense of community.

Communities are also about developing recognizable activities. There are two types of civic group activities. First, there are those activities performing the external functions of the group such as building the house or going to the protest. Second, there are those activities performing the internal functions of the group. Internal functions include all those things about the how the group functions, the climate of the group, and the structure of the group. Internal functions include membership activities, creating logos, writing and enforcing rules, etc. At CouchSurfing.com, activities serving external functions would include sharing housing and participating in tours, and activities serving internal functions involve hosting meetings of members in a particular locale to schedule tours when guests come from other locales and to just socialize. Repeated performance of internal functions leads naturally to the development of instrumental social routines and rituals, similar to other organizations. Involvement in internal functions generally means greater commitment to the group than involvement in only external functions.

Members obtain resources and satisfy needs in two ways. First, the communication among civic engagement group members and between group members and clients provides the opportunities for resources just as any communication would. Secondly, community interactions produce one or more collective resources available to the members of the community. Some of these collective resources, such as a recreational park, might be more permanent than other resources such as a picnic or carnival in the park. Many have used the expression "social capital" to refer to this second set of resources, and some of the earliest work about "virtual communities" such as those created through a blog or online website, has been sensitive to the abilities of these communities to create and sustain unique social capital (Rheingold, 1993). An earlier section noted features of online communities such as Couchsurfing.com.

Differences are important to a community. Members must accommodate each other's differences, and the ability to learn from differences is an essential part of sustaining civic engagement, especially political groups (Kobayashi, Ikeda, & Miyata, 2006). The ability to deal with heterogeneity improves the ability to promote social capital online (Rheingold, 1993).

The differences between groups and communities help to establish recognizable boundaries and the bases for social identities. Two community groups may have similar missions, but the values and routines between the groups will be different. This feature of differences between civic groups or communities is similar to the differences between cultures (Agar, 1994; Salem, 2013).

In an article (1995) and then later a book (2000), Putnam argued that Americans participated less in organized groups, had less trust, and engaged in fewer collective activities. There was less civic engagement. For him, social capital referred to features of social organization, and he described the diminution of dense networks of social interaction that facilitated coordination and cooperation for mutual benefits. Membership in larger associations (e.g., Environmental Defense Fund), nonprofits (a museum association), or personal groups (e.g., support groups), was a poor substitute since membership did not involve the dense social interactions for collective activity or mutual gains for a community. He posited many reasons for the decline of civic engagement, and among these was the "technological transformation of leisure".

> There is reason to believe that deep-seated technological trends are radically "privatizing" or "individualizing" our use of leisure time and thus disrupting many opportunities for social-capital formation. The most obvious and probably the most powerful instrument of this revolution is television. Time-budget studies in the 1960s showed that the growth in time spent watching television dwarfed all other changes in the way Americans passed their days and nights. Television has made our communities (or, rather, what we experience as our communities) wider and shallower. (Putnam, 1995, p. 75)

Wellman (1979) argued that traditional notions of community did not reflect how contemporary individuals organized their lives. Rather than relying on dense interactions bounded by geography, individuals were able to maintain sparse personal networks of strong and weak ties that provided them ample resources. Communication has evolved from door-to-door, to place-to-place, to person-to-person (Wellman, 2002). The previous notions of community consisting of people in little boxes bounded by territory had evolved to glocalization in which people can simultaneously maintain local and global ties through networked individualism (Wellman, 2002).

Combining awareness of social networks, with the Internet revolution, and the mobility revolution produces a new social operating system for how people communicate and behave with each other (Rainie & Wellman, 2012). *Networked individualism* describes how individuals engage with multiple diverse people limiting their involvement in and commitment to any one network (Rainie & Wellman, 2012). Networked individualism means people have partial membership into many networks rather than permanent membership into a few groups. People can obtain many resources through their links in their personal networks, but the networks have effects on them as well.

Putnam was describing the loss of groups and social capitol, and Wellman was describing the emergence of greater network activity as an alternative. Furthermore, Wellman was arguing that personal networks have become communities. Our personal networks are our communities. People may have an active network of around 50 and adding some distant contacts and acquaintances may bring the personal network to between 100 and 200 hundred, but anything beyond 150 just increases the size of the "neighborhood". People may not be members of bowling groups, but people are not bowling alone. They are bowling in "networks of shifting sets of others who happen to be free that week" (Rainie & Wellman, 2012, p. 121).

The change to network individualism places greater responsibility on individuals to obtain resources and greater importance on personal skills, motivation, and knowledge (Rainie & Wellman, 2012). There is also an "audience effect" (Rainie & Wellman, 2012) that includes the problems mentioned earlier as diverse social spaces and the additional problems related to the shorter distances between people. Connecting to any one person means connecting to their network as well, and although this has always been the case, the Internet revolution and mobility make any effects quicker and with greater impact.

Network individualism does not mean the same characteristics of community carry over to our personal network. People's involvement in their personal networks changes daily, and so their commitment to any one person and that person's network is limited. Likewise, the commitment of alters to ego is less than the commitment of group members to each other and their group. People are now in communities of "limited liability" (Rainie & Wellman, 2012). This would mean people less willing to engage in internal group activities, more resources obtained through one-to-one communication and fewer collective resources, and more heterogeneous weak ties that people can change readily. The emergence of networked individualism is an explanation for the inability to sustain civic engagement. It is a realist explanation since it involves both a social feature, the recognition of networks, and technological features, the Internet, and mobility.

HCT **does** provide opportunities to connect to others through BEC, and one of the consequences of many SNSs may be the production of a collective good. Blogs, forums, SNS, wikis, open source sites, forums, rating and review sites, and compilers or aggregators provide different opportunities to upload, comment, post links, vote, or tag. What is posted on the sites becomes a collective good, and the communication that occurs may lead to more tangible collective goods such as political demonstrations and the Ice Bucket challenge. It is as if a BEC site was, in and of itself, a link in a personal network, and people developing a sense of community to the others also linked to the site. What does happen is that people may contribute or observe what is happening on the sites, and then connect with each other through some other HCT. A student in my graduate class met his fiancé through Twitter.

Involvement in BEC sites carries the same greater responsibility on individuals as the networked individualism it supports. Everything posted on BEC sites is not of value, and some collective goods are the fan chatter on Twitter and others are Wikipedia. The individual must discriminate. The individual must bring an already developed set of moral and ethical standards, critical thinking, and communication competence to BEC site participation.

Network individualism suggests the Internet and mobility has led to an explosion of brokerage and a shrinking of closure networks. It may be harder to sustain civic engagement or the construction of a lasting collective good, but it is easier to obtain personal resources. Things are not better or worse, but different.

Are most people using HCT to develop larger and more diverse networks? Are people becoming more like brokers? Are people using technology to enhance the cultural values associated with individualism?

Bishop (2008) argued that people are sorting themselves into homogeneous groups both offline and online.

> Beginning nearly 30 years ago, the people of this country unwittingly began a social experiment. Finding cultural comfort in "people like us," we have migrated into ever narrower communities and churches and political groups. We have created, and are creating, new institutions distinguished by their isolation and single-mindedness. We have replaced a belief in a nation with a trust in ourselves and our carefully chosen surroundings. And we worked quietly and hard to remove any trace of the "constant clashing of opinions" from daily life. It was a social revolution, one that was both profound and, because it consists of people simply going about their lives, entirely unnoticed. In this time, we have reshaped our economies, transformed our businesses, both created and decimated our cities, and altered institutions of faith and fellowship that have withstood centuries. Now more isolated than ever in our private lives, cocooned with our fellows, we approach public life with the sensibility of customers who are always right. (Bishop, 2008, pp. 302-303)

This is consistent with commodifying self and others and resisting differences in personal relationships and with not sustaining arguments online. It also means people can become prone to the deindividuation noted above.

> . . . we increasingly live in hermetically sealed ideological zones that are almost immune to compromise or nuance. Internet algorithms and the proliferation of media have let us surround ourselves with opinions that confirm our biases. We're also segregating geographically into red or blue territories; chances are that our neighbors share our views and magnify them. So, when we come across someone outside these zones, whose views have been summarily dismissed or vilified, our minds are closed. (Reich, 2013)

We seem to be choosing closure.

Barwind, Salem, and Gratz (2014) explained a more complex process that may have produced the grouping. Politicians employ marketing techniques that segment communities, and they design messages, including those on SM, for segments and not the whole. People in many of the segments tend to choose to live near each other. Public media, such as television, also employs marketing techniques that segment communities, and they design messages, programs, and networks for the segments. Public media slants messages to fit the audience and they dramatize programming to gain viewers.

People in many of the segments appear to be similar to members of high uncertainty avoidance cultures - they are suspicious of differences and public process, and they rely on many precise and unwritten rules to maintain social order. Recall that those with less trust will also consume more SM (Smith, 2014). Many people in the segments consume the messages that reinforce their biases, avoiding differences and information. The process is self-reinforcing: politicians and the media give people the messages that reinforce people's biases; the more the media supplies these messages, the more people consume them; the more people consume them, the more the politicians and the media supply them. And so it goes.

> In the quest for "eyeballs," the producers of the news construct dramatic narratives rife with conflict, whether or not that drama overstates the reality it portends to report. Dealing at a high level of abstraction (opinions of opinions) is far more interesting than the event itself. In this way the news reinvents reality and we are left with "all the 'news' that's fit to invent." We participate in the invention by selective exposure to various outlets, and we use our online activity to construct our own inventions and to propagate the inventions we find comforting. We are left with Walt Kelley's admonition expressed in the first Earth Day poster: "We have met the enemy, and he is us." (Barwind, Salem, & Gratz, 2014, p. 22)

If there is segmentation, individual choice is a key part of a complex process.

The Pattern

Traditional notions of civic engagement centered around individuals in groups performing activities for the wider community. The latest data on how people are using HCT suggest more latent civic engagement by individuals and more networked civic engagement through BEC sites, and networked individualism. People appear to be unable to sustain dialogue and argument with people who hold different views. While some people are developing more expanded and diverse personal networks, others are constructing personal networks of higher density as part of subgroups or segments of the larger society. There has been a loss of a sense of community for a larger whole. However, there has been the gain of a more volatile and less committed sense of community for many smaller groups, or a more intense commitment to a smaller group of "people like us". The entire pattern is one of social decentralization and fragmentation.

The Internet and the newer HCTs are "cooler media", and a technological deterministic explanation would be that these newer HCTs are forcing people into a more egalitarian, simpler, but tribal social structure. Alternatively, people's use of HCT may simply be a reflection of current social and economic divisions. A more social construction approach would argue the way we are using technology and talking about technology are different, and if there are problems, the users created them. Several of the scholars noted above have offered explanations that combine social and psychological circumstances with technology changes, realist explanations. A media ecology approach would point to decentralization and fragmentation as unanticipated consequences to altering the overall pattern of our communication.

Complexity theory offers a more comprehensive approach to change than other approaches (Salem, 2013). The newer HCTs represent a change in parameters, a change in the *way* people have been doing what they have always done. Parameters can change to increase the variety within any system, to increase information. The increase in variety can challenge the stability in an already existing structure and generate alternative structures. The disruptions can reach a tipping point where the possibilities include a return to the old structure, modifications in the old structure, the dominance of a new structure, or dissolution of the system entirely. People have been trying to do things for the common good for some time, and there will always be differences within a society. People are using the newer HCTs to reconsider the nature of their communities and the ways in which they engage in them. Societies are approaching tipping points.

References

Abdurraham, S., Mayer, L., Riggler, K., & Sharma, M. (Producers) (2015, January 29). Naming the shooter, the law of the Internet and more. *On the Media* (Radio broadcast and podcast from WNYC and NPR)

(Retrieved at http://www.onthemedia.org/story/on-the-media-2015-01-30).

Agar, M. (1994). *Language shock: Understanding the culture of conversation*. New York: William Moore and Company, Inc.

Allen, N. J., & Meyer, J. P. (1996). Affective, continuance, and normative commitment to the organization: An examination of construct validity. *Journal of Vocational Behavior*, *49*, 252-276.

ALS Association (2014). The ALS Ice Bucket Challenge. (Retrieved at http://www.alsa.org/fight-als/ice-bucket-challenge.html?gclid=Cj0KEQiAr9ymBRDdqYrH6Mj5170BEiQAcRUsi9WTftITof27rznJFdy-EugyYHlUgACoZBfnEOZNYo4aAvOa8P8HAQ).

American Psychological Association. (2010). *Civic engagement*. Retrieved from http://www.apa.org/education/undergrad/civic-engagement.aspx.

Barwind, J. A., Salem, P. J., & Gratz, R. D. (2014). A bigger screen for a narrower view. In K. M. Ryan (Ed.), *The more you know: Law and order, inconvenient truths and how television shapes our worldview* (pp. 11-25). Lexington, MA: Lexington Press.

Bhattacharya, R., Devinney, T. M., & Pillutla, M. M. (1998). A formal model of trust based on outcomes. *Academy of Management Review*, *23*, 459-472.

Bishop, B. (2008). *The big sort: Why the clustering of like-minded America is tearing us apart*. Boston: Houghton Mifflin.

Butterworth, T. (2011, June 11). Speed journalism: Some stories need just a Tweet –Some need real thought," *The Daily*. 49.

Davies, R. (2014). *Social media in election campaigning*. (European Parliamentary Research Service Briefing, March 21, 2014). Retrieved at http://www.europarl.europa.eu/RegData/bibliotheque/briefing/2014/140709/LDM_BRI%282014%29140709_REV1_EN.pdf.

DelReal, J. A. (2014, November, 10). Voter turnout in 2014 was the lowest since WWII. *Washington Post* (Retrieved at http://www.washingtonpost.com/blogs/post-politics/wp/2014/11/10/voter-turnout-in-2014-was-the-lowest-since-wwii).

Ekman, J., & Amna, E. (2012). Political participation and civic engagement: Towards a new typology. *Human Affairs*, *22*, 283-300.

Ellis, D., & Maoz, I. (2007). Online argument between Palestinians and Jews. Human *Communication Research, 33*(3), 291-309.

Galbraith, J. R. (1977). *Organization design*. Boston, MA: Addison-Wesley.

Gallup, Inc. (2013, June). *Confidence in institutions*. Washington, DC: Gallup Inc. Retrieved from http://www.gallup.com/poll/1597/confidence-institutions.aspx.

Gusfield, J.R. (1975). *The community: A critical response*. New York: Harper Colophon.

Hersberger, J. A, Murray A. L., & Rioux K. S. (2007) Examining information exchange and virtual communities: An emergent framework. *Online Information Review, 31*(2): 135–147.

Hofstede, G., & Hofstede, G. J. (2005). *Cultures and organizations: Software for the mind* (rev. 2nd ed.). New York, NY: McGraw-Hill.

Kantor, R. M. (1972). *Commitment and community: Communes and utopias in sociological perspective*. Cambridge, MA: Harvard University Press.

Kietzmann, J. H., Hermkens, K., McCarthy, I. P., & Silvestre, B. S. (2011). Social media? Get serious! Understanding the functional building blocks of social media. *Business Horizons, 54*, 241-251.

Kobayashi, T., Ikeda, K., & Miyata, K. (2006). Social capital online: Collective use of the Internet and reciprocity as lubricants of democracy. *Information, Communication and Society*, *9*, 582-611.

Kohndker, H. H. (2011). The role of new media in Arab Spring. *Globalizations, 8*(5), 675-679.

Lewicki, R. J., McAllister, D. J., & Bies, R. J. (1998). Trust and distrust: New relationships and realities. *Academy of Management Review*, *23*, 439-458.

Mannarini, T., & Ralo, C. (2012). Explaining political and civic long-term engagement. Do group-based activities make a difference? *Psicologia Politica*, *45*, 85-102.

McDonald, M. (2014). United States election project: Voter turnout data. Retrieved at http://www.electproject.org/home/voter-turnout/voter-turnout-data.

McMillan, D. W., & Chavis, D. M. (1986). Sense of community: A definition and theory. *Journal of Community Psychology*, *4*(1), 6-23.

Meyer, J. P., & Allen, N. J. (1991). A three component conceptualization of organizational commitment. *Human Resource Management*, *1*(1), 61-89.

Mihailidis, P. (2014). The civic-social media disconnect: Exploring perceptions of social media for engagement in the daily life of college students. *Information, Communication & Society*, *17*(9), 1059-1071.

Miller, G. R., & Steinberg, M. (1975). *Between people: A new analysis of interpersonal communication.* Palo Alto, CA: Scientific Research Associates.

Miller, S. (2014, August 26). I figured out why I hate the ice bucket challenge. *Time* (Retrieved at http://time.com/3182165/i-figured-out-why-i-hate-the-ice-bucket-challenge).

Morgan, J. (2016, September 26). These charts show exactly how racist and radical the alt-right has gotten this year. *Washington Post*. (Retrieved at https://www.washingtonpost.com/news/the-intersect/wp/2016/09/26/thes...-radical-the-alt-right-has-gotten-this-year/?utm_term=.6a83fbc196dd

Oegema, D., Kleinnijenhuis, J., Anderson, K., & van Hoof, A. (2008). Flaming and blaming: The influence of mass media content on interactions in online discussions. In E. A. Konijin, S. Utz, M. Tanis, & S. B. Barnes (Eds.), *Mediated interpersonal communication* (pp. 331-358). New York: Routledge.

Putnam, R. D. (1995). Bowling alone. *Journal of Democracy, 6*(1), 65–78.

Putnam, R. D. (2000). *Bowling alone: The collapse and revival of American community*. New York, NY: Simon & Schuster.

Rainie, L., & Wellman, B. (2012). *Networked: The new social operating system*. Cambridge, MA: The MIT Press.

Reich, R. (2013, September 23) American bile. *The New York Times*. Retrieved form http://opinionator.blogs.nytimes.com/2013/09/21/american-bile.

Rheingold, H. (1993). *The virtual community: Homesteading on the electronic frontier*. Reading, MA: Addison-Wesley.

Rosen, D., Lafontaine, P. R., & Hendrickson, B. (2011). Belonging and trust in a globally cooperative online social network. *New Media and Society, 13*(6), 981-998.

Rousseau, D. M., Sitkin, S. B., Burt, R. S., & Camerer, C. (1998). Not so different after all: A cross-discipline view of trust. *Academy of Management Review, 23,* 393-404.

Rusbult, C., Martz, J., & Agnew, C. (1998). The investment model scale: Measuring commitment level, satisfaction level, quality of alternatives and investment size. *Personal Relationships, 5,* 357-391.

Salem, P. J. (2012). Civic engagement and communication technology networks. In M. H. Safar, & K. A. Mahdi (Eds.), *Social networking and community behavior modeling: Qualitative and quantitative measures* (pp. 51-66). Hersey, PA: IGI Global.

Salem, P. J. (2013). *The complexity of human communication* (2nd ed.). Cresskill, NJ: Hampton Press.

Smith, A. (2013). *Civic engagement in a digital age*. Report for the Pew Internet and American Life Project, Washington, DC. Retrieved from http://www.pewinternet.org/Reports/2013/Civic-Engagement.aspx.

Smith, A. (2014). *Cellphones, social media and the 2014 campaign*. Report for the Pew Research Center, Washington, DC. Retrieved from http://www.pewinternet.org/2014/11/03/cell-phones-social-media-and-campaign-2014/

Smith, C., & Caporimo, A. (2013, June). Reader's Digest trust poll: The 100 most trusted people in America. *Reader's Digest*. http://www.rd.com/slideshows/readers-digest-trust-poll-heres-what-shocked-us-the-most/#slideshow=slide1.

Stiglitz, J. (2013, December 22). In no one we trust. *New York Times*, SR4.

Tilly, C. (2005a). *Identities, boundaries, and social ties*. Boulder, CO: Paradigm Publishers.

Tilly, C. (2005b). *Trust and rule*. Cambridge: Cambridge University Press.

Wellman, B. (1979). The community question: The intimate networks of East Yorkers. *American Journal of Sociology, 84*(3), 1201-1231.

Wellman, B. (2002). Little boxes, glocalization, and networked individualism. In M. Tanabe, P. von den Besselaar, & T. Ishida (eds.), *Digital cities* (pp. 10-25). Berlin: Springer.

Chapter Eleven:
Reality and Technology

The April 1, 1985 *Sports Illustrated* issue featured an article in the middle of the magazine about Sidd Finch, a new pitching phenomenon for the New York Mets. He could play the French horn, and, thanks to his Buddhist training, he could throw a pitch 168 miles per hour. Today, the average major league fastball is 92 mph. The article featured pictures of Sidd at the Mets spring training camp, including a famous picture of him pitching wearing a working boot on one foot while the other one was barefoot. There were also pictures of Sidd as a child and with his parents, interviews with players and coaches, and a few comments by Sidd. General managers from other teams called the *Sports Illustrated* editors in an effort to learn if Sidd made the Mets final opening day roster or if he was available in a trade or to sign with another team. The entire story was a hoax, an April Fool's day joke (Bean & Poling, 2014). It was not real, although most people, including most of the *Sports Illustrated* staff, thought it was.

Lennay Kekua met a handsome football player from Notre Dame while he was touring the Stanford University campus. She had a Twitter account, and she visited her new boyfriend at his home in Hawaii. On April 28, 2012, she had a near fatal car accident, and then she was diagnosed with leukemia. The sound of her boyfriend's voice seemed to bring her to life, and he wrote her inspirational notes. Finally, she died, within just 24 hours of the death of the boyfriend's grandmother. Pete Thamel reported on the various parts of the story in a series of articles in *Sports Illustrated*. There actually was a Twitter account, and the grandmother did die, but the rest of the story was a fabrication and a hoax. Manny Te'o, a finalist for the Heisman Trophy awarded to college football's best player, and the supposed boyfriend in the stories was the victim of the hoax, but he may also have been complicit in it (Burke & Dickey, 2013). The reporter and most of the people who heard about the initial stories believed they were real.

The reporter, and the public, may have fallen victim to a confirmation bias (Levin, 2013), a tendency for people to select evidence and put data together that confirms already held beliefs (Nickerson, 1998). The reporter may have believed Te'o because it made a good news story. Te'o's tales had "truthiness", and so, the reporter and the rest of us believed the stories because we wanted them to be real. No need to check on the facts; it is what we already believe or want to hear.

People's use of the newer human communication technologies (HCTs) have muddled the lines between reality and fantasy, and the cases noted above demonstrate people may be too willing to accept fiction as fact. In some cases, the results have been tragic. Slenderman is a fictional character originating and popularized on the Internet. While most people recognize Slenderman is fantasy, two Wisconsin middle school girls tried to kill another 12 year-old in an attempt to prove the character was real (Wagner, 2013). Then there was the man in his thirties who threatened his brother and his family with a baseball bat because the brother had killed his online gaming character (Parry, 2015). The actual deaths for reasons like this have led to a Wikipedia entry for "Internet homicide", and a Google search for "Internet murders" produces over 15 million hits.

Advances in artificial intelligence have also challenged people's sense of reality. It is becoming increasingly more difficult to detect when one is interacting with a person or computer. Indeed, there are algorithms that can compose complete news stories and reports, and these stories appear to most to be written by humans (Podolny, 2015). A computer can already use an algorithm to examine the pattern of "likes" on someone's Facebook and make communication style and personality judgments more accurate than the in-person friends of the Facebook users (Youyou, Kosinski, & Stillwell,

2015). Computer agents are now replacing humans as representatives of organizations, and when people learned they were interacting with a computer, some important impressions of the agents did not change (Shank, 2014). People seem to have treated their computers as social actors for some time (Reeves & Nass, 1996), and now they seem to be willing to accept computers as substitutes for humans.

This chapter begins with old problems distinguishing reality, and then moves to the current digital problems. Along the way, there will be references to material already presented, some psychiatric and political material about reality, current problems finding out what "really" happened, and people's involvement in virtual worlds. The journey is a bit like Alice's rabbit hole into Wonderland. A man divorced his virtual wife in MapleStory, an online virtual world, and the woman playing the wife, a 43-year old piano teacher, became so angry she logged into the computer game with the man's password and deleted his digital persona, an avatar. Police arrested her, and transported her 620 miles to face, in person, the man she had "virtually killed". She was facing a stiff fine and up to five years in prison for tampering with the game site (Leach, 2008).

The Reality of Technology

Below is a picture of a mechanical typewriter. I decided I needed to show a picture since most people reading this book may not have used one, and most may not have seen one. People rolled paper into the top of the machine and used the keyboard. By depressing a key, a lever would force a thin arm to send a hard head attached to the lever quickly into a ribbon that was soaked in ink (just above the red line in the picture). The ribbon was next to paper, and so, when the head hit the ribbon, there would be an impression of what was on the head of the lever — "a typeface". Over the years, manufacturers added electricity, got rid of the levers, and made it easier to change the fonts. The latest ones have built in programs or slots to insert programs to improve the experience or the document. Are the latest machines still typewriters? A type of computer devoted to word processing? A word processor?

People still type, but on what? There are physical devices people can attach to a computer, and people still call these keyboards. But the images that appears on your smart phone, the ones you touch with your fingers that result in other images - letters for a text message or email or document – are also "keyboards". People seem to have decided to use "keyboard" for some device you can touch to make letters. You can also make images by changing the font. The images can be sketches, and you can change a key into a cursor. People are changing keyboards or how they use these terms. The objects change, and so do the categories.

Some classic distinctions are a good starting point to help with understanding the reality of technology. *Reality, physical reality, or in real life* (IRL) are unmediated experiences. IRL is what is going on without using digital technology or the use of newer HCTs. There are several problems with this idea, but it is a beginning.

A *simulation* is a representation of something IRL. Games such as a football board game or computer game are often simulations. Simulations are good or bad depending on the fidelity of representing IRL. A person learning to fly using a flight simulator does not want to be surprised when they fly IRL. Simulations of all sorts and games in particular have been a popular way to help organizational members learn a task or make decisions for some time (Davenport, 1997).

Virtual reality is a digital representation of an idea that does not exist IRL. That is, something in virtual reality is a digital "realization of an idea" (Wooley, 1992). The physical reality of a computer, the hardware, exists IRL, but what a computer can do through its software and hardware are the realization of many people's ideas about information, computation, and artificial intelligence (Gleick, 2011; Wooley, 1992).

Hybrid reality is the merging of humans and the new HCTs to create a new reality - a combination of mediated and un-mediated factors leading to an experience users act on as real (Khanna & Khanna, 2012). What happened to those people in the introduction is that they had trouble distinguishing the contours of that hybrid reality. What some had been experiencing may have been simulations (including a hoax) or virtual reality they confused with IRL. What these people experienced was real to them, even though the sources may have been artificial in some way.

What will happen when a computer can learn and think independent of human actions? There are computers that have artificial intelligence, and some can act alone. This can happen through a complexity like effect where advances in computer intelligence multiply with each advance and computers link together. The Singularity is the point at which these advances will lead to artificial intelligence surpassing human intelligence, and, at least one author thinks it will happen in 2045 (Kurzweil, 2005). When this happens, will a computer be a computer or a robot or some other living system comparable to a human being?

The Technology of Reality

There are many philosophical approaches to the nature of reality. Do things exist in and of themselves or do they exist only as people know them? Is what people think about things more important than what might be there even if people believe something might be there? The "realist" and empirical sides of this argument go back to Confucius and Aristotle, and the contrasts were rationalist or idealist arguments from Lao Tzu and Plato. More contemporary positions include descriptions of how people socially construct reality (Berger & Luckman, 1966).

The political implications of different realities are that some people may be able to impose their sense of reality on others. Some argued that traditional ways of knowing have their own discourses that impose a reality on those who might communicate about reality in different ways (Foucault, 1966). People who think they know reality can claim others who disagree are not sane (Watzlawick, 1976). Reality can be a difficult proposition to grasp, and the entire quandary gets more muddled when power is part of the equation.

Chapter One described human information processing (HIP) as a framing process. The process begins with an enactment stage in which a person actively engages in attending to signals to create data. Similarly, the rest of the framing process requires the active participation of humans connecting cues to frames. People create the differences they are uncertain about, and they actively participate in a process to reduce the uncertainty to a comfortable level. The sense that people make is the basis for their actions. The view described in Chapter One presents a description of reality that has some parts that exist without human engagement, but humans access "what is going on" and act on what they have created.

Chapter Two explained communication as a process in which individuals in a social relationship construct messages for each other as part of an ongoing episode. The process is one of assisted HIP. When people end an episode, both leave with a sense of what they have created. What each person contributes depends, in part, on the responses of the others. And so, the entire episode develops coherence as people coordinate their behaviors. What this means is that people's perceptions of reality from communication are sense that relies on other people's cooperation. In this way, the stories we tell ourselves rely on the audiences and the audience reactions. The storyteller may own the story, but the telling of it relies on others. Our sense of reality relies on others.

When people move from conversation to conversation, they can link episodes. The topic of conversation from one episode can be part of another. Themes can chain throughout a network as a community converges around a set of stories and a reality (Bormann, 1982; Rogers & Kincaid, 1981). Everyone in the chain contributes to everyone else's reality.

The dominating stories become the signals people are more likely to access when they start their own individual framing with enactment. Pete Thamel's first stories about Lennay Kekua were part of the conversations he had with others. He may have framed what he heard with a confirmation bias leading to further elaborations of the tale, and one column led to a series of conversations and columns by others that led to another of his own columns and more conversations, etc. One of the great ironies is that the Internet allowed others to check some details, that led to different conversations, and finding a hoax.

The problems distinguishing different parts of hybrid realities are just an extension of the problems people have been having regardless of a particular HCT or mix of HCTs. People have always had problems distinguishing what happened from their sensations of what happened, from their perceptions of what happened, from the language they attach to what happened, and from the way they talk about what happened with one person or another. People use the same words for perceptions, sensations, and events that are different than others experienced, and people use the different words for perceptions, sensations, and events than are similar to what others experienced.

A likely area of confusion is the scope of an idea or statement. There are three kinds of statements people confuse frequently (Haney, 1967; Ross, 1994). An *observation or statement of fact* is a description of something that can be verified by sensation. For example, "John came to work at 8:05 AM", is a statement someone could verify by asking the people who work with John, people who were there when he came to work, or better yet, by being one of those people who was there when he came to work. The statement is a statement reporting a direct experience.

An *inference* connects to or more observations or ideas together in one statement. "John was late" or "John was five minutes late" connects "John came to work at 8:05" with "John's boss regards coming to work any later than 8:00 AM as being late". There is no way to verify "John was late" with a sensation since you can't see, hear, etc. "late". You can logically argue that John was late by providing the separate observations you linked together as evidence for your inference, but you don't have an observation that directly confirms the inference. Linking two inferences together to get a third inference requires even better argument. Claims need evidence, and the evidence for inferences are different than the evidence for observations. Of course, there are those situations when people make a claim and can't explain what led them to that conclusion – the worst situation.

Evaluations are inferences with some critical or judgmental expression. These statements have all of the problems of inferences plus the addition of having to explain criteria. "John was tardy, and he is lazy" is an evaluation. When does being late become tardy or lazy? What are the standards? When someone agrees with an evaluation it suggests the listener and the speaker have similar knowledge and values.

There is nothing wrong with any of these statements, but failing to understand the differences can lead to Lennay Kekua. Having the same values as another may limit your natural tendency to ask a few questions. If you really want Sidd Finch to be a great spring training hope for the Mets, you may not ask any questions. And Sidd Finch happened without the latest HCT.

Today's hybrid reality is an era of big data. There may be so much to process people can forget to ask the big questions. People may settle for reports that are just "true enough" to feed a bias or help people feel they have not missed out (Manjoo, 2008).

Whatever Happened to the News?

On February 27, 2011, CNN aired an interview Fareed Zakaria had with Paul Wolfowitz, a man who held several foreign policy posts for three American presidents. Zakaria asked him about his impressions of the current unrest in the Middle East. In the middle of interview, Zakaria asked this question:

> Now, the people saying things like this are people who one tends
> to think of as allies of yours, that is to say the conservatives have
> had a very mixed view on this. I mean, you have - you know,
> people on the right effectively saying the Obama administration
> junked Mubarak too soon, that they should have - they should
> have supported him more, that they're, you know, allowing for
> the rise of an Islamic caliphate. (Zakaria, 2011).

What is noteworthy about this question is that it comes from a respected journalist posing the question to a recent participant in events similar to the subject of the question. Zakaria was acting as a **reporter** seeking information and opinion from a **person with experiences in events**. One would have expected Zakaria to ask Wolfowitz about events, the reports of events, and the opinions of other people with similar experiences. What is troubling is that he asked Wolfowitz to comment on the opinions expressed by Glenn Beck, an **entertainer**. A caliphate? Really? Zakaria, one of the more astute media journalists, fell into the trap of confusing levels of news coverage.

Traditional news began with an **event**. Something happened. Journalism teachers urge prospective reporters to ask basic questions about the event – who, what, where, when, how, and why. Notice that most of these questions produce observations, but answering the last one necessarily leads to an inference.

The person filing the **news report** is attempting a description of the event. In traditional reporting, the reporter needed several people with similar descriptions before an aspect of the event could make it into the report. The reporter was careful to answer "why" with such expressions as "According to". The goal was accuracy or at least to give as confirmable a report as possible. On contemporary television news, there are few true reports beyond some presentations of those on location as events unfold.

Meta-news consists of reports of other reports. The television news reporter says, "According to the *New York Times*" or "According to the *National Inquirer*". The television reporter is reporting on some other report. If there are several reports of the same event, the television reporter must select one or the television reporter generalizes the reports – "According to published sources." The event and those involved in the event are data sources for the reporter on the scene, but the reports themselves become available data for the television reporter. The old Headline News 30-minute broadcasts were primarily meta-news, and most network news programs are meta-news since reporting staffs have shrunk.

An **editorial** is an evaluation of an event. It is commentary and opinion. There may be expectations that an editorial begins with a report or meta-report, but it is often difficult to distinguish the evaluation from the description, no matter how removed the editorial was from the event. Furthermore, editorial writers often provide their opinions about what should be done about the event. The public seldom asks these writers to account for their errors, but the writers and performers are skilled at strategic ambiguity and often explain their errors as misinterpretations of their advice. Much of the programming on Fox and MSNBC consists of editorials.

Finally, there is entertainment. **Entertainment** is a dramatic media performance. What happens in such a performance is intended to be exaggerated and to challenge an audience's sense of perspective. The traditional extremes of drama are tragedy and comedy. The nightly news anchors are a part of show business and not figures of authority (Dowd, 2015). Fake news such as *The Daily Show* or the old *Colbert Report*, and several skits on *Saturday Night Live* are entertainment parodying news, meta-news, and editorials, but these performances are entertainment.

It is much too easy to confuse these various levels. For example, are Bill O'Reilly or Chris Mathews performing editorials or entertainment? Where is the news in either program? Glen Beck's histrionics should have made it easy to understand him as an entertainer, and Rush Limbaugh often describes himself as an entertainer who makes his audience think. However, Beck appeared on a "fair and balanced" network and he re-dramatizes his own dramatic events such as his Washington rally. Limbaugh becomes part of the event when he appears at political rallies. Keith Olbermann was dismissed from MSNBC for becoming too involved in the events. Donald Trump became president, but the public may have been unable to separate his performances as an entertainer from his potential actions as president. In the end, it is about Lonesome Roads, an Arkansas hobo, in the 1957 film *Face in the Crowd*, and Chauncy Gardner, the mentally challenged orphan of the 1979 film *Being There*. These fictional characters entertained and dealt with complex problems with country ballads and homilies that brought them to the brink of national office. Today, the editorials become entertaining. The performances are disconnected from reports and the events. Zakaria asked Wolfowitz to take a joke seriously.

When presented with five factual statements and five opinions, most Americans correctly classified at least three of each type of statement (Mitchell, Gottfried, Barthel, & Sumida, 2018). But, these percentages were only slightly better than random. Far fewer were able to classify all ten statements, and a quarter missed all of the statements. This suggests systematic error and a lack of critical thinking.

Johnson (1946) described a critical thinking method to sort through various claims. His crap detector involved asking three questions: (1) what does the speaker mean, (2) how does the speaker know, and (3) what is the speaker leaving out. One asks about meaning recognizing that it is the speaker who means and calling attention to what the speaker's biases might be. One asks about evidence recognizing that a speaker's statements may not contain the reports that might suggest inferences and evaluations. One asks about alternative evidence, reports, inferences, and evaluations recognizing that it is impossible to say everything there is about an event. Such critical thinking is important when experiencing an editorial or entertainment.

In a digital environment, people get or read posts online where it may be difficult to identify the source or assess the credibility of the source. People may need an object history. Where did the story originate? Where has it been? How has it changed from the original? Journalists have been asking the large Internet companies (e.g., Google) to use their technology to provide such a history (Ignatius, 2017).

People get news from a variety of sources, in addition to television (Mitchell, Gottfried, Kiley & Weisel, 2014). Over 24% of Americans get their news from Google News and Yahoo News, and these sources ranked ahead of National Public Radio and Public Broadcasting System in America, the British Broadcasting Company, and the *New York Times*. In 2014, 13%

regularly got their news from the *Huffington Post*, an online source, 12%
from the Daily Show, 12 % from the *New York Times*, and 10% from the
Colbert Report. An in-depth study of three communities and how people
learned about local news revealed a mix of technology, including Twitter
and Facebook, as part of a complex news environment (Mitchell, Holcomb,
Hitlin, Gottfried, Matsa, Barthel, & Olmstead, 2015). The percentage of
people who prefer online sources (34%) has increased slightly over two
years, but television is still the preferred platform for news (44%) (Mitchell,
2018).

The reduction in news staffs means that news outlets use more reports
from local citizens as part of gathering data for a story. How reliable is the
average citizen? Law enforcement officials and traditional media obtained
photos and messages from people at the bombing at the Boston Marathon
and other tragedies. The people at the event extended their participation
with the authorities, and these same people became stringers for news
bureaus. Local television stations frequently encourage their viewers to
upload the videos they have taken to expand their capacity for on-the-spot
news coverage. These bits and pieces of "speed journalism" are not enough
to "make the news," since someone must connect them into a sensible
narrative (Butterworth, 2011).

The story can be wrong—inaccurate—as when the *New York Daily News*
continued to run pictures of the wrong people as the Boston Police
Department's primary suspects (Morales & Ford, 2013). One of the men in
the pictures reported over 200 hundred aggressive phone messages within
the day of the publication of the pictures, described people following and
harassing him, and received advice from the Boston Police to take down his
Facebook (Morales & Ford, 2013). The interactions of a tragic event, a
panicked public, multiple amateur sources of data, pressured reports at a
newspaper, station or website, and management and owners competing for
readership had led to cyberbullying and stalking.

A final trend is for people to select news sources that confirm their own biases. Conservatives and liberals in America rely on different news sources (Mitchell, et al., 2015). Various media outlets use market research techniques to provide targeted audiences the stories that reinforce their beliefs and values. People are more likely to correctly distinguish between facts and opinions when the statement comes from a source they trust and when they agree with the statement (Mitchell et al., 2018). Although there are more sources for news, the recursive loop of people increasingly seeking sources for confirmatory data and media increasingly providing stories that reinforce leads to a bigger screen but narrower views (Barwind, Salem & Gratz, 2014). What is *really* going on in the world?

Virtual Humans

It is now possible to turn all sensation into electronic bits, and although the electronic versions are not the same as the originals, our experiences of most of them are the same. Can human intelligence become a set of algorithms? What about personalities? What about the abilities of virtual humans to communicate with humans? Can humans build social relationships with virtual humans? Can virtual humans provide the same resources as humans?

In 1996, Gary Kasparov, the highest rated chess player in history, won a six-game match with Deep Blue, an IBM program. However, he lost the first game when he failed to respond correctly to a poor move by Deep Blue because he believed the computer was "up to something" (Vogel & Jayanti, 2003). In 1997, Deep Blue won a second match. Kasparov would claim the programmers cheated and that Deep Blue had human assistance during the games."

Deep Blue is a program that responds to opponent moves by searching a massive databank full of moves already evaluated as to their strength, given the current position. Deep blue makes decisions on a move-by move-basis, and the only thing Deep Blue could have been "up to" was searching for a move. Kasparov projected intent onto a program. It is comparable to Lars projecting a personality onto the doll he bought (Aubry, Cameron, Kimmel, & Gillespie, 2007), and similar to a person believing they have a relationship with a fictional character or a celebrity even though there has been no communication between them. The introduction noted examples of people making the same mistakes.

Alan Turing (1950) described the imitation game, a challenge computers would need to overcome to prove they had achieved human intelligence. The game was about communication, and an interrogator who must ask questions of two others the interrogator cannot see. In the original description, one of the people was a man and the other was a woman, and the challenge for the interrogator was to correctly identify the sex of the others. Turing then extended the game to having the interrogator ask questions of two others the interrogator could not see, but one was a human and the other was a computer. If interrogators were unable to correctly identify the other, the computer had achieved human intelligence. In 2014, a computer fooled 33% of the judges after a 25-minute conversation (McCoy, 2014). The challenge was the inspiration for computer programmers to create a program that performed Rogerian therapy, and several competitions between different programs to win cash prizes (Epstein, Roberts & Beeber, 2009).

In 2003, Linden Labs developed Second Life, a virtual online world. People create avatars and virtual environments, and they can use their avatars to interact with others and develop relationships. Until recently, people could also design and sell virtual things (e.g., buildings, furniture, clothes). Over the last 10 years, people created over 36 million accounts, spent over 3.6 billion dollars, and spent the equivalent of 217, 266 years on Second Life (Soekel-Walker, 2013). A recent report suggests over 600,000 current members with 300,000 of them also on the Second Life Facebook site (Soekel-Walker, 2013). Second Lifers refer to real life as First Life.

The personae people create in Second Life may be more important to them than the ones they create IRF. But, prioritizing roles had been important before Second Life – role conflict, "Mom likes you best", work-life conflict, etc. People have killed others over petty things before becoming engrossed in a virtual world.

Can virtual humans substitute for humans? The answer from recent movies is "Yes". See *Robot & Frank* (Acord, Bisbee, Bisbee, Neiderhoffer, & Schreier, 2012) and *Thomas in Love* (Elbaum & Renders, 2000). It is possible that people recognize the differences, but, like Theodore in *Her* (Ellison, Jonze, Landay, & Jonze, 2013), people may now prefer a computer companion to a human one. There are popular video games in which people create their ideal romantic partner, and many are choosing to interact with the virtual partners to avoid the "messiness" of romantic relationships IRL (Aiken, 2016).

Virtual environments are just another avenue for bad behavior . . . except that the repercussions can happen more quickly and with greater impact. Police arrested an Oklahoma couple for child abuse and neglect believing the couple spent so much time playing with their Second Life avatars they failed to feed their three-year-old child; the girl weighed 13 pounds (Kemp, 2013). In a similar story, a Korean couple spent so much time caring for a virtual baby online, their real life infant died. One reporter concluded as follows:

> The balance of power between the worlds is shifting. Here and
> there, virtual reality is gaining the upper hand. The clearest
> evidence is death. When people consumed by the digital world
> begin to die and kill in the physical world, flesh is losing its grip.
> It still defines our deaths, but it no longer defines our lives.
> (Saletan, 2010).

It is a dramatic statement, but it points to some cracks in the armor. So do the stories that began this chapter. People are not trending toward the virtual world and away from real life, are they?

A mindless approach to engaging the digital world is one explanation for the problems people are having. Chapter Five described three features of mindlessness (Langer, 1989), and here is how they could apply to problems distinguishing realities. Mindlessness includes using rigid categories, and a person could come to believe his/her reality is the only reality. Since a virtual reality feels real, and since it conforms to that person's sense of reality, there will be no questioning of the limits of a virtual reality. Mindlessness involves acting as if there were only one set of rules, one way to act. Obviously, bringing the way a person acts IRL to a virtual world or thinking the actions of avatars are based and limited by the same rules will lead to problems. Finally, mindlessness involves reflexive behaviors, and so intimacy IRL involves self-disclosure, and when a similar but different virtual situation occurs, people will disclose without hesitating to consider the implications for the virtual world.

In a virtual environment, a mindful person recognizes and appreciates differences. Different people make different realities, and there are many digital realities. Accept and negotiate alternative sets of rules. People need to expect different rules and look for different rules similar to when they visit a different country or a different family. People should be looking for alternative ways to interact and communicate with others in a virtual world. The keys are an appreciation for differences and flexibility. People may be involved in a simulation or virtual world that is part of a hybrid reality, but the communication can have real life consequences.

Of course, none of these concerns are new. Current concerns about distinguishing realities have their literary counterparts.

> Alice caught the baby with some difficulty and it was a queer
> shaped little creature, and held out its arms and legs in all

directions "just like a star fish". . . "If I don't take this child with me," thought Alice, "there are sure to kill it in a day or two: wouldn't it be murder to leave it behind?" She said the last words out loud, and the little thing grunted in reply . . . "Don't grunt," said Alice, that's not at all a proper way of expressing yourself." The baby grunted again, and Alice looked anxiously into its face to see what was the matter with it. There could be no doubt that it had a very turn-up nose, much more like a snout than a real nose; also its eyes were getting extremely small for a baby; altogether Alice did not like the look of the thing at all . . . "If you are going to turn into a pig, my dear," said Alice seriously, "I'll have nothing more to do with you. Mind now!" The poor little thing sobbed again, (or grunted, it was impossible to say which) and they went on for some time in silence. Alice was just beginning to think to herself, "Now, what am I to do with this creature when I get home?" when it grunted so violently, that she looked down into its face with alarm. This time there could be *no* mistake about it: it was neither more or less than a pig, and she felt it would be quite absurd for her to carry it any further. So she let the creature down, and she felt quite relieved to see it trot away quietly into the wood. "If it had grown up," she said, "it would have been a dreadfully ugly child: but it makes rather a handsome pig, I think." And she began to thinking over other children she knew, who might do very well as pigs. (Carroll, 1865/1994, pp. 83-84).

Disrupting Reality

Different HCTs have design features that constrain or afford people's choices or behaviors. Thinking about visiting my sister tomorrow in another part of the country would just be fantasy without the existence of airplanes and the HCT that would enable me to reserve a seat and get to and from airports, or without the existence of HCT that would enable my sister and me to communicate about visiting her. However, the existence of these features does not force me to particular behaviors. Some people use old mobile phones as door stops.

Similarly, social and cultural predispositions and routines might constrain or afford people's choices or behaviors using HCT. There are different greeting rituals in different cultures, for example. However, previous chapters have noted that people use the newer HCT because the old rules do not apply. What is happening with the commodification of people and shallow close relationships is happening in different cultures. Stunted argument happens in different cultures. The couples that starved their children were from Korea and Oklahoma.

Throughout this volume, specific advantages and disadvantages associated with newer HCT were more about the use of HCT than the design features of technology. People construct the worlds they inhabit, and their communication constructs their realities. However, some people have greater success than others, and some have more problems than others. The descriptions of various "idisorders" and the consistent advocacy of being more mindful reinforces a more realist explanation, especially when what is being explained are more personal and local patterns rather than more global or cultural ones.

Hybrid reality is another term for the current media ecology people have created. Of course, there will be unanticipated consequences because people do not make many decisions about or act in the interests of long term or global consequences. Rather, people construct messages as responses to the previous messages or as part of routines they have performed before. Furthermore, one episode is part of a flow of episodes that may produce consequences it would be impossible to recognize for those people involved in a current exchange of text messages occurring in the present.

The newer HCTs change the way we communicate, and so they are a change in parameters. The emerging patterns appear to be greater breadth and less depth for many topics in this volume. A more shallow self, more shallow relationships, and more shallow civic engagement appear to be part of these trends.

Are these trends necessarily bad or tragic? Are these trends just part of the normal disruptions humans have experienced, the kind of disruptions that biology and culture eventually absorb or dismiss as humans return to old patterns or somewhat modified patterns? Perhaps, these trends lead humanity to newer and better ways to accomplish more and to create novel outcomes. Developing models of the possibilities would help understand the complexity of using the newer human communication technologies (Salem, 2013).

References

Acord, L., Bisbee, J. K., Bisbee, S., Neiderhoffer, G. (producers), & Schreier, J. (director). (2012). *Robot & Frank*. United States: Dog Run Pictures, Park Pictures, TBB, & White Hat.

Akin, M. (2016) *The cyber effect*. New York: Spiegel & Grau.

Aubry, S., Cameron, J., Kimmel, S. (producers), & Gillespie, C. (director). (2007). *Lars and the real girl*. Canada: Metro-Goldwyn-Mayer, Sidney Kimmel Entertainment, & Lars Production.

Barwind, J. A., Salem, P. J., & Gratz, R. D. (2014). A bigger screen for a narrower view. In K. M. Ryan (Ed.), *The more you know: Law and order, inconvenient truths and how television shapes our worldview* (pp.11-25). Lexington, MA: Lexington Press.

Bean, T. & Poling, L. (2014, May 16). *American Masters: Plimpton*. New York: Public Broadcasting System.

Berger, P. L., & Luckmann, T. (1966). *The social construction of reality: A treatise on the sociology of knowledge*. New York: Doubleday.

Bormann, E. G. (1982). The symbolic convergence theory of communication: Applications and implications for teachers and consultants. *Journal of Applied Communication Research*, *10*, 50–61.

Burke, T., & Dickey, J. (2013, January 16). Manti Te'o's dead girlfriend, the most heartbreaking and inspirational story of the college football season, is a hoax. *Deadspin* (Sports blog). http://deadspin.com/manti-teos-dead-girlfriend-the-most-heartbreaking-an-5976517.

Butterworth. T. (2011, June 13). Speed journalism: Some stories need just a Tweet – some need real thought. *The Daily*, 49.

Carroll, L. (1994). *Alice in wonderland and through the looking glass*. New York: Quality paperback Book Club. (originally published in 1865 and 1871).

Davenport, T. H. (1997). *Information ecology: Mastering the information and knowledge environment*. New York: Oxford University Press.

Dowd, M. (2015, February 7). *Anchors aweigh*. New York Times, SR11.

Elbaum, D. (producer) & Renders, P. (director). (2000). *Thomas in love*. Belgium and France: Entre Chien et Loup, JBA Production, & Radio Television Belge Francophone.

Ellison, M., Jonze, S., Landay, V. (Producers), & Jonze, S. (Director) (2013). *Her* (Motion picture). United States: Anapurna Pictures.

Epstein, R., Roberts, G., & Beeber, G. (Eds.). (2009). *Parsing the Turing test: Philosophical and methodological issues in the quest for the thinking computer*. New York: Springer.

Foucault, M. (1966/2001). *The order of things: An archeology of the human sciences* (Trans.) (2nd ed.). New York: Routledge.

Gleick, J. (2011). *The information: A history, a theory, a flood*. New York: Pantheon Books.

Haney, W. V. (1967). *Communication and organizational behavior: Text and cases*. Homewood, IL: Irwin

Ignatius, D. (2017, November). How to protect against fake "facts". *Washington Post*. ttps://www.washingtonpost.com/opinions/getting-back-to-facts/2017.

Johnson, W. (1946). *People in quandaries: The semantics of personal adjustment*. NY: Harper & Brothers.

Kemp, J. (2013, October 12). Oklahoma parents so engulfed in Second Life they allegedly starved their real 3-year-old daughter: cops. *The New York Daily News*. http://www.nydailynews.com/news/national/oklahoma-parents-engulfed-online-fantasy-world-allegedly-starved-real-3-year-old-daughter-cops-article-1.1483479.

Khanna, A., & Khanna, J. (2012). *Hybrid reality: Thriving in the merging human-technology civilization*. TED Books. http://www.ted.com/pages/tedbooks_library.

Kurzweil, R. (2005). *The Singularity is near: When humans transcend biology*. New York: Viking.

Langer, E. L.(1989). *Mindfulness*. Cambridge, MA: De Capo Books.

Leach, B. (2008, October 25). Woman arrested after virtual murder. *The Telegraph*. http://www.telegraph.co.uk/news/newstopics/howaboutthat/3257876/Woman-arrested-after-virtual-murder.html.

Levin, J. (2013, January 16). The fake girlfriend experience: Why didn't sportswriters catch on to Manti Te'o's phony relationship? Because they didn't care to look. *Slate*. http://www.slate.com/articles/sports/sports_nut/2013/01/manti_te_o_hoax_lennay_kekua_why_sportswriters_didn_t_catch_on_to_the_notre.html.

Manjoo, F. (2008). *True enough: Learning to live in a post-fact society*. Hoboken, NJ: John Wiley & Sons.

McCoy, T. (2014, June 9). A computer just passed the Turing Test in landmark trial. *Washington Post* http://www.washingtonpost.com/news/morning-mix/wp/2014/06/09/a-computer-just-passed-the-turing-test-in-landmark-trial/

Mitchell, A. (2018). *Americans still prefer watching to reading the news—and mostly still through television.* (report). Washington, DC: Pew Research Center. http://www.journalism.org/2018/12/03/americans-still-prefer-watching-to-reading-the-news-and-mostly-still-through-television/.

Mitchel, A., Gottfried, J., Barthel, M., & Sumida, N. (2018). *Distinguishing between factual and opinion statements in the news.* (report). Washington, DC: Pew Research Center. http://www.journalism.org/2018/06/18/distinguishing-between-factual-and-opinion-statements-in-the-news/

Mitchel, A., Gottfried, J., Kiley, J., & Weisel, R. (2014). *Political polarization and media habits: From Fox News to Facebook, how liberals and conservatives keep up with politics* (report). Washington, DC: Pew Research Center. http://www.journalism.org/files/2014/10/Political-Polarization-and-Media-Habits-FINAL-REPORT-11-10-14-2.pdf.

Mitchell, A., Holcomb, J, Hitlin, P., Gottfried, J., Matsa, K. E., Barthel, M., & Olmstead, K. (2015). *Local news in a digital age* (report). Washington, DC: Pew Research Center. http://www.journalism.org/files/2015/03/PJ_MediaEcology_complete_report.pdf.

Morales. M., & Ford, B. (2013, April 18). Boston Marathon spectator Salah Barhoum, who was interviewed by authorities following the bombings, swears he 'didn't do it'." *New York Daily News.*

http://www.nydailynews.com/news/national/hs-track-star-speaks-didn-article-1.1320766?print.

Nickerson, R. S. (1998). Confirmation bias: A ubiquitous phenomenon in many guises. *Review of General Psychology, 2*(2), 175–220.

Parry, H. (2015, March 21). Grand Theft Auto gamer was so upset when his brother killed his character in online session he drove 50 miles to threaten him with a baseball bat. *The Daily Mail.* http://www.dailymail.co.uk/news/article-3005278/Grand-Theft-Auto-gamer-upset-brother-killed-character-online-session-drove-50-miles-threaten-baseball-bat.html#ixzz3WRYY3Yw2.

Podolny, S. (2015, March 7). If an algorithm wrote this, how would you know? *New York Times*, SR6.

Reeves, B., & Nass, C. (1996). *The media equation*. Stanford, CA: CSLI Publications, Cambridge University Press.

Rogers, E. M., & Kincaid, D. L. (1981). *Communication networks: Toward a new paradigm for research*. New York: The Free Press.

Ross, R. B. (1994). The ladder of abstraction. In P. Senge, C. Roberts, R. Ross, B. J Smith, & & A. Kleiner, *The fifth discipline fieldbook: Strategies and tools for building a learning organization* (pp. 242-261). NY: Doubleday.

Salem, P. J. (2013). *The complexity of human communication* (2nd ed.). Cresskill, NJ: Hampton Press.

Saletan, W. (2010, March 10). Game over: A baby starves to death while the parents play online. *Slate.* http://www.slate.com/articles/health_and_science/human_nature/2010/03/game_over.html.

Shank, D. B. (2014). Impressions of computer and human agents after interaction: Computer identity weakens power but not goodness impressions. *International Journal of Human-Computer Studies, 72*(10-11), 747-756.

Stokel-Walker, C. (2013, September 24). Second Life's strange second life: In Linden Lab's strange experiment, the end has no end. *The Verge*. http://www.theverge.com/2013/9/24/4698382/second-lifes-strange-second-life.

Turing, A. M. (1950). Computing machinery and intelligence. *Mind, 50*, 433-460.

Vogel, H. (producer) & Jayanti, V. (director) (2003). *Game over: Kasparov and the machine*. Canada and the United Kingdom: Alliance Atlantic Communications & National Film Board of Canada.

Wagner, M/ (2014, June 3). What is Slenderman, and what does it have to do with the Wisconsin murder plot? *New York Daily News*. http://www.nydailynews.com/news/national/slenderman-wisc-stabbing-article-1.1815135.

Watzlawick, P. (1976). *How real is real: Confusion, disinformation, communication*. New York: Random House.

Wooley, B. (1992). *Virtual worlds*. Oxford: Blackwell Publishers.

Youyou, W., Kosinski, M., & Stilwell, D. (2015). Computer-based personality judgments are more accurate than those made by humans. *Proceedings of the National Academy of Sciences, 112*(4), 1036-1040.

Zakaria, F. (2011, February 27). *Fareed Zakaria GPS: Interview with Paul Wolfowitz* (Transcript). New York: Cable News Network International.

Index

CPSIA information can be obtained
at www.ICGtesting.com
Printed in the USA
LVHW071726150121
676574LV00004B/123